LANCASTER COUNTY COOKBOOK

LANCASTER COUNTY COOKBOOK

LOUISE STOLTZFUS AND JAN MAST

Good Books

Intercourse, PA 17534
800/762-7171
www.goodbks.com

Photo Credits
Photographs on pages 28a, 92a, and 220a by Dawn J. Ranck;
pages 28b, 156b and 220b by Richard Reinhold; page 92b by Huddle Images;
and page 156a by John P. Herr

Cover Illustration by Cheryl Benner
Design by Dawn J. Ranck

LANCASTER COUNTY COOKBOOK
Copyright © 1993, 2003 by Good Books, Intercourse, Pennsylvania, 17534
International Standard Book Number: 1-56148-092-4 (paperback edition)
International Standard Book Number: 1-56148-412-1 (comb-bound paperback edition)
Library of Congress Catalog Card Number: 93-30020

Library of Congress Cataloging-In-Publication Data
Stoltzfus, Louise
    Lancaster County cookbook / Louise Stoltzfus and Jan Mast.
        p.cm.
    Includes index.
    1. Cookery--Pennsylvania--Lancaster County. 2. Cookery, German
I Mast, Jan. II. Title.
TX721.S76 1993
641-59748' 15--dc20   93-30020
                                                                    CIP

Table of Contents

Introduction

A place deeply rooted in its rural farm beginnings, the fertile land of Lancaster County, Pennsylvania yields hundreds of acres of crops and produce each year. Gardens abound. Truck farms thrive. Traditional corn, hay, and cattle farmers run their machinery alongside suburban housing developments and growing towns and boroughs. Many of these farmers have expanded their operations to include cottage industries—quilt shops, roadside vegetable and fruit stands, health and bulk food stores, and larger ventures such as furniture or farm equipment manufacturing plants.

The people who live in Lancaster County today reflect years of tradition as well as an increasing diversity and multiculturalism. The thriving city of Lancaster, founded in 1729-30, is home to persons of many different cultural understandings and practices. Art galleries, women's and men's specialty stores, delis and cafes often give the city a cosmopolitan feel.

Many of the villages, towns, and boroughs scattered throughout the County also have a particular history, often revolving around specific national or religious groupings. Places such as Lititz, Manheim, Strasburg, and Columbia date to the mid-1700s, within fifty years of the establishment of Lancaster County and the arrival of the first European settlers.

The area's proximity to the vast eastern seaboard cities makes it a natural vacation hub. Visitors come to experience the unique and living story of Amish and Mennonite culture. They return to participate in a slower pace of life and to drive along winding back country roads where few cars pass and neighbors all know each other. They also come back to enjoy concerts in the park, downtown festivals, and the abundance of autumn auctions and farmers' fairs.

From the various neighborhoods in Lancaster City, from towns and villages such as Adamstown, Peach Bottom, Bainbridge, Kirkwood, and Mount Joy, cooks and lovers of food throughout the County share their favorite recipes, as well as short vignettes about their lives. Widely known for their Pennsylvania Dutch food heritage, many Lancaster Countians have made room for other ways of cooking, including a greater health consciousness and willingness to experiment with different food traditions.

The seven sweets and seven sours of Pennsylvania Dutch cooking are in this collection. Chicken potpie, shoofly pie, and funnel cakes still please many a Lancastrian's palate. However, stromboli and burritos and egg rolls also often find their way onto the tables of Lancaster homes—reflecting the variety of peoples who now live in the County—and recipes for such foods also are included here.

To the many people from all parts of the County who gave of their valuable time and energy to collect recipes and to help test them, we express our grateful thanks. We also wish to thank the men and women of various volunteer fire companies and auxiliaries, as well as those of other community centers throughout Lancaster County, who graciously answered our questions and helped spread the word about our project. The recipes and stories in this book provide a way for people everywhere to share in the vibrant life and treasured history of those of us who call Lancaster County, Pennsylvania, home. We thank you for helping make that possible.

—Louise Stoltzfus and Jan Mast

Lancaster County Towns Profiled in this Cookbook

Directory of Town Profiles

Appetizers and Snacks

Round Pumpernickel with Dried Beef Spread

Deb Lied
Akron, PA

Makes 4½ cups spread

1 large loaf round pumpernickel bread
1 pint sour cream
1 pint mayonnaise
2 tsp. dill seed
2 Tbsp. minced onion
2 Tbsp. parsley flakes
2 pkgs. dried beef, diced

1. Remove center of pumpernickel loaf and cut bread into cubes. Cover tightly and set aside.
2. Combine all remaining ingredients and mix well. Spoon dip into hollowed out loaf of pumpernickel.
3. Spread bread cubes around edge of plate and serve.

Party Rye Bread with Bavarian Spread

Carolyn Burns
Lancaster, PA

Makes 28 appetizer servings

8 ozs. sauerkraut, well drained and snipped
½ cup finely shredded cheddar cheese
½ cup finely chopped turkey ham
¼ cup mayonnaise
¼ cup saltine cracker crumbs
1 Tbsp. chopped pimento
1 Tbsp. snipped parsley
2 tsp. finely chopped onion
½ cup sour cream
28 slices party rye bread

1. In large mixing bowl combine all ingredients except bread. Shape into big mound. Cover and chill.
2. Spoon 1 Tbsp. Bavarian spread over each piece party rye bread. Serve.

*H*ummus with Pita Bread

Sarah Ellen Myers
Mount Joy, PA

Makes 2 cups

1 cup chickpeas
3 cups water
2 cloves garlic
2 Tbsp. olive oil
⅓ cup tahini (purée of sesame seeds)
2 Tbsp. lemon juice
1 tsp. honey
¼ cup yogurt
¾ tsp. salt
½ tsp. cayenne pepper
½ tsp. chopped parsley

1. Soak chickpeas overnight in water. Add garlic and bring to a boil. Lower heat and simmer 2½-3 hours.

2. To chickpeas add oil, tahini, lemon juice, honey, yogurt, and salt and cook until smooth, stirring frequently. Add cooking water as needed. Cool.

3. Spread into serving dish. Top with a little olive oil. Sprinkle lightly with cayenne pepper and chopped parsley.

4. Serve with pita bread.

Variation: During the summer I often serve fresh tomatoes stuffed with hummus.

Bird-in-Hand

*C*alled Enterprise as late as the 1880s, Bird-in-Hand served the surrounding Mennonite and Amish farm community as a stop on the Pennsylvania Railroad line. Built around the area where the railroad crossed the Old Philadelphia Pike (Route 340), the hamlet eventually became more easily identified with the local hotel and tavern which practiced under the bird-in-hand sign.

In 1910 the fire company witnessed some significant excitement when lightning struck Jake and Fannie Beiler's barn on a stormy summer afternoon. Jake had taken a load of wheat to the railroad station. While he sat waiting to unload, a neighbor galloped into town with the message that his barn was on fire. Unhitching his horses from the load of wheat, Jake ran over to the local firehouse and hitched them to the firewagon. At breakneck speed he dashed the mile-and-a-half east to his farm on Weavertown Road. In spite of his heroic efforts, Jake Beiler was unable to save his barn.

Today, the Bird-in-Hand Fire Company serves the surrounding community with its busy volunteer fire organization, which includes many local Amish men and women. Well known for its annual fall ham supper, the company recently built a new addition, bringing its firehouse and shining modern fire engines into the twenty-first century.

Stretching east along Route 340 from Mill Creek as far as Ronks Road, where open Amish farmland takes over the landscape, Bird-in-Hand embraces a popular local restaurant and motel on its eastern edge as well as a manufacturing complex on its western edge. At the village center a sprawling farmer's market and several small gift and curiosity shops line the busy highway which bisects the town.

Surprise Spread
Julia Mowrer
Quarryville, PA

Makes 3 cups dip

8-oz. pkg. cream cheese
½ cup sour cream
¼ cup mayonnaise
2 4¼-oz. cans fine shrimp, well drained
1 cup seafood cocktail sauce
2 cups grated mozzarella cheese
1 green pepper, chopped
2 green onions, chopped
1 small tomato, chopped
1 large pkg. tortilla chips

1. Cream together cream cheese, sour cream, and mayonnaise. Spread over large meat platter.
2. Scatter drained shrimp over cheese mixture.
3. Layer remaining ingredients except tortilla chips over shrimp and cheese in order given. Cover and chill until ready to serve.
4. Serve with tortilla chips.

Hot and Spicy Cheese Dip
Valerie Voran
Ephrata, PA

Makes 4 cups dip

8 ozs. mozzarella cheese, shredded
8 ozs. cheddar cheese, shredded
1 cup cottage cheese
¼ tsp. salt
¼ tsp. celery salt
3 Tbsp. pizza sauce
2 Tbsp. chili sauce
1 Tbsp. hot taco sauce

¾ cup mayonnaise
4-6 apples
1 large pkg. tortilla chips

1. Combine all ingredients except apples and tortilla chips in a small crockpot or fondue pot and heat until melted.
2. After dip is heated through, prepare apples. Arrange apples and tortilla chips on platter.
3. Serve immediately with warm dip.

Taco Salad Dip
Susanne Brubaker
Lancaster, PA

Makes 10-12 servings

2 8-oz. pkgs. cream cheese
16-oz. carton cottage cheese
2 8-oz. jars taco sauce
½ green pepper, diced
½ onion, diced
2-3 tomatoes, diced
Chopped lettuce
1 lb. cheddar cheese, shredded
Black olives (optional)
2 medium bags tortilla chips

1. Mix cream cheese and cottage cheese together. Spread onto large tray or platter. Layer with remaining ingredients except tortilla chips in order given.
2. Refrigerate at least 8 hours before serving. Serve with tortilla chips.

Shrimp Dip
Deb Lied
Akron, PA

Makes 2 cups dip

4¼-oz. can fine shrimp
8-oz. pkg. cream cheese, softened
1 small onion, finely chopped
¼ cup mayonnaise
¼ cup milk
Pinch garlic salt
Pinch pepper

1. Using a wire whisk, mix all ingredients until shrimp is shredded. Chill.
2. Serve with choice of crackers and potato chips.

Deviled Ham Picnic Dip
Norma I. Gehman
Kinzers, PA

Makes 3 cups dip

2 4¼-oz. cans deviled ham
12 ozs. cream cheese, softened
2 Tbsp. Worcestershire sauce
⅛ tsp. cayenne pepper
⅔ cup finely chopped green pepper

1. In small mixing bowl beat together ham, cream cheese, Worcestershire sauce, and cayenne pepper until creamy. Fold in green pepper.
2. Cover and refrigerate for 1 hour or until ready to serve. Serve with choice of crackers or fresh vegetables.

Vegetable Dip
Barbara Hummel, Brownstown, PA
Margaret G. Layton, New Holland, PA

Makes 1½ cups dip

1 cup sour cream
½ cup mayonnaise
1 tsp. finely chopped onion
1 tsp. parsley
1 tsp. dill seed
¾ tsp. seasoned salt

1. Combine all ingredients and mix well.
2. Refrigerate and chill at least 2 hours before serving.
3. Serve with choice of sliced, raw vegetables.

Zesty Dip
Marie Splain
Maytown, PA

Makes 1 cup dip

2 beef bouillon cubes
¼ cup hot water
8-oz. pkg. cream cheese, softened
1 small onion, minced
3 tsp. mayonnaise
½ tsp. herb seasoning

1. Dissolve beef cubes in hot water. Combine beef bouillon mixture, cream cheese, onion, 2 tsp. mayonnaise, and herb seasoning and mix until smooth.
2. Immediately before serving, add remaining 1 tsp. mayonnaise and mix well.
3. Serve with choice of raw vegetables.

Crab Puffs

Betty Pellman
Millersville, PA

Makes 12 servings

½ lb. Velveeta cheese
6 Tbsp. butter *or* margarine
1½ tsp. Worcestershire sauce
1 lb. crab meat, carefully cleaned
1 tray Pepperidge Farm Party Rolls

1. In a saucepan melt cheese, butter, and Worcestershire sauce over low heat. Fold in crab meat and cool.
2. Cut rolls in half lengthwise. Spread even amounts of crab meat mixture on each roll and arrange on cookie sheet.
3. Bake at 350° for 10 minutes, watching carefully to prevent burning.

Herb Veggie Dip

Cathy Rohrer
Willow Street, PA

Makes 1½ cups dip

⅔ cup mayonnaise
⅔ cup sour cream
1 Tbsp. onion flakes
1 Tbsp. chopped fresh chives
1 Tbsp. chopped fresh parsley
1 tsp. seasoned salt
1 tsp. dill weed
½ tsp. Worcestershire sauce

1. Cream together mayonnaise and sour cream. By hand crumble spices into mixture and stir until smooth. Add Worcestershire sauce and mix well.
2. Refrigerate to chill. Serve with choice of raw vegetables.

An Itinerant Artist in Rural Lancaster County

In the 1920s our rural neighborhood always looked forward to the summertime arrival of the itinerant artist whom we called Moudrum. Moudrum painted, inscribed, and designed mailboxes. He also entered births, weddings, and deaths in the family Bible in careful fraktur-like script. Because he usually bartered for his services, our family regularly gave him a chicken, which he added to his collection in the chicken coop attached to the back of his covered market wagon. In my childhood mind, he was an unusual creature, using his talent and enjoying his life.

—*Anne H. Strickler, Lititz, PA*

Hot Olive Puffs

Gina Burkhart
Landisville, PA

Makes 8 servings

1 cup shredded cheddar cheese
3 Tbsp. butter, softened
½ cup flour
1 tsp. paprika
½ tsp. Worcestershire sauce
Dash cayenne pepper
Dash salt
24 medium green olives

1. Cream together cheddar cheese and butter. Blend in flour, paprika, Worcestershire sauce, pepper, and salt.
2. Mold a rounded teaspoon of dough around each olive. Arrange on ungreased cookie sheet.
3. Bake at 400° for 12 minutes or until golden brown. Serve.

Mozzarella Cheese Sticks

Debra Hoover
Paradise, PA

Makes about 3 dozen cheese sticks

16-oz. piece mozzarella cheese
1 cup milk
1 cup flour
½ tsp. salt
1 cup fine, dry, seasoned bread crumbs
1 cup Parmesan cheese
1 quart cooking oil

1. Cut mozzarella cheese into desired-sized pieces.
2. Pour milk into shallow dish.
3. Combine flour and salt in another dish.
4. In third dish stir together bread crumbs and Parmesan cheese.
5. Heat cooking oil to 375° in heavy 3-quart saucepan or deep fryer.
6. Meanwhile dip cheese pieces, one at a time, in milk, flour mixture, and bread crumb mixture. Repeat.
7. Carefully drop breaded cheese sticks, a few at a time, into hot oil. Deep fry about 30 seconds or just until they start to sizzle. Remove from oil and drain on paper towels. Serve immediately.

Note: *Cheese sticks may be frozen. Immediately before serving, reheat in hot oil, deep frying until cheese is soft but not melted.*

Cheese Logs

Barbara A. Kurtz
Gap, PA

Makes 3 cheese logs

1 lb. sharp cheddar cheese, grated
3 8-oz. pkgs. cream cheese, softened
2 pkgs. bacon and onion dip mix
2 cups finely chopped pecans

1. Combine all ingredients except pecans and form into logs. Roll each log into pecan meal until completely covered.
2. Wrap in plastic and chill before serving.

Cheese Straws

Rhoda H. Lind
Lititz, PA

Makes 6-8 servings

1 cup flour
½ tsp. salt
3 Tbsp. butter
1 cup grated sharp cheese
Water (optional)

1. Combine flour and salt and cut in butter until well mixed. Stir in cheese and mix well. Knead slightly. Add a little bit of water if needed to make dough roll out more easily.
2. Roll out and cut into strips. Arrange on greased cookie sheet.
3. Bake at 350° for 20-25 minutes, until golden brown.

Mount Hope

*A*long the northeastern edge of Lancaster County, about a mile-and-a-half south of the Lebanon County line on Route 72, stands Mount Hope, a Victorian estate and winery. Formerly, the summer home of nineteenth century iron ore barons, the Grubb family, the estate once stood near the village of Mount Hope, which became a ghost town with the collapse of the iron industry.

The only surviving public buildings on the original village site are the Mount Hope Church, an Episcopal church founded in 1848, and a secluded stone mansion, The Inn at Mount Hope, a bed and breakfast establishment.

When the nearby Grubb family mansion was purchased in 1980, the resulting renovation with its working winery began to bring the area around Mount Hope back to life. Today the home and grounds burst into life with the beginning of the Pennsylvania Renaissance Faire each Fourth of July weekend. The Faire, which began in 1980 as a single weekend of jousting events on the winery's parking lot, has evolved into a full-scale 30-acre Tudor Village with eleven staging areas, including a reproduction of Shakespeare's Globe Theatre and a jousting arena with a capacity of 7000 people. Hundreds of 16th century costumed characters roam the grounds every weekend from July 4 through mid-October.

The Faire's culinary delights include giant roasted turkey legs, fish and chips, spuds, and scones, all available inside the stone castle walls in the company of jugglers and jesters, swordsmen and mercenaries, and madrigals and magicians. Thus, for a few enchanting weekends each summer and fall Mount Hope transports its visitors several centuries back in time to Merrie Olde England.

Cheese Crisps

Lucy Moore Bomberger
Lancaster, PA

Makes 12-16 servings

8 Tbsp. butter
1 cup grated sharp cheese
1 cup flour
1½ cups Rice Krispies
Dash red pepper

1. Let butter and cheese soften. Work by hand and add flour, a little at a time. Add Rice Krispies and red pepper, working by hand.
2. Form into small balls. Arrange on greased cookie sheet. Press down with fork.
3. Bake at 350° for 10-12 minutes. Watch closely. Serve.

Ranch Pretzels

Erma J. Frey
Leola, PA

Makes many snack servings

½ cup cooking oil
1 tsp. dill weed
1 pkg. Hidden Valley Ranch dressing mix
1-lb. pkg. small pretzels

1. Combine oil, dill weed, and dressing mix and mix well.
2. Stir together. Add pretzels and stir until dressing covers pretzels.
3. Serve at a cookout or picnic.

Variation: Substitute no-salt pretzels for a less salty snack.

Onion-Flavored Pretzels
Katie Beiler
Leola, PA

Makes many snack servings

8 Tbsp. butter
1 pkg. dry onion soup mix
1-lb. pkg. broken pretzels

1. Melt butter. Add soup mix and mix well.
2. Pour over pretzels and stir until well coated.
3. Bake at 200° for 1 hour, stirring every 15 minutes.

Jnack Crackers
Betty Eberly
Denver, PA

Makes many snack servings

1-lb. box club crackers
8 ozs. sliced almonds
1 cup butter
$\frac{2}{3}$ cup sugar

1. Line 10" x 15" jelly roll pan with aluminum foil and arrange crackers to fill bottom of pan. Spread almonds evenly over crackers.
2. In a saucepan melt butter. Add sugar and stir until sugar dissolves. Pour evenly over nuts and crackers in thin stream.
3. Bake at 300° for 20-25 minutes or until nicely browned. Remove from oven and let cool. While still slightly warm, break into squares. Serve.

The Gordonville Sale

Each spring the Gordonville Fire Company holds an auction which has become immensely popular, drawing people from far and wide. Our 25th annual sale was postponed when it happened to fall on the weekend of the Blizzard of '93. While a few hardy souls made it to the auction site that second Saturday in March, most people waited for the rescheduled date.
—*Lydia Smoker, Gordonville, PA*

Fruit Dip
Orpha Kilheffer
Lititz, PA

Makes 1 pint dip

8-oz. pkg. cream cheese
7-oz. jar marshmallow cream
2 Tbsp. orange juice
1 tsp. grated orange rind
Dash ginger

1. Cream together cream cheese, marshmallow cream, and orange juice.
2. Fold in orange rind and ginger and mix well.
3. Serve with choice of fresh, sliced fruit pieces.

Variation: *Combine cream cheese, marshmallow cream, and 1 tsp. vanilla and mix until creamy. Serve with choice of fresh fruit.*
—*Betty Brightbill, Sinking Spring, PA*

*B*reads, Rolls, and *M*uffins

*A*mish Friendship Bread
Norma I. Gehman
Kinzers, PA

Starter:
1 cup flour
1 cup warm water
$\frac{1}{2}$ cup sugar
1 pkg. yeast

Add on Fifth Day:
1 cup flour
1 cup milk
1 cup sugar

Add on Tenth Day:
1 cup flour
1 cup milk
1 cup sugar

1. Mix all starter ingredients well and place in medium-sized glass bowl. Cover with dinner plate so as not to cover too tightly. Let stand overnight in warm place. Stir down each day for 4 days. (Important: Do *not* refrigerate batter at any time.)

2. On the fifth day add flour, milk, and sugar and stir. Stir down each day until tenth day.

3. On the tenth day add flour, milk, and sugar and measure out 3 separate cups starter. Give 1 cup starter and a copy of the instructions to each of 3 friends.

4. Use remaining dough to bake choice of bread or use in streusel recipe which follows this one.

Friendship Starter Streusel

Norma I. Gehman

Kinzers, PA

Makes 12-16 servings

Batter:
⅔ cup cooking oil
1 cup sugar
2 cups flour
2 tsp. baking soda
½ tsp. salt
3 eggs
Starter

Streusel:
⅓ cup margarine, melted
½ cup white sugar
½ cup brown sugar
½ cup quick oats
1 cup nuts (optional)

1. After sharing 3 cups starter with friends mix oil, sugar, flour, baking soda, salt, and eggs with remaining starter. Mix well and spoon ½ of batter into greased and floured 9" x 13" baking pan.

2. To prepare streusel combine all ingredients and mix well. Sprinkle ½ of streusel over batter. Cover with remaining batter and remaining streusel.

3. Bake at 350° for 35-40 minutes.

Whole Wheat Bread

Florence Nolt

New Holland, PA

Makes 3-4 small loaves

1 cup milk
1 cup water
⅓ cup molasses *or* honey
⅓ cup melted butter and cooking oil
1½ cups cold water
3 cups white bread flour
3 cups whole wheat flour
1½ Tbsp. yeast
2 tsp. salt

1. Heat milk and water to just below boiling point. Add molasses and ⅓ cup butter and cooking oil (half of each to make ⅓ cup). Add cold water to bring to workable temperature.

2. Combine flours, yeast, and salt. Gradually add dry ingredients to liquid.

3. Finish by kneading in more white and whole wheat flour until dough is right consistency. (Knead at least 8-10 minutes until dough no longer sticks to hands.)

4. Let rise 1 hour or until doubled in size. Knead again, working out bubbles. (The more you work dough the nicer bread will be.)

5. Shape into 3 or 4 small greased loaf pans. Let rise again until doubled in size. (Letting it rise too long makes it crumbly and produces air bubbles; letting it rise too little makes it more solid.)

6. Bake at 400° for 10 minutes. Reduce oven temperature to 350° and bake 20 minutes longer.

Homemade Bread

Susie S. Stoltzfus
Ronks, PA

Makes 3 loaves

1½ Tbsp. yeast
½ cup lukewarm water
1 Tbsp. salt
⅓ cup brown sugar
¼ cup cooking oil
2 cups hot water
2 cups whole wheat flour
5 cups bread flour

1. In a large bowl combine yeast and lukewarm water. Let rest for 10 minutes.
2. Add salt, brown sugar, and oil. Add hot water and stir well. Add whole wheat flour and mix well.
3. Add bread flour, 1 cup at a time, and mix well. Knead by hand for at least 5 minutes or until the dough no longer sticks to hands. (Add a little more flour if necessary.)
4. Cover and let rise in warm place for 2 hours. Knead down, cover, and let rise another hour.
5. Knead down and divide dough into equal pieces, arrange in 3 greased loaf pans, and let rise 1¼ hours.
6. Bake at 350° for 22 minutes. Brush tops with cooking oil. Cool on racks at least ½ hour before storing in plastic bags.

Note: It is very important to use a good brand bread flour. Many people have been frustrated when making bread simply because they were not using a bread flour.

Raisin Bread

Emma King
Gordonville, PA

Makes 2 loaves

1 cup raisins
2 cups hot water
1 pkg. yeast
⅓ cup warm water
½ cup sugar
1 tsp. salt
1 tsp. cinnamon
⅓ cup melted margarine *or* cooking oil
2 tsp. molasses
6 cups bread flour

1. Soak raisins in 2 cups hot water. Set aside.
2. Dissolve yeast in ⅓ cup warm water. Set aside.
3. Drain and reserve water from raisins. Add enough water to make 2 cups liquid.
4. Mix together sugar, salt, cinnamon, margarine, molasses, hot raisin water, and 4 cups bread flour.
5. Stir in raisins, yeast mixture, and remaining flour. Knead about 10 minutes. Let rise 2-3 hours.
6. Knead down dough. Separate and put into 2 greased loaf pans. Let rise again until doubled in size.
7. Bake at 350° for 35-40 minutes.

English Muffin Bread

Marcene Becker
Manheim, PA

Makes 2 loaves

6 cups flour
2 pkgs. yeast
1 Tbsp. sugar
2 tsp. salt
¼ tsp. baking soda
2 cups milk
½ cup water
Cornmeal

1. In a large bowl combine 3 cups flour, yeast, sugar, salt, and baking soda.
2. In a saucepan heat milk and water until scalding. Add milk mixture to the dry ingredients. Beat well.
3. Stir in remaining 3 cups flour to make a stiff batter. Spoon into two loaf pans which have been greased and sprinkled with cornmeal.
4. Cover and let rise in a warm place for 45 minutes.
5. Bake at 400° for 20-25 minutes. Remove from pans immediately to cool.

Whole Wheat Crescent Rolls

Sarah Ellen Myers
Mount Joy, PA

Makes 24 rolls

2 pkgs. yeast
1 Tbsp. brown sugar
2 cups warm water
⅓ cup honey
3 Tbsp. shortening *or* cooking oil
2 tsp. salt
2½ cups whole wheat flour
2½ cups white flour
Softened butter *or* margarine

1. Dissolve yeast and brown sugar in warm (105°-115°) water.
2. Add honey, shortening, salt, whole wheat flour, and enough white flour to make a stiff dough. Knead on a lightly floured surface for 10 minutes and place in a greased bowl.
3. Cover and let rise about 1½ hours.
4. Knead down and divide into 3 equal pieces. Shape into balls. Cover and let rest for 12 minutes.
5. Roll out each ball of dough into 12-inch circle. Spread with butter. Cut each circle into 12 wedges.
6. To shape crescent rolls, begin at the wide end of the wedge and roll toward point. Arrange rolls, point side down, on greased baking sheet. Cover and let rise 20-30 minutes.
7. Bake at 375° for 12 minutes.

Dinner Rolls
Esther Gingrich
Lancaster, PA

Makes 2 dozen rolls

1½ Tbsp. yeast
3 Tbsp. warm water
1 tsp. sugar
1½ cups hot water
⅓ cup sugar
1½ tsp. salt
2 Tbsp. margarine
1 large egg
4½ cups flour *or* more

1. Put yeast, 3 Tbsp. water, and 1 tsp. sugar into a bowl. Mix slightly. (This will make a sponge and rise rapidly.)

2. In large bowl combine 1½ cups water, ⅓ cup sugar, salt, and margarine and mix until dissolved. Add egg and beat. Add 2 cups flour and yeast mixture and beat until smooth. Use spoon to stir in remaining flour. Knead in additional flour until dough is soft, but not sticky.

3. Place in greased bowl and let rise in warm place until doubled in size.

4. Knead slightly to work out air bubbles. Pat or roll to ½-inch thickness. Cut with 2-inch round cutter and arrange rolls on baking sheets. Let rise until doubled in size.

5. Bake at 325°-350° for 15-20 minutes or until golden. Do not overbake.

Vanilla Buns or Rolls
Ruth Good
Ephrata, PA

Makes 20-24 rolls

2 cups scalded milk
½ cup shortening
2 cakes yeast
½ cup warm water
3 Tbsp. sugar
6½ cups bread flour *or* more
2 eggs, beaten
¾ cup sugar
1 tsp. salt

1. Pour scalded milk over shortening.

2. Dissolve yeast in warm water with 3 Tbsp. sugar. Let rise.

3. When both milk and yeast mixtures are lukewarm, mix them together. Add 3 cups flour and beat until smooth. Let rise in a warm place for 1 hour.

4. Stir in well beaten eggs, ¾ cup sugar, and salt and beat well. Gradually add remaining flour. Add more flour if needed to make a stiff dough. Knead with buttered hands about 8-10 minutes or until dough seems like a ball. Place in greased bowl and let rise in warm place for 2 hours or until doubled in size.

5. With a spoon cut out pieces of dough and shape into desired-sized rolls. Arrange on greased baking pan. Let rise in warm place until doubled in size.

6. Bake at 300° for 30-35 minutes or until light and golden.

The City of Lancaster

*O*ne of the more ethnically diverse cities of its size, Lancaster lies near the geographic center of the County from which it inherited its name. Today, this thriving metropolis boasts beautiful, residential streets lined with azalea, forsythia, dogwood, and mock pear trees. While its downtown business district continues to battle the fall-out of a mid-twentieth-century mass exodus of retail stores, most Lancastrians love their sometimes quiet, sometimes bustling, city.

At the heart of downtown, Lancaster's only skyscraper, the eleven-story Griest Building towers above Penn Square. Along with the Griest, Central Market, a flourishing farmer's market, anchors the square's northwest corner. Across the way, The Bonton—Watt and Shand, a regal art deco department store, bravely continues its long tradition, stocking everything from housewares to dresses to greeting cards. The two remaining corners are secured by Mellon Bank headquarters and Fulton Bank headquarters. At high noon the square bursts with energy. Office workers pour out of their buildings for a quick rest in Steinman Park, a pocket park maintained by the Lancaster Newspapers franchise, or a break at one of the many restaurants serving the downtown lunch crowd. By early evening when people head for their neighborhood or suburban homes, the city center settles into a quiet peace with occasional stirrings around Windows on Steinman Park, an upscale dining establishment, or the Fulton Opera House, a 150-year-old fine arts theater.

The Northwest neighborhoods around College Hill surround Buchanan Park, Franklin and Marshall College, and St. Joseph's Hospital. The close, but single unit homes have a palatial quality with stunning glass and iron work as well as quiet, tree-shaded backyards. People from various backgrounds inhabit the more affordable rowhouses found east of Lancaster Theological Seminary. Restaurants as dissimilar as the Asian Restaurant, a Vietnamese eatery at the corner of Pine and Frederick, the Neptune Diner, a roadside diner on North Prince Street, and Checkers, a yuppie bar with Friday night crowds, herald the Northwest neighborhoods' historic, yet vital flavor.

*R*aised Doughnuts

Jeanette Oberholtzer, Akron, PA
Joanne Gestewitz, Akron, PA

Makes about 5 dozen doughnuts

Doughnuts:
1 pkg. yeast
1 cup warm water
1 cup mashed potatoes, cooled
1 cup white sugar
2 eggs, beaten
½ cup shortening, melted
5-6 cups all-purpose flour
Shortening *or* lard

Filling:
2 egg whites
2 tsp. vanilla
4 cups powdered sugar
4 Tbsp. milk
1 cup shortening

1. To prepare doughnuts dissolve yeast in warm water. Combine yeast, mashed potatoes, and sugar and mix well. Let stand overnight.

2. In the morning add eggs and ½ cup shortening. Gradually add flour, working until soft and doughy. Knead 10 minutes.

South of St. Joseph's Hospital, the gentle climb into the rolling streets around Cabbage Hill reveals a working class population with roots in Lancaster's large German population. St Mary's Catholic Church, established in 1741, stands on the northeast edge of the Cabbage Hill neighborhood where it has served many generations of German, Irish, and Hispanic immigrants. Strawberry Hill Restaurant, with its unusual combination of French, Italian, and American cuisine caters to Lancaster's cultural crowd. Four blocks southwest of Strawberry Hill, O'Halloran's Irish Pub draws a more casual clientele.

East of Prince Street and south of King, the Seventh Ward neighborhoods slope toward the banks of Conestoga Creek, which caresses the southeast edge of the city with its long, gentle curves. Corner groceries and restaurants, featuring everything from African-American to Puerto Rican to Chinese food, demonstrate the ethnic diversity of the Ward. Churches such as South Christian Street Mennonite, Bright Side Baptist and Spanish Assembly of God dot the landscape. And block after block of red-brick rowhouses line the teeming streets. Most people who live in the Ward embrace a centuries-old tradition of neighbors visiting on front porch stoops and watching out for each other.

North of King Street and east of Queen, the East End neighborhoods surround the diamond-shaped Lancaster Cemetery which interrupts the straight east-west flow of numerous streets in the area. Southwest of the cemetery, rows of elegant, stately, old homes line North Queen, North Duke, and North Lime Streets. From the 1870s when North Duke Street was considered the finest residential neighborhood in the fledgling city, these stone and brick structures with classic lines and spacious interiors have been home to some of Lancaster's most renowned citizens. Tucked into various corners of the East End are cozy oases like Musser Park, tiny Triangle Park, and the more imposing Sixth Ward Park. Middle class neighborhoods fill the streets north and east of the cemetery. The Horse Inn, where stalls serve as booths; Molly's Pub, where Molly, the owner's dog, reigns supreme; Quips, where fish & chips come wrapped in the *London Times;* and Carlos and Charlie's, where Mexican fare and margaritas meld; distinguish Lancaster's East End with their fine food and distinctive flavors.

Let rise until doubled in size.

3. Work dough down and roll out to ½-inch thickness. Cut into pieces with round doughnut cutter. Cover and let rise until doubled in size.

4. Heat shortening or lard in kettle. Deep fry doughnuts until lightly browned. Drain on absorbent paper.

5. To prepare filling beat egg whites until well mixed but not stiff. Add vanilla and 2 cups powdered sugar and mix well. Beat in milk and 2 more cups powdered sugar. Beat in 1 cup shortening and mix until creamy.

6. Carefully split each doughnut and fill with filling. Serve.

Overnight Cinnamon Rolls
Shirley Hoover
Lancaster, PA

Makes 10-12 rolls

Rolls:
1 pkg. yeast
1 cup warm water
¼ cup white sugar
1 tsp. salt
2 Tbsp. margarine
1 egg
3 cups flour
Butter
Brown sugar
Cinnamon

Topping:
⅓ cup butter
½ cup brown sugar
½ cup white sugar
½ tsp. cornstarch
3 Tbsp. milk
½ cup chopped nuts
2 tsp. cinnamon

1. Dissolve yeast in warm water. Add ¼ cup sugar, salt, and margarine and mix well. Beat egg and add to mixture. Add flour and knead until well mixed.
2. Put in greased bowl, grease top of dough, and cover. Refrigerate overnight.
3. In the morning roll out dough to ½-inch thickness on lightly floured surface. Spread with butter and sprinkle with brown sugar and cinnamon.
4. Roll up and cut into 2-inch slices. Set aside.
5. To prepare topping melt butter in a saucepan. Add sugars, cornstarch, milk, and nuts. Heat through, stirring frequently.
6. Pour heated syrup mixture into baking pan. Set rolls into syrup and cover. Let rise 1 hour.
7. Bake at 375° for 20 minutes. Invert rolls onto serving dish and serve.

Cinnamon Rolls
Susie S. Stoltzfus
Ronks, PA

Makes approximately 2 dozen rolls

Rolls:
1½ Tbsp. yeast
½ cup lukewarm water
1 Tbsp. salt
⅓ cup brown sugar
¼ cup cooking oil
½ cup boiling water
3 eggs, beaten
Milk
1 tsp. cinnamon
1 cup whole wheat flour
6 cups bread flour
1 Tbsp. cooking oil
2 Tbsp. cinnamon
¾ cup brown sugar
½ cup chopped nuts

Syrup:
1½ cups water
1½ cups brown sugar
1½ cups molasses

1. In a large bowl combine yeast and lukewarm water. Let rest for 10 minutes.
2. Add salt, brown sugar, ¼ cup cooking oil, and boiling water and mix well.
3. Add enough milk to beaten eggs to make 1½ cups liquid. Add to batter and mix well. Add 1 tsp. cinnamon and whole wheat flour and stir well.
4. Add bread flour, 1 cup at a time, and mix well. Knead by hand at least 5 minutes or until dough no longer sticks to hands.

(Add a little more flour if necessary.)

5. Cover and let rise in warm place for 2 hours. Knead down, cover, and let rise another hour.

6. Roll dough out into large (12" x 20") rectangle. Brush with oil. Sprinkle with cinnamon, brown sugar, and nuts. Roll up as for jelly roll.

7. Cut dough into ¾-inch pieces. Arrange rolls in 3 9" x 13" baking pans, spacing them evenly apart. (They will fill up pan after rising.) Let rise 1¼ hours.

8. Meanwhile, prepare syrup by combining all ingredients in medium saucepan. Heat until dissolved, stirring frequently. Pour even amount of syrup into each pan of rolls.

9. Bake at 350° for 15 minutes. Let cool for at least 45 minutes before serving.

Note: To achieve success with this recipe, it is essential to use bread flour.

Easy Sticky Buns
Margaret G. Layton
New Holland, PA

Makes 10 servings

2 Tbsp. butter *or* margarine
¼ cup corn syrup
¼ cup brown sugar
1 cup chopped nuts *or* raisins
10-serving pkg. refrigerator biscuits

1. Melt butter in a glass pie plate. Add syrup, brown sugar, and nuts or raisins and stir.

2. Arrange refrigerator biscuits on top of syrup, sugar, and nuts/raisins mixture.

3. Bake at 350° for 10 minutes or until done. Invert onto serving plate and serve warm.

Zucchini Bread
Ida E. Winters, Lititz, PA
Rosie Stoltzfus, Ronks, PA

Makes 2 loaves bread

3 eggs
2 cups sugar
1 cup cooking oil
2 tsp. vanilla
3 cups flour
1 tsp. baking soda
1 tsp. baking powder
1 tsp. salt
1 tsp. cinnamon
3 cups grated zucchini
½ chopped nuts *or* raisins (optional)

1. In large bowl beat together eggs and sugar. Add oil and vanilla and mix well.

2. In separate bowl combine all dry ingredients. Add dry ingredients to creamed mixture, alternating with grated zucchini. Fold in nuts or raisins if desired. Spoon into 2 greased loaf pans.

3. Bake at 350° for 1 hour.

Rhubarb Bread

Darlene Harding
Sinking Spring, PA

Makes 2 loaves

1½ cups brown sugar
⅔ cup cooking oil
1 egg
1 cup sour milk
1 tsp. baking soda
1 tsp. salt
1 tsp. vanilla
2½ cups sifted flour
2 cups diced rhubarb
1 cup chopped nuts
½ cup sugar
1 Tbsp. butter

1. Combine brown sugar, oil, and egg and mix well.
2. In separate bowl combine sour milk and baking soda. Stir sour milk mixture into creamed mixture. Add salt, vanilla, and flour and mix well. Fold in rhubarb and nuts. Spoon into 2 greased and floured loaf pans.
3. Combine sugar and butter and mix until crumbly. Sprinkle evenly over batter in both pans.
4. Bake at 325° for 50-60 minutes. This bread can be frozen.

Pumpkin Bread

Betty Brightbill
Sinking Spring, PA

Makes 3 loaves

Bread:
3½ cups flour
3 cups sugar
½ tsp. baking powder
2 tsp. baking soda
1 tsp. cinnamon
1 tsp. nutmeg
1 tsp. cloves
1½ tsp. salt
4 eggs, slightly beaten
2 cups pumpkin
1 cup cooking oil
⅔ cup warm water
1 cup raisins *or* chopped walnuts

Crumb Topping:
½ cup sugar
1 cup flour
⅓ cup butter *or* margarine

1. In a medium bowl combine flour, sugar, baking powder, baking soda, cinnamon, nutmeg, cloves, and salt.
2. In a large bowl combine eggs, pumpkin, oil, water, and raisins. Stir in dry ingredients and mix well. Spoon batter evenly into 3 small greased and floured loaf pans.
3. Combine all topping ingredients until crumbly. Sprinkle evenly over pumpkin mixture in each pan.
4. Bake at 350° for about 40 minutes. Serve.

Spiced Applesauce Raisin Bread

Jeanette Barr
Stevens, PA

Makes 1 loaf

¾ **cup fiber cereal**
1¾ **cups flour**
½ **cup white sugar**
½ **cup brown sugar, packed**
1 **cup applesauce**
½ **cup skim milk**
¼ **cup cooking oil**
3 **tsp. baking powder**
¾ **tsp. cinnamon**
½ **tsp. allspice**
½ **tsp. salt**
¼ **tsp. ground cloves**
1 **egg** *or* 2 **egg whites**
½ **cup raisins**

1. Crunch cereal in blender. Mix all ingredients except raisins in large bowl and beat about 30 seconds. Fold in raisins. Spoon into greased 9-inch loaf pan.

2. Bake at 350° for 50-55 minutes or until toothpick inserted in center comes out clean. Cool 10 minutes and remove from pan. Cool completely before slicing. Serve.

Traditional Shortbread

Reba I. Hillard
Narvon, PA

Makes about 5 dozen shortbreads

2 **cups butter**
1 **cup sugar**
1 **tsp. vanilla**
½ **tsp. salt**
4 **cups flour**

1. Cream together butter and sugar; add vanilla.

2. Combine salt and flour and work into butter mixture with finger tips. Knead gently until smooth. Pat into a large ball, wrap in plastic, and refrigerate at least 30 minutes (may be refrigerated overnight).

3. Roll out to ⅜-inch thickness onto floured surface. Cut into 1" x 2½" rectangles with a knife. Arrange on ungreased cookie sheet and prick each shortbread several times with a fork.

4. Bake at 300° for 30 minutes or until golden.

Scotch Shortbread

Carmen Watson
Lititz, PA

Makes 12-16 small servings

1 cup soft margarine
½ cup white sugar
2 cups sifted flour
½ cup cornstarch

1. Cream together margarine and sugar.
2. Combine flour and cornstarch. Add to creamed mixture until very crumbly.
3. Press mixture into 8-inch square baking pan. Press with fingers turned into fist-like shape until mixture is reasonably smooth.
4. Bake at 325° for 1 hour. Cut into squares while still hot. Sprinkle with white sugar and serve.

Corn Bread

Sarah Ellen Myers
Mount Joy, PA

Makes 12-16 servings

2 cups cornmeal
2½ cups white flour
½ tsp. salt
2 tsp. baking soda
½ cup butter *or* margarine, melted
1¼ cups brown sugar
2 eggs, beaten
1½ cups sour milk, buttermilk, *or* yogurt

1. Sift together dry ingredients.
2. Cream together butter, brown sugar, eggs, and milk.
3. Combine dry and liquid ingredients. Spoon into greased 9" x 13" baking pan.
4. Bake at 350° for 25-30 minutes.

Onion Cheese Bread

Twila D. Wallace
New Holland, PA

Makes 1 loaf

2 cups sliced onion
3 Tbsp. butter
2 cups flour
2 Tbsp. baking powder
1 tsp. salt
¼ cup shortening
2 Tbsp. parsley *or* ½ tsp. caraway seeds
1 cup milk
½ cup grated Parmesan cheese

1. Sauté onions in butter until soft. Set aside to cool.
2. Sift together dry ingredients. Cut in shortening until mixture has coarse meal consistency. Add parsley and milk and stir just until moistened. Pat out dough into a rectangle. Spread 1½ cups onion and ¼ cup cheese over dough. Roll up like jelly roll and place into greased baking pan.
3. Spread remaining onions over top and sprinkle with remaining cheese.
4. Bake at 425° for 30 minutes or until done.

Buttermilk Biscuits
Joyce E. Zercher
Holtwood, PA

Makes 15-20 biscuits

2 cups all-purpose flour
2¼ tsp. baking powder
¼ tsp. baking soda
1 tsp. salt
⅓ cup + 2 tsp. shortening
¾ cup thick buttermilk

1. Sift flour. Measure and sift again with baking powder, baking soda, and salt. Cut shortening into flour mixture with a pastry blender or 2 knives.
2. Add buttermilk and stir briskly with a fork until thoroughly blended. Turn onto lightly floured surface and knead 8-10 times. Roll or pat out to ½-inch thickness.
3. Cut out biscuits with round, floured cutter. Arrange in greased, shallow baking pan.
4. Bake at 450°-500° for 10-15 minutes.

Blueberry Muffins
Mary N. Nolt, New Holland, PA
Gladys A. Zimmerman, Ephrata, PA

Makes 20-24 muffins

3 cups flour
4 tsp. baking powder
1 tsp. salt
1 cup sugar
2 eggs
1 cup milk
½ cup cooking oil
2 cups blueberries

1. Sift flour. Measure and add baking powder, salt, and sugar.
2. Beat together eggs, milk, and oil. Add dry ingredients and stir lightly to blend. Fold in blueberries.
3. Drop by tablespoonsful into greased muffin tins.
4. Bake at 375° for 25 minutes.

Happy Day Muffins
Anne Nolt
Reinholds, PA

Makes 12 muffins

1 egg
½ cup milk
¼ cup cooking oil
1½ cups flour
½ cup sugar
2 tsp. baking powder
½ tsp. salt
½ tsp. vanilla
¾ cup halved cranberries

1. Beat together egg, milk, and oil. Add all remaining ingredients and stir just until flour is moistened. (Batter should be lumpy.)
2. Fill greased or lined muffin cups ⅔ full.
3. Bake at 400° for 20-25 minutes. Serve warm.

Variation: Substitute blueberry or cherry halves for cranberries.

Learning from My Grandmother

My grandmother, Mary Ann Benedict Cauler, gave me the recipe for veal shin soup, included on page 29 in this book. Born near Rock Hill, Pennsylvania in 1879, she loved to cook and bake.

Every summer of my childhood I would spend a week or so with her on Hazel Street in the Cabbage Hill neighborhood of Lancaster City. My favorite day was always Friday because we would get up and ride the city bus to Southern Market. Grandmother enjoyed getting fresh vegetables directly from the farmers who came to market.

It was on one such trip that she introduced me to one of my favorite foods—chocolate eclairs. In those days they sold for 10 cents each.

—*Mary C. Sage, Pequea, PA*

*L*ittle Applesauce Muffins

Barbara A. Kurtz

Gap, PA

Makes 3 dozen small muffins

½ **cup margarine**
½ **cup sugar**
2 **eggs**
¾ **cup applesauce**
1¾ **cups flour**
1 **Tbsp. baking powder**
½ **tsp. salt**
½ **cup margarine**
1 **cup sugar**
½ **tsp. cinnamon**

1. In large bowl cream together ½ cup margarine and ½ cup sugar. Beat in eggs, one at a time. Beat in applesauce.
2. In separate bowl combine flour, baking powder, and salt. Add dry ingredients to creamed ingredients and stir just enough to moisten. Spoon into greased, miniature muffin cups.
3. Bake at 425° for 15 minutes.
4. Melt ½ cup margarine and pour into small bowl.
5. Combine 1 cup sugar and cinnamon and pour into another bowl.
6. While muffins are still warm, dip tops into melted butter and cinnamon sugar. Serve warm.

*P*ineapple Bran Muffins

Tammy Groff

Quarryville, PA

Makes 12 muffins

1¼ **cups all-purpose flour**
1 **Tbsp. baking powder**
½ **tsp. salt**
3 **Tbsp. brown sugar, firmly packed**
1 **egg**
2 **cups bran cereal**
⅓ **cup milk**
¼ **cup cooking oil**
8-oz. **can crushed pineapple with juice**

1. Stir together flour, baking powder, salt, and brown sugar. Set aside.
2. Beat egg slightly. Add cereal, milk, oil, and pineapple, including juice. Stir to combine. Let stand about 10 minutes or until cereal has softened. Stir again.
3. Add flour mixture, stirring only until combined. Spoon batter evenly into 12 greased muffin cups.
4. Bake at 400° about 20 minutes or until muffins are golden brown. Serve warm.

Bran Muffins

Marilyn Langeman
Akron, PA

Makes 12 large muffins

1 cup buttermilk
1½ cups wheat bran
⅓ cup cooking oil
1 egg
⅔ cup brown sugar
½ tsp. vanilla
1 cup flour
1 tsp. baking soda
1 tsp. baking powder
½ tsp. salt
½ cup raisins *or* chopped dates (optional)

1. Mix together buttermilk and wheat bran. Let stand while beating together oil, egg, brown sugar, and vanilla.
2. Add creamed mixture to buttermilk and bran mixture and beat well.
3. Sift together all dry ingredients. Quickly stir into bran mixture. Fold in raisins.
4. Spoon into greased or lined muffin tins.
5. Bake at 400° for 15-20 minutes.

Bareville Ladies' Auxiliary

The Bareville Ladies' Auxiliary meets the second Monday of each month. We plan the year's events, including our January chicken corn soup supper, our March quilting days, our May charcoal steak dinner, and our November Christmas craft show.

We also operate a food trailer which we set up regularly at local farm and household auctions.

—*Erma J. Frey, Leola, PA*

Cornmeal Muffins

Ruth G. Frackman
Paradise, PA

Makes 12 muffins

¾ cup cornmeal
¾ cup flour
½ cup sugar
1½ tsp. baking powder
¾ cup milk
¼ cup butter, melted
1 egg

1. Combine all ingredients and mix well. Spoon into greased muffin tins.
2. Bake at 350° for 25-30 minutes.

*S*oups

*C*hicken Corn Soup
Dorothy Galebach
Manheim, PA

Makes 8 servings

4 cups fresh *or* frozen corn
2½ cups diced, cooked chicken
46-oz. can chicken broth *or* 6 cups
    homemade broth
2 cups water
Pinch saffron
⅛ tsp. salt
Pepper to taste
1 cup flour
1 raw egg
3 hard-boiled eggs, chopped

   1. Combine corn, chicken, broth, water,
and seasonings in a kettle. Heat to boiling.
Reduce heat and cook 3-4 minutes until
corn is tender.
   2. Meanwhile combine flour and raw
egg to make rivels. Mix by hand until
consistency of pie dough crumbs. Add
extra flour if dough is too sticky.
   3. Slowly add rivels to boiling soup by
crumbling into soup with hands while
stirring constantly. Cook about 5 minutes
and stir in hard-boiled eggs. Serve.

*R*ivel Soup
Ruth Weaver, Reinholds, PA
Cathy Rohrer, Willow Street, PA

Makes 6-8 servings

8 cups chicken broth
1 onion, diced
2 Tbsp. parsley flakes
2 cups flour
1 tsp. salt
2 eggs, beaten
1 pint whole kernel corn
2 cups diced, cooked chicken (optional)

   1. Bring broth to boil.
   2. In a bowl combine flour, salt, and
eggs until mixture is crumbly. Drop small
clumps of rivels into boiling broth. Add
corn and cook about 10 minutes.
   3. If desired, stir in diced chicken
immediately before serving.

Veal Shin Soup

Mary C. Sage
Pequea, PA

Makes 6-8 servings

Soup:
1 meaty veal shin
4 quarts water
Salt and pepper to taste
1 pint diced potatoes
1 pint diced celery
1 cup diced onions
1 cup diced carrots

Dough Balls:
1 Tbsp. margarine
1 cup flour
Pinch salt
¼ tsp. baking powder, rounded
2-3 Tbsp. water *or* more

1. Cook veal shin with water until meat is very soft. Cool, bone, and chop meat into bite-sized pieces. Set aside.

2. Strain broth. Add salt and pepper to taste. Add potatoes, celery, onions, and carrots. Cook on medium heat for about 15 minutes.

3. Meanwhile prepare dough balls by cutting margarine into sifted dry ingredients. Add just enough water to make a stiff dough. (Add water carefully to make sure dough will be stiff.) Work dough with floured hands and form into pea-sized balls.

4. When all dough balls are made, add to boiling soup and cook about 25 minutes longer.

5. Add meat, stir, and serve.

Sporting Hill

On a rise in the road from Manheim to Mount Joy, travelers encounter one of the many small residential villages typical of present-day Lancaster County. So residential that it has no restaurant, no grocery store, no gas station, and no post office, Sporting Hill is a place where people live, not where they shop or conduct business.

Jack Haas, a resident of the nearby village of Manheim, remembers the day when Sporting Hill did have its own general store and gas station. The store stocked the traditional fare of such establishments, and the station pumped gas for local folks from several old-style pumps. As they have in many small Lancaster County villages, these Sporting Hill points of interest have been swallowed up by super grocery chains and multiple-pump gas emporiums in nearby suburban strip malls. Village residents have become completely dependent on automobiles.

Other than the neatly-kept dwellings, the most interesting spots in town today are a plaque commemorating the birth of John Seybert, a Methodist circuit riding preacher, the Kauffman Cemetery on the east end of town, Sporting Hill Elementary School, and Sporting Hill Mennonite School.

Vegetable Beef Soup
Christina L. Rohrer
East Petersburg, PA

Makes 6 servings

2 lbs. beef cubes
2 Tbsp. cooking oil
4 cups water
2 carrots, diced
2 stalks celery, diced
1 small onion, chopped
1½ cups diced tomatoes
½ cup peas
½ cup corn
½ cup green beans
5 beef bouillon cubes
2 tsp. salt
½ tsp. parsley flakes
¼ tsp. oregano
¼ tsp. thyme
¼ tsp. pepper
2 bay leaves
Dash sage
3 medium potatoes, diced

1. In large Dutch oven over medium heat, brown meat in oil.
2. Add all remaining ingredients except potatoes. Cover and simmer for 1 hour.
3. Add potatoes and simmer for 1 more hour or until meat is tender. Discard bay leaves and serve.

Upstate Minestrone Soup
Sandy Huber
Holtwood, PA

Makes approximately 3 quarts

1 lb. Italian sausage
1 Tbsp. cooking oil
1 cup chopped onions
1 clove garlic, minced
1 cup sliced carrots
1 tsp. basil
2 small zucchini, sliced
1 quart fresh *or* canned tomatoes
2 10¾-oz. cans beef broth
2 cups shredded cabbage
1 tsp. salt
¼ tsp. pepper
16-oz. can Great Northern beans
¼ cup chopped fresh parsley

1. Dice sausage into small pieces in soup kettle and brown lightly in oil. Drain excess fat.
2. Add onions, garlic, carrots, and basil and cook for 5 minutes. Add zucchini, tomatoes, broth, cabbage, salt, and pepper and bring to boil.
3. Simmer for 30-40 minutes. Add beans and cook 20 minutes longer. Garnish with parsley and serve.

Hearty Minestrone
Marion Witmer
Manheim, PA

Makes 4 servings

¾ lb. link sausage
1 Tbsp. cooking oil
½ cup sliced carrots
½ cup sliced celery
10¾-oz. can beef broth
10¾-oz. can Italian tomato soup
1½ cups water
1 cup uncooked, bow-shaped pasta

1. Slice sausage into ¼-inch pieces. In soup kettle brown lightly in oil, stirring frequently. Drain any excess fat.
2. Add vegetables and cook 5 minutes, stirring often. Add broth, tomato soup, and

water and heat to boiling.

3. Stir in pasta and reduce heat to low. Simmer about 15 minutes or until pasta is done, stirring occasionally.

*M*ennonite-Style Chili
Dawn Ranck
Strasburg, PA

Makes 6 servings

1 lb. ground beef
2 medium onions, minced
16-oz. can kidney beans
1 quart home-canned tomatoes *or*
    2 16-oz. cans tomatoes
1 tsp. salt
¼ tsp. pepper
1 tsp. chili powder
Water

1. Brown ground beef and onion. Drain excess fat.

2. Add all remaining ingredients except water and simmer for 15 minutes.

3. Add water to obtain desired consistency and heat through. Serve.

*Ch*ili
Arlene Eaves
Strasburg, PA

Makes 6 servings

1 medium onion, finely chopped
1 stalk celery, finely chopped
1 Tbsp. cooking oil
1½ lbs. ground beef
16-oz. can kidney beans
20-oz. can baked beans
16-oz. can whole tomatoes, chopped
8-oz. can tomato sauce

8-oz. can tomato paste
Dash oregano
Dash garlic powder
Salt and pepper to taste
1-2 Tbsp. chili powder
Water

1. Sauté onion and celery in cooking oil. Add ground beef and brown. Drain all excess fat.

2. Add kidney beans, baked beans, tomatoes, tomato sauce, tomato paste, oregano, garlic powder, salt, and pepper. Heat through.

3. Add chili powder to desired taste. Add small amount of water and simmer about 30 minutes. (Add more water if chili seems too thick.) Serve.

*H*earty Cabbage Soup
Patti Smith
Columbia, PA

Makes 6 servings

1 lb. ground beef
½ medium head cabbage, diced
6 cups chicken stock
1 large onion, chopped
3 Tbsp. sugar
1 tsp. salt
3 peppercorns
1 bay leaf
4 allspice berries (optional)
2 Tbsp. Worcestershire sauce
2 6-oz. cans tomato paste

1. Combine all ingredients except tomato paste. Bring to a boil and simmer 1 hour. Remove peppercorns, bay leaf and allspice berries.

2. Stir in tomato paste and cook 15 minutes longer. Serve.

Cream of Crab Broccoli Soup
Rachel Pellman
Lancaster, PA

Makes 4-6 servings

8-oz. pkg. frozen Alaskan King crab, thawed
10-oz. pkg. frozen, chopped broccoli
1/2 cup chopped onion
3 Tbsp. butter
2 Tbsp. flour
2 cups milk
2 cups half-and-half
2 chicken bouillon cubes
1/2 tsp. salt
1/8 tsp. black pepper
1/8 tsp. cayenne pepper
1/8 tsp. thyme
1 Tbsp. Worcestershire sauce
4-6 Tbsp. sherry

1. Drain and slice crab. Set aside.
2. Cook broccoli according to package directions. Set aside.
3. Sauté onion in butter and blend in flour. Add milk and half-and-half and cook until thickened and smooth, stirring constantly. Dissolve bouillon cubes in hot soup.
4. Add salt, peppers, thyme, Worcestershire sauce, crab, and broccoli and heat through.
5. Pour 1-2 Tbsp. sherry into each soup bowl. Ladle soup into bowls and serve immediately.

Ham and Bean Soup with Rivels
Ginny Lausch
Akron, PA

Makes 10 servings

4 ham hocks
Water to cover
2 stalks celery, chopped
1 large onion, chopped
3 16-oz. cans Great Northern beans
2 28-oz. cans whole tomatoes
Water

Rivels:
2 cups flour
2 eggs, slightly beaten
Pinch salt and pepper

1. Cook ham hocks in water to cover until meat is very soft. Strain off broth. Add celery and onion to broth and cook until vegetables are tender. Add beans and tomatoes and simmer. Add water to desired consistency.

2. Meanwhile prepare rivels by combining flour, beaten eggs, salt, and pepper in a bowl. Rub with hands until little balls form.

3. Bring soup to a slight boil. Add rivels and keep stirring. Dice ham meat and stir into soup. Turn to low and cook 5-10 minutes longer. Serve.

Old-Fashioned Bean Soup
Miriam Stoltzfus
Ronks, PA

Makes 6-8 servings

6 strips bacon
½ cup chopped celery
½ cup chopped onion
1 medium tomato, chunked
1 cup water
41-oz. can white northern beans
2 cups milk

1. Cut bacon into small pieces.
2. In a large saucepan combine bacon, celery, onion, tomato, and water and cook until vegetables are soft. Stir in beans and milk and heat to scalding. Serve.

Lentil Soup
Ruby Bontrager
Kinzers, PA

Makes 10 servings

2 cups uncooked lentils
1 cup diced celery
1 large onion, diced
2 Tbsp. chopped, fresh parsley
2 Tbsp. cooking oil
3 quarts cold water
1 ham hock

6-oz. can tomato paste
Salt and pepper to taste

1. Wash lentils and set aside.
2. In a soup kettle sauté celery, onion, and parsley in oil until soft. Add water, ham hock, tomato paste, salt, pepper, and lentils. Bring to a boil and simmer about 2½ hours. Add more water if needed. Heat through and serve.

Fresh Tomato Soup
Sadie S. Nolt
East Earl, PA

Makes 6-8 servings

¼ cup butter
1 small onion, chopped
1 cup chopped celery
1 large carrot, grated
4½ cups chicken broth
1 quart diced fresh tomatoes
½ tsp. salt
¼ tsp. pepper
4 tsp. sugar
¼ cup flour
Water

1. Melt butter in large saucepan. Sauté onion, celery, and carrot until just softened. Add chicken broth, tomatoes, salt, pepper, and sugar and heat to boiling. Reduce heat and simmer for 15-20 minutes.
2. Blend flour with a little water and gradually stir into soup. Cook until slightly thickened, stirring frequently. Serve.

Short History of the Stevens Fire Company

On July 30, 1914 a group of men met at the Stevens Post Office to organize a local fire company. By October 29 of that year the Stevens Fire Company had obtained a charter, purchased a lot for $195, secured a Howe Fire Engine for $650, and organized an orchestra.

Today, our all-volunteer operation manages yearly fund raisers such as a carnival in August, spaghetti suppers, craft shows, and sandwich sales. We thank God for the good men and women who devote themselves to volunteer work of this type.
—*Elsie Kauffman, Stevens, PA*

Cream of Tomato Soup
Yvonne Sensenig
Akron, PA

Makes 4 servings

16-oz. can whole tomatoes with juice
½ cup chopped onion
1 Tbsp. chopped parsley
½ tsp. sugar
¼ tsp. crushed basil
⅛ tsp. pepper
2 Tbsp. butter *or* margarine
1½ Tbsp. all-purpose flour
1 cup chicken broth
½ cup milk

1. In a saucepan combine tomatoes and juice with onion, parsley, sugar, basil, and pepper. Bring to a boil and simmer for 20 minutes.
2. Pour hot mixture into a blender or food processor and blend for 30 seconds.
3. Melt butter in saucepan. Stir in broth, return to heat, and bring to a boil, stirring constantly. Add blended tomato mixture and simmer 5 minutes. Stir in milk and cook 1 minute longer.

Tomato Soup
Betty Pellman
Millersville, PA

Makes 4 servings

2 cups tomato juice
½ tsp. baking soda
1 quart milk
1 tsp. salt
Dash pepper
2 Tbsp. butter

1. Heat tomato juice in 2-quart saucepan. After juice boils, add baking soda and stir because mixture foams. Remove from heat.
2. Heat milk in 3-quart saucepan, watching carefully so it does *not* come to a boil. Add salt, pepper, and butter.
3. Stir tomato mixture into milk and serve immediately with crackers or toast.

Note: I use home-canned tomato juice with peppers, onions, and celery.

Potato Chowder
Julie Weaver
Reinholds, PA

Makes 8-10 servings

4 cups peeled, diced potatoes
½ cup finely chopped onion
1 cup grated carrots
1 tsp. salt
¼ tsp. pepper
1 Tbsp. dried parsley flakes

4 chicken bouillon cubes
Water to cover
6 cups milk
2 Tbsp. butter
½ cup flour

1. In a large Dutch oven or kettle combine potatoes, onion, carrots, salt, pepper, parsley flakes, and bouillon cubes. Add just enough water to cover vegetables.

2. Cook about 15 minutes or until vegetables are tender. Do not drain.

3. In a separate saucepan scald milk. Remove 1½ cups scalded milk from saucepan and set aside.

4. Stir butter and flour into remaining milk in saucepan and heat, stirring constantly with wire whisk.

5. Stir 1½ cups reserved milk into undrained vegetables. Immediately add milk, which has been thickened with flour, to vegetables and stir until well blended. Simmer on low heat for 15 minutes.

6. Serve hot with crackers.

*C*heesy Potato Soup
Ruth Ann Becker
Manheim, PA

Makes 10-12 servings

6 cups peeled, diced potatoes
8 ozs. prepared cheese spread
12 slices bacon
1½ cups carrots, diced
1 small onion, diced
4 Tbsp. margarine
4-6 hard-boiled eggs, chopped
2 10¾-oz. cans potato soup
6 cups milk
¼ cup bacon drippings

1. Cook potatoes until tender and drain. While potatoes are hot, put prepared cheese spread over them until cheese melts.

2. Fry bacon. Reserve ¼ cup drippings and set aside. Crumble bacon and set aside.

3. Sauté carrots and onion in margarine until softened.

4. Combine all ingredients in large soup kettle. Heat slowly and serve. (Be sure soup does not come to a boil.)

*C*heese Soup
Norma I. Martin
Lititz, PA

Makes 8 servings

1½-2 quarts water
4 chicken bouillon cubes
2½ cups diced potatoes
1 cup chopped celery
½ cup chopped onion
20-oz. pkg. frozen mixed vegetables
2 10¾-oz. cans cream of chicken soup
1 lb. Velveeta cheese, cut into chunks

1. In a heavy saucepan combine water, bouillon cubes, potatoes, celery, and onion and bring to a boil. Cook for 20 minutes or until vegetables have softened.

2. Stir in frozen vegetables, cream of chicken soup, and cheese. Cook at medium heat until cheese melts, stirring frequently. Serve.

Orange Carrot Soup
Susanne Brubaker
Lancaster, PA

Makes 4-6 servings

2 Tbsp. butter
1 lb. carrots
3 medium onions, coarsely chopped
2 garlic cloves, chopped
$\frac{1}{3}$ cup flour
4 cups chicken stock
1 tsp. sugar
Juice of 1 orange
1 cup heavy cream
Pinch cayenne pepper
Salt and pepper to taste
1 cup chopped watercress

1. Melt butter in large, heavy saucepan.
2. Cut carrots into 2-inch slices. Add carrots, onions, and garlic to saucepan and sauté 5 minutes. Add flour and stir well.
3. Gradually add chicken stock and bring to a boil, stirring constantly. Cover and simmer for about 20 minutes. Add sugar and simmer 10 minutes longer.
4. Remove from heat and purée in food processor. Return soup to saucepan and add orange juice and cream. Season with cayenne pepper, salt, and pepper. Reheat gently, but do not bring to a boil.
5. Garnish with watercress and serve.

Gazpacho
Marian E. Going
Lancaster, PA

Makes 8 servings

1 onion
1 medium yellow squash
1 medium zucchini
1 cucumber
16-oz. can chopped tomatoes
1 quart tomato juice
1 handful chopped cilantro
1 Tbsp. olive oil
1 Tbsp. balsamic vinegar

1. Chop all vegetables into bite-sized pieces. In a large bowl combine with chopped tomatoes, tomato juice, cilantro, oil, and vinegar.
2. Refrigerate at least 2 hours or overnight. Serve.

Note: I often serve this in tortilla cups garnished with black pepper.

$\mathcal{S}$alads

$\mathcal{E}$gg Salad with Chives
Esther Gingrich
Lancaster, PA

Makes 3-4 servings

6 hard-boiled eggs
¼ tsp. salt
Dash pepper
½ tsp. prepared mustard
¼ cup mayonnaise
1 Tbsp. fresh, chopped chives

1. Mash eggs with a fork. Add remaining ingredients and mix well. Chill thoroughly.
2. Serve on bread or rolls.

$\mathcal{R}$ed Beet Eggs
Jennifer Trimble
Denver, PA

Makes 24 servings

2 quarts red beets
1½ cups cider vinegar
2½ cups sugar
2 dozen hard-boiled eggs

1. In a saucepan bring beets, vinegar, and sugar to a boil. Remove from heat.
2. Peel eggs. Add eggs to beet mixture when still hot. Cool and refrigerate several hours or overnight. Serve.

Dijon Herb Chicken Salad
Sue Steffy
Leola, PA

Makes 6-8 servings

Salad:
2 cups chopped, cooked chicken
½ cup chopped celery
½ cup chopped onion
2 Tbsp. cilantro

Dressing:
2 Tbsp. Dijon mustard
4 Tbsp. red wine vinegar
¼ tsp. salt
2 cloves garlic, chopped
1 tsp. dry basil
1 tsp. dry savory
½ tsp. oregano
⅛ tsp. pepper
2 drops Tabasco
1 Tbsp. minced onion
¼ cup cooking oil
¼ cup water

1. Combine all salad ingredients in bowl.
2. Blend all dressing ingredients in blender on high. Pour over salad ingredients and mix well. Refrigerate and chill for 1 hour.

Note: Serve with lettuce on rolls, croissants, pita bread, or rye bread.

Taco Salad
June M. Charles
Lancaster, PA

Makes 10-12 servings

Salad:
1 lb. ground beef
1 head lettuce, chopped
4 medium tomatoes, chopped
1 medium cucumber, diced
1 medium bag taco chips
16-oz. can kidney beans, drained

Dressing:
1 small onion, chopped
1 tsp. salt
½ tsp. pepper
⅓ cup vinegar
1 cup cooking oil
3 tsp. dry mustard
1 tsp. celery seed
1 cup sugar

1. In large skillet brown ground beef. Drain all excess fat. Combine all salad ingredients in large bowl and mix well.
2. Combine all dressing ingredients in blender and blend until thickened.
3. Serve with dressing on the side.

Taco Salad Variation
Anna Mae Conley
Mount Joy, PA

Makes 12-16 servings

1 lb. ground beef
1 Tbsp. taco sauce
1 pkg. dry taco seasoning
1 medium head lettuce, chopped
4 tomatoes, chopped
1 medium onion, chopped
8 ozs. longhorn cheese, grated

16-oz. can kidney beans, drained
8-oz. bottle Thousand Island dressing
¼ cup sugar
1 medium pkg. taco chips *or* corn chips

1. Brown ground beef with taco sauce and taco seasoning, reserving 1 Tbsp. taco seasoning for dressing. Drain excess fat.
2. Toss together lettuce, tomatoes, onion, and cheese. Add beans.
3. To prepare dressing combine Thousand Island dressing, reserved taco seasoning, and sugar and mix well.
4. Crush taco chips. Immediately before serving, add to salad. Pour dressing over salad and toss.

*M*eat and Potato Salad
Doris Becker
Manheim, PA

Makes 6-8 servings

4 cups cubed, cooked potatoes
1½ cups sliced celery
¼ cup chopped onions
¼ cup thinly sliced radishes
3 hard-boiled eggs, chopped
1 cup mayonnaise
2 Tbsp. vinegar
2 tsp. dry mustard
½ tsp. salt
1 cup diced ham

1. Mix potatoes, celery, onions, radishes, and eggs in serving dish.
2. In a bowl combine mayonnaise, vinegar, mustard, and salt. Stir dressing into salad until lightly mixed. Cover and chill several hours or overnight.
3. Immediately before serving, fold in diced ham.

*P*otato Salad
Alberta Gehman
Terre Hill, PA

Makes 10-12 servings

Salad:
8-10 medium potatoes
1 cup celery, chopped
1 cup onion, chopped
8 hard-boiled eggs, diced

Dressing:
4 eggs
1 cup sugar
½ cup vinegar
2 Tbsp. mayonnaise
2 tsp. prepared mustard

1. Cook potatoes. When cooled, peel and dice into serving dish. Add celery, onion, and diced eggs.
2. To prepare dressing combine eggs, sugar, and vinegar in double boiler and cook until it thickens, stirring occasionally. Add mayonnaise and mustard and mix well.
3. While still warm, pour dressing over potatoes. Serve.

Churchtown

*A*long the base of the small eastern triangle of Lancaster County, intersected by Route 23, lies the quiet village of Churchtown. In the early 1700s a group of industrious Welsh settlers came to the area and became active in the iron industry. According to local lore, the Bangor Episcopal Church, established in 1732-33, once owned the town, gradually selling off lots. Consequently, the area became known as "The Church Town."

At the foot of the hill approaching the village's western edge, stands the magnificent 1770s Pool Forge Mansion. In his day, Cyrus Jacobs, the ironmaster who built the forge, had lots of company. Churchtown was the summer resort home for a group of wealthy iron barons. Local legends maintain fancily-dressed ladies accompanied by top-hatted gentlemen could often be seen promenading along Main Street from mansion to mansion.

Today, many of the mansions are being carefully maintained by people as different from each other as local Amish families and out-of-towners who have turned the dwellings into bed-and-breakfast havens, antique shops, and private homes.

The town's firehall and the Bangor Church anchor its eastern edge. Each spring and fall the firehall serves a turkey supper widely considered the best in the region. In addition to the historic Episcopal church, worshipers gather at various other local churches on Sunday morning.

*O*vernight Potato Salad

Lois Nafziger
Lancaster, PA

Makes 10 servings

Salad:
6 medium potatoes
2-3 hard-boiled eggs, diced
1 medium onion, minced
2-3 stalks celery, chopped

Dressing:
1 cup sugar
1 Tbsp. cornstarch
½ tsp. salt
⅛ tsp. pepper
½ cup water
½ cup vinegar
2 eggs, beaten
1 tsp. prepared mustard
½ cup salad dressing

1. Cook potatoes and cube them.
2. Toss together all salad ingredients. Set aside.
3. To prepare dressing combine all dry ingredients in a saucepan. Gradually add water and vinegar to make a smooth paste, stirring constantly. Add eggs and cook until thickened, stirring occasionally.
4. Remove from heat and add mustard and salad dressing. Pour hot dressing over warm potato mixture and toss.
5. Chill overnight and serve.

Old-Fashioned Potato Salad

Janice Horning
Mohnton, PA

Makes 20-24 servings

Salad:
4 lbs. potatoes
12 hard-boiled eggs, diced
⅓ cup chopped onion
2 cups chopped celery

Dressing:
3 cups salad dressing
2 cups sugar
3 Tbsp. prepared mustard
¼ cup vinegar
4 tsp. salt*Bl*orless
½ cup milk

1. Cook potatoes. When cool, peel and dice. Combine potatoes, eggs, onion, and celery in serving dish.
2. To prepare dressing combine all ingredients and mix well. Pour dressing over salad ingredients and mix lightly. Refrigerate and chill several hours or overnight. Serve.

Macaroni Salad

Janet M. Schwert, Mountville, PA
Janet Rettew, Denver, PA

Makes 15-20 servings

Salad:
1 lb. uncooked macaroni
1 cup chopped celery
1 carrot, grated
½ cup diced onion
4 hard-boiled eggs, separated

Dressing:
4 egg yolks
3 Tbsp. prepared mustard
1½ cups white sugar
1 cup salad dressing
5-oz. can evaporated milk
⅓ cup vinegar
¼ tsp. salt

1. Cook macaroni according to package directions. Drain, rinse, and cool. Stir celery, carrot, and onion into macaroni.
2. Dice whites of eggs into salad.
3. To prepare dressing mash egg yolks with mustard and blend well. Add sugar, salad dressing, milk, vinegar, and salt to egg and mustard mixture. Pour over macaroni and vegetables (mixture will appear soupy). Chill well before serving.

Variation: Add ¼ cup diced red pepper to salad ingredients.

—*Jennie Horst, Denver, PA*

Make-Ahead Macaroni Salad
Emma Reiff
Ephrata, PA

Makes 8-10 servings

Salad:
3 cups cooked macaroni
2 hard-boiled eggs, finely chopped
1 cup chopped celery
1 small onion, chopped
1 cup shredded carrots

Dressing:
1 cup sugar
½ cup vinegar
1 tsp. dry mustard
1 tsp. butter
2 eggs, beaten
⅔ cup mayonnaise

1. Combine all salad ingredients in a serving bowl and set aside.
2. To prepare dressing combine all ingredients except mayonnaise and bring to a boil. Cook for 3 minutes, stirring constantly. Cool. Add mayonnaise and stir well. Pour dressing over salad ingredients and refrigerate.

Note: This salad should be made 2 days before you want to serve it. The time for flavors to blend is very important.

Macaroni Tomato Salad
Miriam Stoltzfus
Ronks, PA

Makes 15-20 servings

Dressing:
1½ cups mayonnaise
½ cup Italian dressing
¼ cup sugar

Salad:
1 lb. uncooked macaroni
1 cup chopped celery
¼ cup chopped onion
2 medium tomatoes, chunked
½ lb. Longhorn cheese, cubed
Salt and pepper to taste
1 Tbsp. dill seed

1. Blend all dressing ingredients together and let stand while preparing salad.
2. Cook macaroni according to directions. Drain, rinse, and cool.
3. Combine all salad ingredients and mix well. Pour dressing over salad and stir to blend thoroughly. Serve.

Italian Salad
Mabel Eshleman
Landisville, PA

Makes 12 servings

Salad:
1-lb. uncooked macaroni shells
3 stalks celery, diced
3 large tomatoes, chopped
½ lb. provolone *or* mozzarella cheese, cubed
4-oz. jar green olives
16-oz. can black olives, halved
¼ lb. pepperoni, cubed (optional)

Dressing:
$\frac{1}{2}$ cup cooking oil
$\frac{2}{3}$ cup vinegar
1 Tbsp. oregano
$\frac{1}{2}$-1 Tbsp. crushed red pepper
1 tsp. black pepper
2 drops Tabasco

1. Cook macaroni shells according to directions. Drain, rinse, and set aside.
2. While macaroni shells cool, mix all dressing ingredients until thoroughly blended.
3. In large bowl combine macaroni shells, dressing, and all remaining ingredients. Refrigerate.
4. Let stand at room temperature for an hour or so before serving.

Note: This salad is best when made a day ahead of time.

Mountville Fire Company Auxiliary

In addition to catering weddings, banquets and Lion's Club dinners, our auxiliary sponsors a New Year's Dance at the beginning of each year. We usually serve our special macaroni salad (see page 41) and through the years have received many requests for the recipe.

After the dance on New Year's Eve 1992-1993, a major fire broke out in our neighboring community of Silver Spring. At three o'clock on New Year's morning, we loaded up the leftover food from the dance (including the macaroni salad) and took it to the Silver Spring Auxiliary to feed the hungry fire fighters. Everything tasted especially good to those tired, hungry men!
—*Janet M. Schwert, Mountville, PA*

End of Garden Salad
Miriam Stoltzfus
Ronks, PA

Makes 6-8 servings

6 tomatoes
$\frac{1}{2}$ cup chopped celery
$\frac{1}{2}$ cup chopped onion
1 large green pepper, chopped
1 large red pepper, chopped
$\frac{1}{2}$ cup chopped radishes
$\frac{1}{2}$ head lettuce, chopped
$\frac{1}{2}$ cup sugar
$\frac{1}{2}$ cup vinegar

1. Chunk tomatoes into serving bowl. Add celery, onions, peppers, radishes, and lettuce and mix well.
2. Mix together sugar and vinegar and stir into vegetables. Chill and serve.

Tomatoes with Dressing
Elaine Gibbel
Lititz, PA

Makes 8-10 servings

4 large tomatoes, sliced
3 Tbsp. olive oil
1 Tbsp. wine vinegar
1 tsp. salt
1 tsp. Tabasco *or less*
1 Tbsp. lemon *or lime* juice
$\frac{1}{2}$ tsp. garlic powder
1 onion, sliced (optional)
1 green pepper, sliced (optional)

1. Slice tomatoes into large serving bowl.
2. Combine all other ingredients and pour over tomatoes. Mix to distribute dressing.
3. Refrigerate about 1 hour and serve.

Spinach Salad

Julie Weaver
Reinholds, PA

Makes 6 servings

1 lb. fresh spinach
½ lb. bacon (optional)
4 Tbsp. cooking oil
2 Tbsp. sugar
2 Tbsp. vinegar
2 tsp. prepared mustard
4 hard-boiled eggs, sliced

1. Wash spinach and set aside to drain.
2. Fry, drain, and crumble bacon. Set aside.
3. In a saucepan combine cooking oil, sugar, vinegar, and mustard and heat slightly, stirring constantly.
4. Tear spinach into serving bowl. Toss dressing with spinach. Garnish with eggs and bacon, if desired. Serve immediately.

Broccoli Salad

Kimberly L. Firestone, Denver, PA
Diane K. Gehman, Stevens, PA

Makes 6-8 servings

1 large head broccoli
6-8 pieces bacon
1 medium onion, diced
½ cup grated cheddar cheese
½ cup white *or* dark raisins
½ cup chopped walnuts (optional)

Dressing:
1 cup mayonnaise
⅓ cup sugar
2 tsp. vinegar

1. Cut broccoli flowers and stalk into bite-sized pieces.
2. Fry, drain, and crumble bacon.

3. Combine all salad ingredients in serving bowl.
4. Combine all dressing ingredients in small bowl and mix well. Pour dressing over salad and mix lightly. Refrigerate several hours or overnight before serving.

Layer Salad

June M. Charles
Lancaster, PA

Makes 10-12 servings

1 head lettuce
3 medium carrots, shredded
1 medium green pepper, diced
1 small onion, diced
10-oz. pkg. frozen peas
1½ cups mayonnaise
1 lb. bacon
8 hard-boiled eggs
1 cup grated cheese
1 tsp. paprika

1. Wash and shred lettuce. Form layer of lettuce in bottom of large bowl. Add layers of carrots, green pepper, onion, and frozen peas.
2. Spread mayonnaise over vegetables.
3. Fry and drain bacon. Crumble over mayonnaise. Slice hard-boiled eggs over bacon. Sprinkle with cheese and paprika. Serve.

Kidney Bean Salad
Elsie Kauffman
Stevens, PA

Makes 6 servings

Salad:
4 hard-boiled eggs
¾ cup finely diced celery
1-2 onions, minced
2½ cups kidney beans, drained
6 leaves lettuce

Dressing:
½ tsp. salt
3 Tbsp. sugar
3 Tbsp. vinegar
2 Tbsp. cream
¼ cup mayonnaise

1. Chop eggs and combine with celery and onions. Add beans and mix well.
2. Combine all dressing ingredients and mix well. Refrigerate to chill. Blend dressing through mixed vegetables.
3. Arrange salad on individual serving dishes on bed of lettuce.

Cabbage Slaw to Freeze
Maribelle M. Steffy
Leola, PA

Makes 6-8 servings

Slaw:
1 medium head cabbage
1 large carrot
1 green pepper
1 small onion (optional)
1 tsp. salt

Dressing:
1 tsp. mustard seed
1 cup vinegar

¼ cup water
2 cups sugar
1 tsp. celery seed

1. Shred together cabbage, carrot, pepper, and onion. Add salt and let stand 1 hour.
2. Combine all dressing ingredients in a saucepan and bring to a boil. Boil 1 minute. Set aside to cool.
3. Drain cabbage well and stir in dressing. Mix thoroughly. Freeze to enjoy later.

Coleslaw
Elaine W. Good
Lititz, PA

Makes 8-10 servings

1 small to medium head cabbage
1 cup mayonnaise
½ cup sugar
½ tsp. prepared mustard
1 Tbsp. vinegar
Pinch salt
1 tsp. celery seed (optional)

1. Chop cabbage in blender and drain all juices off.
2. Combine all remaining ingredients and mix well. Stir dressing into well-drained cabbage and chill. Serve.

Confetti Coleslaw
Alice Whitman
Lititz, PA

Makes 8-10 servings

½ large head cabbage
2 Tbsp. milk
2 Tbsp. vinegar
1 heaping Tbsp. sugar
½ cup mayonnaise
½ tsp. celery seed
Salt and pepper to taste
Dash celery seed
Dash paprika

1. Shred cabbage very fine. Drain all excess juice.
2. Combine milk, vinegar, sugar, mayonnaise, ½ tsp. celery seed, salt, and pepper and mix until well blended. Stir into shredded cabbage.
3. Chill at least 2-3 hours. Immediately before serving, stir well and sprinkle with dashes celery seed and paprika.

Creamy Coleslaw
Jaci Rettew
Denver, PA

Makes 6-8 servings

1 small head cabbage, shredded
1 medium carrot, grated
½ cup white sugar
¼ cup vinegar
1 tsp. salt
½ cup evaported milk
½ cup mayonnaise

1. Combine all ingredients in serving dish and mix well.
2. Refrigerate at least 1 hour before serving.

Pickled Cabbage Salad
Miriam E. Lefever
East Petersburg, PA

Makes 1 gallon salad

2 large heads cabbage
2 Tbsp. salt *or* less
4 cups sugar
2½ cups vinegar
1½ cups water
1 Tbsp. celery seed
1 Tbsp. dry mustard
1 onion, finely chopped
2 carrots, shredded
2 cups diced celery
½ cup diced red *or* green pepper

1. Shred cabbage and work salt into cabbage. Let stand for 2 hours. Drain thoroughly.
2. In a saucepan heat sugar, vinegar, and water to boiling. Remove from heat and add spices. Refrigerate to chill.
3. Add onion, carrots, celery, and green pepper to dressing and mix well. Stir into drained cabbage and mix thoroughly.
4. Freeze or keep 3-4 weeks in refrigerator. Serve as needed.

Pepper Cabbage
Darlene Harding
Sinking Spring, PA

Makes 10-12 servings

Salad:
8 cups shredded cabbage
1 large red *or* reen pepper, diced
1 cup celery, diced
1 carrot, shredded
¼ onion, shredded
Salt to taste

Dressing:
2 cups sugar
1 cup vinegar
$\frac{1}{2}$ cup water
1 tsp. celery seed
1 tsp. mustard seed

1. Mix cabbage, pepper, celery, carrot, and onion. Sprinkle with salt and toss.
2. In a saucepan mix all dressing ingredients and bring to a boil. Boil for 1 minute. Cool until lukewarm. Pour dressing over salad and mix thoroughly.
3. Will keep in refrigerator for a long time.

Apple Salad
Kathryn M. Horst
New Holland, PA

Makes 8 servings

Salad:
8 apples, diced
2 bananas, sliced
$\frac{1}{2}$ cup chopped celery
$\frac{1}{2}$ cup raisins
$\frac{1}{4}$ cup coconut
$\frac{1}{2}$ cup chopped peanuts
$\frac{1}{2}$ cup chopped walnuts
Juice of $\frac{1}{2}$ lemon

Dressing:
$\frac{1}{4}$ cup peanut butter
$\frac{1}{4}$ cup cream
$\frac{1}{2}$ cup sugar
$\frac{1}{2}$ cup mayonnaise

1. Combine all salad ingredients in serving bowl.
2. Beat together all dressing ingredients and pour over salad ingredients, mixing well. Chill and serve.

Deluxe Applesauce Salad
Marian E. Smith
Bainbridge, PA

Makes 6-8 servings

3-oz. pkg. raspberry *or* cherry gelatin
1 cup boiling water
$1\frac{1}{2}$ cups applesauce
1 tsp. lemon juice

1. Dissolve gelatin in boiling water. Blend in applesauce and lemon juice. Pour into lightly greased mold or serving dish. Chill until firm.
2. Unmold and serve with sour cream or mayonnaise.

Fruited Slaw
Marion Witmer
Manheim, PA

Makes 9-10 servings

Slaw:
6 cups shredded cabbage
2 cups seedless grapes, halved
8-oz. can crushed pineapple, drained

Dressing:
1 cup mayonnaise
$\frac{1}{2}$ cup sugar
2 Tbsp. vinegar

1. Combine all slaw ingredients. Set aside.
2. Combine all dressing ingredients and mix well. Pour over cabbage. Refrigerate at least 1 hour before serving.

Cinnamon Apple Sauce
Rhoda Kilheffer
Manheim, PA

Makes 6 servings

¼ cup red cinnamon candies
1 cup water
3-oz. pkg. orange *or* strawberry gelatin
Dash salt
3 cups applesauce

1. Cook candies in water until they are melted. Add gelatin and dissolve. Bring mixture to a boil, add salt and applesauce, and mix well.
2. Remove from heat, pour into serving dish, and cool before serving.

Cranberry Relish
Elsie Houser
Lampeter, PA

Makes 10-12 servings

1 lb. fresh cranberries
3 large apples, cored and sliced
15¼-oz. can crushed pineapple, drained
3 oranges, peeled and diced
2 cups sugar

1. Grind together cranberries and apples in food chopper. Add all remaining ingredients and mix well.
2. Refrigerate at least 10 hours before serving.

Cranberry Salad
Eva Brubaker
East Earl, PA

Makes 8 servings

1 cup ground cranberries
1 cup sugar
¼ cup water
3-oz. pkg. cherry gelatin
1¼ cups boiling water
2 cups grated apples
1 cup crushed pineapple

1. In a saucepan combine cranberries, sugar, and ¼ cup water and heat through, stirring occasionally. Cool slightly.
2. Meanwhile dissolve cherry gelatin in boiling water. Cool slightly. Stir in cranberry mixture, apples, and pineapple. Pour into serving dish.
3. Chill until firm. Serve.

Blueberry Salad
Orpha S. Kilheffer
Lititz, PA

Makes 2 quarts

6-oz. pkg. raspberry gelatin
1 cup boiling water
21-oz. can blueberry pie filling
20-oz. can crushed pineapple
4-oz. container whipped topping
½ cup chopped nuts (optional)

1. Dissolve gelatin in boiling water. Stir in pie filling and pineapple with juice. Refrigerate until slightly thickened.
2. Fold in topping and nuts and pour into lightly greased mold. Chill until firm.
3. Unmold and serve.

Grape Juice Bavarian Salad

Jeanette Oberholtzer

Akron, PA

Makes 6 servings

3-oz. pkg. lemon gelatin
$\frac{1}{4}$ cup sugar
1 cup boiling water
1 cup grape juice
1 cup whipping cream

1. Dissolve gelatin and sugar in boiling water. Add grape juice and stir well. Refrigerate and chill until slightly thickened.
2. Whip cream until thickened and stir into slightly thickened gelatin. Pour into lightly greased mold, refrigerate, and chill until firm.
3. Unmold and serve.

Red Ruby Salad

Jean Barnes

Peach Bottom, PA

Makes 10 servings

6-oz. pkg. strawberry gelatin
2 cups hot water
2 cups cold water
8-oz. pkg. cream cheese, softened
2-3 Tbsp. lemon juice
$\frac{1}{4}$ cup orange juice
2 cups whipped topping

1. Dissolve gelatin in hot water. Add cold water and set aside until partially set.
2. Beat cream cheese and juices into gelatin.
3. Fold in whipped topping and pour into serving dish. Refrigerate to set. Serve.

Red Gelatin Salad

Darlene Rohrer-Meck

Lancaster, PA

Makes 8 servings

3-oz. pkg. lemon gelatin
12 large marshmallows
2 cups boiling water
2 cups whipped topping
8-oz. pkg. cream cheese
1 cup crushed pineapple, drained
6-oz. pkg. strawberry *or* cherry gelatin

1. Dissolve lemon gelatin and marshmallows in boiling water. Set aside to gel.
2. Cream together whipped topping and cream cheese and beat until smooth.
3. Combine lemon gelatin mixture, cream cheese mixture, and pineapple and whip with a beater. Spoon into serving dish and refrigerate to set.
4. Meanwhile prepare strawberry or cherry gelatin according to package directions. Before strawberry gelatin sets, pour over lemon gelatin mixture. Chill to set and serve.

Lemon Gelatin Salad

Dawn Ranck
Strasburg, PA

Makes 8-10 servings

Gelatin:
6-oz. pkg. lemon gelatin
1 cup boiling water
8 large marshmallows
2 bananas, sliced
1 cup crushed pineapple

Topping:
1 egg, beaten
½ cup sugar
1 cup pineapple juice
2 Tbsp. flour
2 Tbsp. butter
2 cups whipped topping

Garnish:
½ cup finely chopped nuts
Lettuce

1. Dissolve lemon gelatin and marshmallows in boiling water. Let cool.
2. Drain crushed pineapple and reserve 1 cup juice for topping.
3. Add bananas and crushed pineapple to partially set gelatin. Pour into 8-inch square pan and chill until firm.
4. To prepare topping combine all ingredients except whipped topping in saucepan and cook until thickened, stirring frequently. Cool. Fold in whipped topping. Spread over firm layer of gelatin.
5. Sprinkle with nuts, cut into squares, and serve on beds of lettuce.

Lime Gelatin Salad

Audrey Landis
Ronks, PA

Makes 8-10 servings

Layer 1:
2 3-oz. pkgs. lime gelatin
2 cups boiling water
2 cups cold water
20-oz. can crushed pineapple

Layer 2:
2 cups whipped topping
8-oz. pkg. cream cheese

Layer 3:
2 cups pineapple juice
¾ cup sugar
¼ cup flour
3 egg yolks

1. To prepare layer 1 combine gelatin with hot and cold water. Pour into large serving bowl or 9" x 13" pan. Refrigerate to set.
2. Drain pineapple, reserving juice. Arrange pineapple over lime gelatin.
3. To prepare layer 2 combine whipped topping and softened cream cheese and beat until smooth. Pour over pineapple and gelatin layers.
4. To prepare layer 3 add enough water to reserved pineapple juice to make 2 cups. In a saucepan stir together pineapple juice, sugar, flour, and egg yolks and cook until thickened, stirring occasionally. Let cool.
5. Pour topping over cream cheese layer and refrigerate to chill. Serve.

Variation: Substitute lemon gelatin for the lime gelatin in the first layer.
—*Tammy Groff, Quarryville, PA*

Gelatin Treat

Diana Russell
Holtwood, PA

Makes 6-8 servings

3-oz. pkg. lime gelatin
1 cup boiling water
8-oz. can diced pineapple
1½ cups chopped walnuts
1 banana, sliced
1 apple, diced
11-oz. can mandarin oranges, diced
1 cup pineapple syrup

1. Dissolve gelatin in boiling water.
2. Drain pineapples, reserving juice. Add enough water to make 1 cup liquid.
3. Combine all ingredients and pour into serving dish. Chill until firm. Serve.

Lemon Orange Gelatin Delight

Susan H. King
Lancaster, PA

Makes 10-12 servings

3-oz. pkg. orange gelatin
3-oz. pkg. lemon gelatin
2 cups hot water
15-oz. can mandarin oranges
20-oz. can crushed pineapple
21-oz. can lemon pie filling

1. Dissolve gelatins in hot water. Cool.
2. Drain oranges and pineapple. Add enough water to juices to make 1 cup. Stir into gelatin. Add lemon pie filling and blend with whisk until smooth. Fold in orange slices and pineapple.
3. Pour into lightly greased, large mold and chill until firm. Unmold and serve.

Orange Salad

Carolyn Espigh
Terre Hill, PA

Makes 8-10 servings

2 3-oz. pkgs. orange gelatin
1 cup hot water
8-oz. pkg. cream cheese, softened
15¼-oz. can crushed pineapple, drained
11-oz. can mandarin oranges with juice
14-oz. bottle orange soda

1. Dissolve gelatin in hot water.
2. Beat cream cheese until smooth. Stir cream cheese, pineapple, mandarin oranges with juice, and orange soda into gelatin. Pour into serving dish.
3. Refrigerate until gelatin sets. Serve.

Variation: Substitute 1 cup miniature marshmallows for cream cheese. Melt marshmallows with gelatin and hot water. Do not drain pineapple. Substitute 1 pint orange sherbet for orange soda. Immediately before pouring into serving dish, fold in 4-oz. carton whipped topping. Continue with step 3.
—Mary Louise Kurtz, Ephrata, PA

Manheim

$\mathcal{A}$long the busy Route 72 corridor from the Pennsylvania Turnpike to the city of Lancaster lies one of Lancaster County's oldest towns. Founded in 1762 by the famed glass merchant, Henry William Stiegel, the borough of Manheim is home to some 5000 people.

According to Manheim historian, John Kendig, Stiegel's extravagant lifestyle was the talk of the town in the 1700s. Legend claims he would shoot off a small cannon when he was several miles from town, signaling his private band to gather on the balcony of his home and serenade his arrival. Kendig remarked, "He lived like a baron."

Today, the former residence of Baron Stiegel, as he preferred to be called, houses a Subway Shop on the east side of Market Square. The square is at the center of town, intersecting with Route 72. From the Evangelical Congregational Church on its west side to the municipal offices on its east side, private homes on the square mingle with businesses as different from each other as Jacob Ruhl Insurance Brokers and an aging Italian pizzeria. Free parking lines the middle of the street, inviting the casual visitor to stay awhile.

A burg of churches and homes, where only an occasional corner grocery store or restaurant survive, one of Manheim's main dining attractions today is the Cat's Meow, an American-style gourmet restaurant near the railroad tracks on the south side of town.

About 150 years after Henry William Stiegel, Manheim also was home to a person of quite different talents. According to Kendig, "With the exception of Stiegel, Jack Fasig is Manheim's most legendary character." Sometimes called "the monster of Manheim," Fasig lived in a dirt-floor shack on the northern edge of town. About seven feet tall and strong as an ox, he was known as a small-time professional boxer who had made some money at the sport, only to squander it in later life. People remember seeing him carry hundred-pound sacks of feed under each arm from the feed mill on the south side of town to his home on the north side. Others tell stories of him lifting cars out of ditches or lifting horses off their feet.

$\mathcal{G}$inger Ale Salad
Gladys A. Zimmerman
Ephrata, PA

Makes 8 servings

Salad:
2 envelopes plain gelatin
2 Tbsp. cold water
1 cup hot water
$\frac{3}{4}$ cup sugar
Juice of 1 lemon
1 pint ginger ale
15$\frac{1}{4}$-oz. can diced pineapple, drained
1 cup red grapes, halved

Dressing:
2 Tbsp. flour
$\frac{1}{2}$ cup sugar
2 eggs, well beaten
1$\frac{1}{2}$ Tbsp. melted butter
Juice from pineapple
1 cup whipped topping

1. Dissolve gelatin in cold water. Add hot water and stir well.
2. Add sugar, lemon juice, and ginger ale. Chill until partially set.
3. Stir in pineapples and grapes and mix well. Pour into lightly greased mold.
4. To prepare dressing combine flour and sugar in a saucepan and mix well. Add

eggs, butter, and pineapple juice. Cook until thickened, stirring occasionally. Cool and fold in whipped topping.

5. Spoon dressing over gelatin in mold. Refrigerate to chill completely. Serve.

Seven-Up Salad
Marian E. Smith
Bainbridge, PA

Makes 6 servings

3-oz. pkg. lime gelatin
8-oz. pkg. cream cheese, softened
1 cup hot water
¼ cup sugar
1 cup 7-Up
1 tsp. vanilla
8-oz. can crushed pineapple, drained
1 cup chopped walnuts (optional)

1. Beat together gelatin, cream cheese, water, and sugar until creamy. Cool slightly and add 7-Up and vanilla. Chill until partially set.

2. Stir in pineapple and walnuts. Pour into mold or serving dish. Chill until firm and serve.

Yum Yum Salad
Elsie Stoltzfus
Gap, PA

Makes 10-12 servings

12-oz. can evaporated milk
15¼-oz. can crushed pineapple with
    juice
½ cup sugar
3-oz. pkg. strawberry gelatin
8-oz. pkg. cream cheese

1. Chill milk overnight.

2. In a saucepan combine pineapple with juice and sugar. Bring to a slow boil and cook for 5 minutes. Add gelatin and stir until dissolved. Let cool.

3. Beat chilled milk with cream cheese until smooth and fluffy. Fold into pineapple and gelatin mixture. Pour into mold and chill until firm. Serve.

Carrot and Pineapple Salad
Ethel M. Brendle
Lititz, PA

Makes 4-6 servings

3-oz. pkg. orange gelatin
1 cup pineapple juice
1 cup boiling water
1 cup crushed pineapple
1½ cups grated carrots
½ cup chopped nuts (optional)
4-6 lettuce leaves
½ cup mayonnaise

1. Dissolve gelatin in hot water. Add pineapple juice. Chill in refrigerator until partially set.

2. Add pineapple, carrots, and nuts. Pour mixture into a mold or dish and chill until set.

3. Serve on bed of lettuce with dollop of mayonnaise.

The Long-Horned Steer of Lititz

When I was about ten years old, a local farmer bought some long-horned steer from out West. When they were unloaded at his farm, one steer escaped and ran wild in the area just west of Lititz. It hid in the corn during the day. At night it sought out watering troughs such as the one on our farm.

Whenever it started to get dark, I always felt great fear about going outside to do an errand. After repeated efforts to catch the steer, the owner finally agreed to shoot the animal because it was so impossible to corner. I remember feeling sorry but also feeling great relief that the long-horned steer was finally gone.

—*Millie Eisemann, Ephrata, PA*

Carrot Relish Salad
Ida E. Winters
Lititz, PA

Makes 8 servings

3-oz. pkg. orange gelatin
¼ cup sugar
1½ cups boiling water
8-oz. pkg. cream cheese, softened
½ cup orange juice
1 cup shredded carrots
1 cup chopped apples

1. Dissolve gelatin and sugar in boiling water. Add softened cream cheese and beat smooth with mixer or blender. Stir in orange juice. Chill until partially set.
2. Add carrots and apples and pour into serving dish. Chill until firm and serve.

Strawberry Pretzel Salad
Marlene Weaver
Ephrata, PA

Makes 12-15 servings

2 cups crushed pretzels
¾ cup melted butter
8-oz. pkg. cream cheese
12-oz. container whipped topping
6-oz. pkg. strawberry gelatin
1 cup boiling water
1 pint fresh strawberries, sliced
20-oz. can crushed pineapple

1. Combine crushed pretzels and melted butter and press into 9" x 13" baking pan.
2. Bake at 400° for 7 minutes. Set aside to cool.
3. Meanwhile, cream together cream cheese and whipped topping. Spread over cooled crust and chill.
4. Dissolve gelatin in boiling water. Add strawberries and pineapple and chill until almost set but still pourable.
5. Pour over cream cheese mixture and chill until set. Serve.

Vegetables

Creamed Cabbage

Gladys Stoesz
Akron, PA

Makes 8 servings

1 head cabbage
Salt and pepper to taste
1 Tbsp. butter
¼ cup water
1 egg, beaten
1 Tbsp. flour
3 tsp. sugar
1 cup cream
½ cup vinegar

1. Cut cabbage into fine pieces. In a saucepan combine cabbage, salt, pepper, butter, and water and steam until tender.
2. Meanwhile combine egg, flour, sugar, and cream. Pour over cabbage and bring to a boil. Add vinegar and remove from heat immediately. Serve.

Baked Cabbage

Gina Burkhart
Landisville, PA

Makes 6 servings

1 medium head cabbage, chopped
1 Tbsp. sugar
2 Tbsp. flour
1 cup condensed milk
Salt and pepper to taste
6 strips bacon

1. Combine all ingredients except bacon and spoon into greased casserole dish. Spread bacon strips over cabbage.
2. Cover and bake at 350° for 40 minutes. Uncover and bake 10 minutes longer.

Scalloped Cabbage
Jean R. Ressel
Quarryville, PA

Makes 8-10 servings

1 head cabbage, shredded
1 cup grated cheese
10¾-oz. can cream of celery soup
Buttered bread crumbs

1. Cook cabbage in boiling water about 8-10 minutes. Drain.
2. In a greased casserole dish, alternate layers of cabbage and grated cheese. Pour soup over all. Top with buttered crumbs.
3. Bake at 400° for 30 minutes or until bubbly and brown.

Cabbage, Carrots, and Onions
Betty Pellman
Millersville, PA

Makes 4 servings

½ medium head cabbage
2 carrots, thinly sliced
1 large onion, thinly sliced
4 Tbsp. margarine

1. Slice cabbage thinly into 3-quart kettle. Layer with carrots and onions. Add margarine.
2. Cover tightly and steam about 20 minutes or until tender.

Note: If using a heavy kettle, water clinging to vegetables after washing them will be sufficient for steaming. If not, add small amount of water.

Zucchini Cakes
Julia Mowrer
Quarryville, PA

Makes 6-8 servings

2½ cups grated zucchini
1 egg, beaten
1 Tbsp. butter, melted
2 cups bread crumbs
1½ tsp. Old Bay seasoning
1 tsp. prepared mustard
1 Tbsp. minced onion
1 tsp. dried parsley
Cooking oil

1. Combine zucchini, egg, and melted butter. Add 1 cup bread crumbs, seasoning, mustard, onion, and parsley and mix well.
2. Form into cakes and roll into remaining bread crumbs.
3. Chill for 24 hours.
4. Fry in cooking oil until browned on both sides.

Veggie Casserole
Helen Stoltzfus
Gap, PA

Makes 6-8 servings

16-oz. pkg. frozen broccoli, carrots, and cauliflower
10¾-oz. can cream of mushroom soup
1 cup grated cheese
⅓ cup sour cream
1 small can French Fried onions
Pepper to taste

1. Combine vegetables, soup, ½ cup cheese, sour cream, and ½ can French Fried onions and spoon into casserole dish.

2. Bake at 350° for 40 minutes. Top with remaining cheese and remaining ½ can onions. Return to oven for 5-10 minutes until cheese melts.

Broccoli Casserole
Verna Douts
Quarryville, PA

Makes 6-8 servings

2 10-oz. pkgs. frozen broccoli
10¾-oz. can cream of mushroom soup
2 eggs, slightly beaten
⅔ cup mayonnaise
1 cup grated cheese
1 Tbsp. minced onion

1. Cook broccoli according to directions. Drain.
2. Combine broccoli, mushroom soup, eggs, mayonnaise, cheese, and onion. Spoon into greased casserole dish.
3. Bake at 350° for 30 minutes.

Broccoli Puff
Sandi Crills
Akron, PA

Makes 6 servings

2 10-oz. pkgs. frozen chopped broccoli
1 cup biscuit mix
1 cup milk
2 eggs
½ tsp. salt
1 cup shredded cheddar cheese

1. Cook broccoli according to package directions and drain.
2. Beat together biscuit mix, milk, egg, and salt until smooth.
3. Stir in broccoli and cheese and spoon into greased casserole dish.
4. Bake at 350° for about 50-60 minutes or until knife inserted into center comes out clean.

Mascot

Surrounded by Amish farms, the tiny mill crossroads of Mascot stands at the corner of Stumptown Road and Newport Road in Upper Leacock Township. There along Mill Creek, Jacob Becker built a water-powered flour mill in 1760. About 70 years later in 1835 a general store was established on the hill above the mill. The corner became known as Groff's Store, which it remained until the 1890s.

According to local legend, the owner of the mill in the 1890s, Jacob Ressler, spent his honeymoon in New York City where he and his bride attended a stage play. One of the play's characters was a small dog named Mascot. When the Resslers returned to Groff's Store and the mill operation, they petitioned the postmaster general to set up a post office in their mill. The general requested a short and different name, and the Resslers settled on Mascot.

Today the 230-year-old stone mill, with its adjoining house and barn, welcomes visitors during the summer months. Pleasant, well-informed guides turn on the water-powered rollers installed at the mill in 1906 and demonstrate how corn and wheat were ground for local Amish farmers. During the winter months, the mill closes to the public and local Amish farmers again bring in their corn and wheat to be ground into cornmeal and flour.

Carrot Delight

Rhoda H. Lind, Lititz, PA
Esther W. Sensenig, New Holland, PA

Makes 6-8 servings

4 cups sliced carrots
1 medium onion, chopped
3 Tbsp. butter
10¾-oz. can cream of celery soup
½ tsp. salt
⅛ tsp. pepper
1 cup grated sharp cheese
1 cup bread crumbs
⅓ cup butter, melted

1. Cook carrots until just tender. Drain.
2. Sauté onion in 3 Tbsp. butter.
3. In a bowl combine celery soup, salt, pepper, and cheese. Fold in carrots and onion and mix well. Spoon into greased baking dish.
4. Sprinkle bread crumbs and melted butter over carrot mixture.
5. Bake at 350° for 20 minutes or until hot and bubbly.

Baked Corn

Mary E. Kunkel, Lancaster, PA
Kimberly L. Firestone, Denver, PA
Jane L. Creamer, Lancaster, PA
Catherine Shirk, Ephrata, PA

Makes 6-8 servings

2 cups fresh *or* frozen corn
2 eggs
1 cup milk
2 Tbsp. sugar
1 tsp. salt
2 Tbsp. melted butter *or* margarine
1 Tbsp. flour
¼ tsp. baking powder

1. Put all ingredients in a blender and mix well. Spoon into greased 2-quart casserole dish.
2. Bake at 375° for 1 hour.

Corn Fritters

Joanne Gestewitz
Akron, PA

Makes 4-6 servings

3 large eggs, separated
1½ cups fresh *or* canned corn
½ cup all-purpose flour
½ tsp. salt
Pepper to taste
Cooking oil

1. In a large bowl beat egg yolks until light yellow. Add the corn, flour, salt, and pepper.
2. In another large bowl, using a hand-held electric mixer set at medium-high speed, beat the egg whites until they just start to form stiff peaks. Using a rubber spatula, fold one-third of the beaten egg whites into the corn mixture to lighten it. Fold in the remaining egg whites.
3. Heat oil to 375° in a deep-fat fryer or heavy saucepan. Drop the batter by tablespoonsful into the oil, 5-6 at a time.
4. Turn fritters occasionally so they brown evenly. Using a slatted spoon, remove fritters to several layers of paper towels to drain. Keep warm in a 250° oven until ready to serve.

Making Apple Butter

I remember as a young girl we often made apple butter. The evening before we always invited the neighbors to come and help peel the twenty-some bushels of apples. About four o'clock in the morning, someone had to get up and light the fire in the large fireplace. We would combine cider and water in a large copper kettle and cook the liquid down until it thickened somewhat. Then we poured in the apples and sugar. I remember pushing the long, round pole back and forth to stir the apple butter. We took turns stirring until about three o'clock in the afternoon when the apple butter was put into crocks. We sealed them tightly with waxed paper and stored them in the attic. In those crocks, our apple butter kept as long as two to three years.

—Janice Horning, Mohnton, PA

Scalloped Eggplant
Sandy Shaub
Lancaster, PA

Makes 4-5 servings

2 cups peeled, cubed eggplant
$^1/_2$ cup water
$^1/_2$ cup coarse graham cracker crumbs
4 Tbsp. minced onion
3 ozs. cheddar cheese, shredded
1 egg, beaten
$^1/_2$ cup milk
2 Tbsp. butter

1. In a saucepan cook eggplant with water about 8 minutes or until tender. Drain.
2. In a greased casserole dish layer 1 cup cooked eggplant, $^1/_4$ cup graham cracker crumbs, 2 Tbsp. onion, and $1^1/_2$ ozs. cheese.

Repeat with remaining eggplant, onion, and cheese.
3. In a bowl combine egg and milk. Pour over layered ingredients. Dot with butter. Sprinkle with remaining cracker crumbs.
4. Bake at 350° for 30 minutes.

Eggplant Supreme
Twila D. Wallace
New Holland, PA

Makes 4 servings

$^1/_2$ large eggplant, cubed
4 Tbsp. butter
16-oz. can tomatoes
Dash oregano
1 bay leaf
Salt and pepper to taste
$^1/_2$ onion, sliced
$^1/_2$-1 cup grated cheese
$^1/_2$-1 cup bread crumbs

1. Sauté eggplant in butter for about 5 minutes.
2. In a saucepan combine tomatoes, oregano, bay leaf, salt, and pepper and simmer for 15 minutes. Remove bay leaf.
3. Layer eggplant and onion in a greased casserole dish. Pour tomato sauce mixture over top of eggplant and onion. Sprinkle with desired amount cheese and bread crumbs.
4. Bake at 375° for 35 minutes.

Eggplant Patties
Jo Zimmerman
New Holland, PA

Makes 4 servings

1 medium eggplant, peeled and cubed
20 Ritz crackers, crushed
1¼ cups grated sharp cheddar cheese
2 eggs, lightly beaten
2 Tbsp. snipped parsley
2 Tbsp. sliced green onion
1 clove garlic, minced
½ tsp. salt
⅛ tsp. pepper
2 Tbsp. cooking oil *or* more

1. In covered saucepan cook eggplant in boiling water about 5 minutes or until tender. Drain very well and mash. Stir in cracker crumbs, cheese, eggs, parsley, onion, garlic, salt, and pepper and mix well.
2. Shape into 8 patties about 3 inches in diameter. Heat oil in frying pan. Cook eggplant patties 3 minutes on each side or until golden brown.

Note: Use non-stick frying pan or add more cooking oil if needed.

Cooked Celery
Susan Stoltzfus
Gap, PA

Makes 4 servings

1 quart diced celery
¼ cup sugar
¼ cup water
1½ Tbsp. vinegar
½ tsp. salt
1 Tbsp. butter
12-oz. can evaporated milk
½ cup sugar
1½ Tbsp. flour

1. Combine celery, ¼ cup sugar, water, vinegar, salt, and butter in a saucepan. Cook until celery has softened.
2. Mix together milk, ½ cup sugar, and flour. Stir into cooked celery and heat through, stirring frequently. Do not bring to a boil. Serve.

Note: This traditional Lancaster County Amish dish is usually served for one of the meals at an Amish wedding.

Asparagus Stir-Fry
Marilyn E. Weaver
New Holland, PA

Makes 6 servings

1 lb. fresh asparagus
1 Tbsp. cold water
1 tsp. cornstarch
2 tsp. soy sauce
¼ tsp. salt
1 Tbsp. cooking oil
4 green onions, diced
1½ cups sliced fresh mushrooms
2 small tomatoes, cut in thin wedges

1. Slice the asparagus crosswise into 1-inch lengths.
2. In a small bowl blend water into cornstarch. Stir in soy sauce and salt. Set aside.
3. Preheat a wok or large, heavy skillet over high heat a few minutes; add cooking oil and heat about a minute more. Stir-fry asparagus, onions, mushrooms, and tomatoes to desired tenderness.
4. Push vegetables to sides of wok or skillet and pour cornstarch mixture into

center. Heat until mixture bubbles slightly and stir into vegetables. Cook until mixture thickens, stirring frequently.

5. Serve at once with cooked rice, if desired.

Mushroom Pilaf
Anne H. Strickler
Lititz, PA

Makes 6-8 servings

2 Tbsp. margarine
2 cups sliced mushrooms
$\frac{1}{2}$ cup chopped onion
2 cloves garlic, crushed
2 Tbsp. chopped parsley
1 tsp. basil leaves, crushed
$\frac{1}{2}$ tsp. salt
$\frac{1}{8}$ tsp. pepper
$\frac{2}{3}$ cup uncooked rice
$1\frac{1}{3}$ cups water
$\frac{1}{3}$ cup chopped almonds

1. In a saucepan sauté mushrooms, onion, garlic, parsley, basil, salt, and pepper in margarine for about 5 minutes, stirring frequently.

2. Stir in rice and water and bring to a boil over high heat. Cover, reduce heat, and simmer until liquid is absorbed, about 25 minutes. Do not peek.

3. Stir in almonds and serve.

Three Bean Mix
Tina Snyder, Manheim, PA
Diana Russell, Holtwood, PA
Phyllis Gamber, Lancaster, PA

Makes 6 servings

8 strips bacon
2 large onions
$1\frac{1}{2}$ tsp. garlic powder
1 tsp. dry mustard
$\frac{1}{2}$ cup brown sugar
$\frac{1}{4}$ cup vinegar
16-oz. can kidney beans, drained
16-oz. can baked beans
16-oz. can lima beans, drained

1. Fry, drain, and crumble bacon. Set aside.

2. Slice onions into rings. In large skillet combine onion rings, garlic powder, mustard, brown sugar, and vinegar. Cover and cook over medium heat for 20 minutes.

3. Combine beans in 3-quart casserole dish. Stir in bacon pieces and onion ring mixture.

4. Cover and bake at 350° for 45 minutes.

Strasburg

About six miles southeast of Lancaster City, the village of Strasburg with its graciously restored homes welcomes visitors. Where Main Street meets Decatur Street, locals and tourists alike gather on summer evenings to watch the Strasburg Creamery employees dish up various flavors of ice cream on homemade waffle cones. Many other small businesses, such as a vintage baseball card shop, an herb shop, a video store, a bakery, and an aging pizza place, fan out from the square.

On the east end of town, the Strasburg Railroad runs regular trains through the nearby Amish countryside. The track from Strasburg to Paradise, built in the 1830s to connect the growing village with the Main Line of the Pennsylvania Railroad, now carries passengers roundtrip in authentically restored railroad cars pulled by steam-powered engines. Across Route 741 from the station, the Railroad Museum of Pennsylvania preserves railroad artifacts and lore. The Toy Train Museum, along a nearby country road, and the Choo Choo Barn, a half mile west of the station along 741, feature toy train layouts complete with scenery, buildings, people, and animals.

West of town lies Village Greens Miniature Golf Course. With its towering trees, meandering waterways, and fourteen thousand bedding plants, this magnificent spot attracts serious miniature golfers and families looking for fun, as well as gardeners and plant lovers.

Each year at Christmas, residents, churches, and businesses join to make Strasburg one of the most festive spots in Lancaster County. People wait for hours to attend the oldest, consecutively held Christmas pageant in the County at Wesley United Methodist Church. They line up in droves to walk through the Village Greens display with its more than 50,000 lights, life-sized figures of reindeer, sleds, and skaters, and a Nativity complete with a stable, corral, and live animals. They hop aboard the special "Ride the Rails with Santa" on the Strasburg Railroad. Or they may only drive through the village to admire the many ways residents decorate their historic and contemporary homes.

Baked Pork and Beans

Catherine Zimmerman
Ephrata, PA

Makes 8-10 servings

1 lb. Great Northern beans
1 tsp. salt
½ tsp. baking soda
½ lb. bacon
1 small onion, minced
2 Tbsp. molasses
½ cup brown sugar
½ cup ketchup

1. Rinse and sort beans. Cover with 3 inches water and soak overnight. In the morning add salt and baking soda and bring beans to a boil. Cook for ½ hour or until tender. Add more water if needed.

2. Fry, drain, and crumble bacon.

3. Pour beans into 2-quart casserole dish, add remaining ingredients, and stir well. If desired, add bacon drippings for additional flavoring.

4. Cover and bake at 350° for 1½-2 hours.

Home Baked Beans
Tammy Foltz
Mountville, PA

Makes 8 servings

½ lb. bacon, drained
40-oz. can white beans, drained
1 cup sugar *or* less
1 Tbsp. prepared mustard
3 Tbsp. molasses
Salt and pepper to taste

1. Fry, drain, and crumble bacon.
2. Combine all ingredients in a casserole dish and mix well.
3. Bake at 350° for 1 hour.

Super Duper Beans
Sandy Huber
Holtwood, PA

Makes 12-15 servings

½ lb. bacon
1½ lbs. ground meat *or* less
1 cup chopped onions
5 16-oz. cans pork and beans
1 cup lentils
3 cups frozen green beans
1½ cups frozen lima beans
1½ cups ketchup
1 cup brown sugar

1. Fry, drain, and crumble bacon.
2. In same skillet brown ground meat and onions.
3. In a saucepan cook lentils, green beans, and lima beans until tender. Add these beans and all remaining ingredients to meat mixture and simmer 1 hour. Serve.

Using Our Green Tomatoes

My husband was a master gardener. When fall came each year, he always had lots of green tomatoes hanging on the vines. We learned to enjoy various ways of using green tomatoes, including relishes and sandwich spreads as well as the Green Tomato Pie on page 122.
—*Anna N. Buckwalter, Ronks, PA*

Hobo Beans
Colette Carrow
Akron, PA

Makes 12-15 servings

½ lb. ground meat
1 small onion, chopped
½ lb. bacon
16-oz. can kidney beans, drained
16-oz. can pork and beans
16-oz. can butter beans, drained
1 cup ketchup
1 cup brown sugar
1 Tbsp. prepared mustard
1 Tbsp. vinegar

1. Brown ground meat with chopped onion and drain all excess fat.
2. Fry, drain, and crumble bacon.
3. Spoon ground meat and bacon into 9" x 13" baking pan. Stir in all beans. Add ketchup, brown sugar, mustard, and vinegar and mix well.
4. Bake, uncovered, at 350° for 1 hour.

Dream Street Scalloped Potatoes

Alice Whitman
Lititz, PA

Makes 4-6 servings

6 medium-large boiled potatoes, sliced
1 tsp. salt
1 Tbsp. butter
2 hard-boiled eggs, sliced
1 cup sour cream
1 cup chopped ham
½ cup milk
1 cup buttered bread crumbs

1. Arrange ½ of potato slices in greased casserole dish. Season lightly with salt and dabs of butter. Cover with egg slices. Spread ½ of sour cream over eggs. Add remaining potatoes and cover with ham.

2. Mix remaining sour cream with milk and pour over casserole ingredients. Top with buttered bread crumbs.

3. Bake at 350° for 30 minutes or until top has browned.

Scalloped Potatoes

Margaret G. Layton, New Holland, PA
Jennie Horst, Denver, PA
Rose Scantling, Ephrata, PA

Makes 4-6 servings

6 medium potatoes
1 medium onion, diced
1 tsp. celery seed
3 Tbsp. butter
2 Tbsp. flour
1 tsp. salt
⅛ tsp. pepper
1¾ cups milk

1. Peel and slice a layer of potatoes into casserole dish and sprinkle with onion and celery seed. Continue this pattern until casserole is full.

2. Melt butter in skillet. Add flour, salt, and pepper and cook until bubbly, stirring constantly. Blend in milk and bring to a boil, stirring constantly. Pour white sauce over potatoes.

3. Bake at 350° for 1 hour.

Confetti Scalloped Potatoes

Julia S. Horst
Gordonville, PA

Makes 6-8 servings

½ cup butter *or* margarine
½ cup chopped onion
16-oz. pkg. frozen hash browns
10¾-oz. can mushroom soup
1 soup can milk
1 cup shredded cheddar cheese
1 small green pepper, chopped
2 Tbsp. chopped pimento
Dash pepper
1 cup crushed cheese crackers

1. In a skillet melt butter over medium heat. Sauté onion until tender. Stir in hash browns, mushroom soup, and milk and mix well. Add cheese, green pepper, pimento, pepper, and ½ cup crushed crackers.

2. Spoon into shallow casserole dish. Top with remaining ½ cup crushed crackers.

3. Bake at 375° for 35-40 minutes.

Potatoes Au Gratin

Denise Martin, Lancaster, PA
Esther W. Sensenig, New Holland, PA

Makes 6 servings

6 medium potatoes
¼ cup diced onions
¼ cup diced red peppers (optional)
¼ cup butter
1 tsp. dry mustard
1 tsp. salt
¼ tsp. pepper
¼ cup milk
¼ lb. yellow American cheese, cubed

1. Cook and grate potatoes. Arrange in greased casserole dish.
2. Sauté onions and red peppers in butter. Add all other ingredients and heat until cheese melts, stirring constantly. Pour over potatoes.
3. Bake at 350° for 45 minutes.

Refrigerator Mashed Potatoes

Maribelle M. Steffy, Leola, PA
Louise Weaver, Denver, PA
Jennifer Martin, Stevens, PA

Makes 8 servings

9 large potatoes
2 3-oz. pkgs. cream cheese
1 cup sour cream
2 tsp. onion salt *or* seasoned salt
¼ tsp. pepper
4 Tbsp. butter

1. Peel and cook potatoes until tender. Drain and mash. Add cream cheese, sour cream, salt, pepper, and 2 Tbsp. butter and beat until light and fluffy. Cool and refrigerate. This recipe will keep in refrigerator up to 10 days.

2. To prepare place desired amount potato mixture in greased casserole dish.
3. In a skillet brown 2 Tbsp. butter. Smooth potato mixture into a mound with table knife or spatula. Make indentation in center and add browned butter, allowing to run down ridges.
4. Bake at 350° for 30 minutes.

Variation: I add 1 cup milk to the potatoes when I mash them.
—Edna Smucker, New Holland, PA

Potato and Cheese Bake

Wanda Eby
Denver, PA

Makes 4 servings

4 medium potatoes
1 clove garlic, minced
½ cup thinly sliced green onion
2 Tbsp. butter *or* margarine
4 ozs. cream cheese, softened
½ cup half-and-half
¾ tsp. salt
¼ tsp. pepper
8 ozs. cold Brie *or* Camembert cheese

1. Peel potatoes and dice into 1-inch cubes. Cook in boiling, salted water for 15 minutes or until tender. Drain well.
2. Meanwhile sauté garlic and green onion in butter for 2 minutes or until softened.
3. Mash potatoes. Beat in garlic butter mixture, cream cheese, half-and-half, salt, and pepper and mix well.
4. Remove rind from Brie or Camembert and dice into ½-inch pieces. Fold into mashed potato mixture. Spoon into 1½-quart casserole dish.
5. Bake at 450° for 15 minutes or until top begins to lightly brown. Serve at once.

Gourmet Potatoes

Debra McComsey, Christiana, PA
Norma I. Martin, Lititz, PA

Makes 8-10 servings

8-10 medium potatoes
¼ cup butter
⅓ cup chopped onion
2 cups grated cheddar cheese
1½ cups sour cream
1 tsp. salt (optional)
¼ tsp. pepper
2 Tbsp. butter
4 slices bacon
Paprika

1. Cook potatoes in skins. Cool, peel, and shred coarsely.
2. In saucepan over low heat sauté onion with ¼ cup butter for 8-10 minutes. Do not brown. Add cheese and cook until almost melted, stirring constantly. Remove from heat and blend in sour cream, salt, and pepper.
3. Fold in potatoes and turn into greased 9" x 13" baking pan. Dot with 2 Tbsp. butter.
4. Fry, drain, and crumble bacon. Sprinkle bacon and paprika over potato mixture.
5. Bake at 350° for 25 minutes or until heated through.

Note: This recipe may be prepared ahead and refrigerated or frozen.

Holiday Potatoes

Donella King
Cochranville, PA

Makes 12 servings

12 medium potatoes
1 cup onion, chopped
4 Tbsp. margarine
10¾-oz. can cream of celery soup
1 pint sour cream
1 tsp. salt
1½ cups grated cheddar cheese
3 Tbsp. butter, melted
½ cup crushed cornflakes

1. Cook potatoes. Cool, peel, and shred into bowl.
2. Sauté onion with margarine. Remove from heat and stir in soup, sour cream, and salt. Pour over potatoes and mix well.
3. Fold in cheese. Turn into greased 9" x 13" baking dish. Cover and refrigerate overnight.
4. Melt butter and stir in cornflakes. Sprinkle over potato mixture.
5. Bake at 350° for 1 hour.

Potato Surprise

Phyllis Gamber
Lancaster, PA

Makes 2-4 servings

4 medium potatoes, sliced
5 strips bacon
1 medium onion, sliced
½ cup grated cheese
Salt and pepper to taste
2 Tbsp. butter *or* margarine

1. Arrange sliced potatoes on large piece of aluminum foil.

2. Fry, drain, and crumble bacon.

3. Arrange bacon and onion slices over potatoes. Spread cheese over top and season to taste. Dot with butter. Wrap foil to seal.

4. Bake at 350° for 1 hour.

Crusty Baked Potatoes
Joyce Eby
Denver, PA

Makes 6 servings

6 small *or* medium potatoes
4 Tbsp. melted butter
½ cup cracker crumbs
1 tsp. salt *or* other seasoning

1. Peel potatoes. Slice into halves or quarters.

2. Roll potato slices in melted butter.

3. Combine cracker crumbs and seasoning and roll potatoes in mixture. Arrange in greased casserole or baking pan.

4. Bake at 350° for 1 hour.

Cheddar-Baked Potato Slices
Joanne Gestewitz
Akron, PA

Makes 6-8 servings

10¾-oz can cream of mushroom soup
½ tsp. paprika
½ tsp. pepper
4 medium potatoes
1 cup shredded cheddar cheese

1. Combine soup, paprika, and pepper in small bowl.

2. Cut potatoes into ¼-inch slices. Arrange in overlapping rows in a greased

2-quart oblong baking dish. Sprinkle with cheese and spoon soup mixture over cheese.

3. Cover and bake at 400° for 45 minutes. Uncover and bake 10 minutes longer or until potatoes are tender.

Oven-Fried Potatoes
Joy Layton
Quarryville, PA

Makes 4 servings

4 large potatoes
¼ cup cooking oil
1-2 Tbsp. grated Parmesan cheese
½ tsp. salt
¼ tsp. garlic powder
¼ tsp. paprika
⅛ tsp. pepper

1. Cut each unpeeled potato lengthwise into 4 wedges. Place wedges, peel side down, in a 9" x 13" baking dish.

2. In a bowl combine oil, Parmesan cheese, salt, garlic powder, paprika, and pepper and mix well. Brush mixture over potatoes.

3. Bake at 375° for 45 minutes, basting every 15 minutes with cheese mixture. Turn potatoes and bake 15 minutes longer.

Potato Puffs

Elsie M. Beachy, Lancaster, PA
Martha L. Stoner, Leola, PA

Makes 6 servings

1½ **cups leftover mashed potatoes**
1 **cup flour**
2 **tsp. baking powder**
2 **eggs, lightly beaten**
2 **Tbsp. milk**
¼ **tsp. salt**
Cooking oil

1. Combine all ingredients except cooking oil and mix well.
2. Bring enough oil to deep-fry potato puffs to 380° in kettle.
3. Drop potato mixture by large teaspoonsful into deep fat. Turn until browned on all sides. Drain and keep hot in 250° oven.
4. Serve with molasses, syrup, or ketchup.

Caramelized Sweet Potatoes

Annetta Frackman
Paradise, PA

Makes 5 servings

5 **medium sweet potatoes**
3 **Tbsp. flour**
1 **cup brown sugar**
1 **tsp. salt**
2 **Tbsp. butter**
8 **marshmallows**
1 **cup thin cream**

1. Cook sweet potatoes until tender. Peel potatoes when slightly cooled. Cut in halves lengthwise and arrange in greased baking dish.
2. Combine flour, sugar, and salt and sprinkle evenly over potatoes. Dot with butter and marshmallows. Pour cream over all.
3. Bake at 350° for 45-50 minutes.

Sweet Potato Delight

Jean Barnes
Peach Bottom, PA

Makes 10 servings

Sweet Potatoes:
3 **cups cooked, mashed sweet potatoes**
⅓ **cup sugar** *or* **less**
2 **eggs**
1 **tsp. vanilla**
½ **cup milk**
½ **cup melted margarine** *or* **butter**

Topping:
1 **cup brown sugar** *or* **less**
⅓ **cup flour**
⅓ **cup margarine** *or* **butter**
¾ **cup pecans**

1. Beat together all sweet potato ingredients until well mixed. Spoon into greased casserole dish.
2. Combine all topping ingredients until crumbly. Sprinkle on top of potato mixture.
3. Bake at 350° for 30 minutes.

Sweet Potato and Apple Combo

Ethel M. Brendle
Lititz, PA

Makes 6-8 servings

4-6 medium sweet potatoes
⅓ cup firmly packed brown sugar
½ tsp. ground ginger
⅛ tsp. salt
2 apples, sliced thinly
2 Tbsp. butter
½ cup orange juice
¼ cup chopped nuts *or* marshmallow bits

1. Cook sweet potatoes until soft. Cool, peel, and cut into ½-inch slices.
2. In small bowl combine brown sugar, ginger, and salt. Set aside.
3. Arrange sweet potatoes and apples in alternating layers in greased 1-quart shallow baking dish. Sprinkle each layer with the brown sugar and ginger mixture. Dot with butter and pour the orange juice over layers. Sprinkle with chopped nuts or marshmallows.
4. Bake at 350° for 35 minutes.

Meats and Meat Dishes

Tasty Turkey in Sauce
Marilyn Langeman
Akron, PA

Makes 6 servings

2 lbs. skinless turkey thighs
2 onions, chopped
⅓ cup molasses
⅓ cup vinegar
⅓ cup ketchup
2 Tbsp. Worcestershire sauce
½ tsp. salt
¼ tsp. pepper
½ tsp. liquid smoke
2 Tbsp. cornstarch
2-3 Tbsp. cold water

1. Cut turkey thighs into 1-inch chunks. Put all ingredients except cornstarch and water into crockpot.
2. Cook on low for 8-12 hours.
3. Combine cornstarch and water and stir into turkey mixture to thicken slightly. Cook on high at least 15 minutes.
4. Serve with cooked rice.

Mexican Turkey Loaf
Esther Becker
Gap, PA

Makes 4-6 servings

1 lb. ground turkey
1 medium onion, finely chopped
1 clove garlic, minced
1 green chili, finely chopped
3 Tbsp. cornmeal
1 egg, lightly beaten
2 tsp. chili powder
½ tsp. salt
¼ tsp. oregano, crumbled
2-3 drops Tabasco

1. Mix together all ingredients and shape into loaf. Place loaf in greased baking pan.
2. Bake at 375° for 45 minutes.

Chicken and Filling Roast
Susie S. Stoltzfus
Ronks, PA

Makes 8-10 servings

2 3-lb. whole chickens
1½ loaves bread
⅔ lb. butter
2 cups chopped celery
½ cup chopped onion
4 eggs
¾ cup water
1½ tsp. salt
¼ tsp. pepper
¼ tsp. celery salt
½ cup water

1. Arrange two whole chickens in roaster and bake at 350° for 1 hour. Cool and debone chickens. Reserve and dice hearts and livers.

2. Meanwhile cube bread and let dry about ½ day.

3. In a small saucepan melt butter, cooking until browned. Add celery, onion, and diced hearts and livers and cook for about 15 minutes. Add mixture to bread cubes and mix well.

4. In small bowl beat eggs, ¾ cup water, salt, pepper, and celery salt. Add to bread cubes and mix by hand. Add chicken pieces and mix well. Arrange mixture in well-greased roaster. Pour about ½ cup water around edges.

5. Cover and bake at 350° for 1 hour. About halfway through baking time, stir well.

Chicken Pot Pie with Corn
Jennifer Trimble
Denver, PA

Makes 8-10 servings

Chicken Broth:
4-lb. whole chicken
2 quarts water
1 tsp. salt
5 potatoes, diced
2 cups corn
1 medium onion, diced
1 small pkg. saffron

Pot Pie Dough:
2 cups flour
½ tsp. salt
2 eggs
4 Tbsp. water

1. Cook chicken in 2 quarts salt water until soft. Cool and remove meat from the bones. Set aside chicken pieces.

2. To the boiling broth add potatoes, corn, onion, and saffron. Cook for 10 minutes.

3. To prepare potpie dough combine flour and salt. Beat eggs with 4 Tbsp. water. Work into flour and salt until you have a stiff dough. (Add more water if mixture is too dry.) Roll dough out onto floured surface until thin. Cut into squares.

4. Drop pot pie dough into boiling broth and cook about 20 minutes.

5. Stir chicken pieces into pot pie mixture. Heat through and serve immediately.

Akron

*S*prawling across a hill overlooking the Cocalico Creek valley and the larger town of Ephrata, the borough of Akron quietly goes about its daily business. Rows and rows of unassuming middle-class homes line the streets which meander up and down all sides of the hill.

Odena Detweiler has lived in Akron since 1952. She and her husband, Willis, came to the town to work for the growing Mennonite relief organization, Mennonite Central Committee (MCC). They built a house near the corner of Broad and 12th Street. Eight years later on August 5, 1960, MCC moved its headquarters from Main Street to a brand-new building directly across the street from the Detweilers.

In the years since the Detweilers' arrival in Akron, the borough has changed a great deal. "When we came, MCC was a small operation. It has grown tremendously since 1952." Indeed, the organization has expanded its 12th Street building several times through the years. It also purchased and renovated the former Miller Hess Shoe Factory, converting it into office and storage space for SELFHELP Crafts of the World, a nonprofit MCC program. SELFHELP provides low-income people of the world's developing countries with a way to earn a living by selling their handicrafts in shops across North America.

Detweiler also remembers the day when the Akron Restaurant served meals from a small Main Street eatery. "They got too big and famous, so they moved to a larger space down on Route 272." People still drive from miles around to dine at the popular family spot. Seven local churches, a volunteer fire organization, and a spacious park help make Akron a nice place to live and work.

Chicken Pot Pie with Carrots

Darlene Redcay
Goodville, PA

Makes 10-12 servings

Pot Pie Dough:
3 cups flour
2 eggs
1 Tbsp. shortening
½-¾ cup water

Chicken Broth:
3-lb. whole chicken
2 quarts water
4-6 medium potatoes, diced
2 cups diced celery
1 cup diced carrots
1 small onion, diced
Parsley (optional)
Salt and pepper to taste
1 tsp. saffron (optional)

1. To prepare pot pie dough combine flour, eggs, and shortening. Work with hands, adding water until dough holds together. Roll out into thin sheet on floured surface and cut into 2-inch squares. Let dry at least 1 hour.

2. Meanwhile cook chicken in 2 quarts water until tender. Cool and debone chicken. Set aside chicken pieces.

3. Add all remaining chicken mixture ingredients to boiling broth and cook about 10 minutes.

4. Drop pot pie squares into boiling broth, turn to medium heat, and cook about 30 minutes, stirring frequently.

5. Add chicken pieces to broth, heat through, and serve immediately.

Pot Pie Dough
Jaci Rettew
Denver, PA

Makes enough to serve with 3-lb. chicken

1½ cups flour
3 Tbsp. butter *or* margarine
¼ cup milk
½ tsp. salt
1 egg

1. Combine all ingredients and work by hand until dough holds together. Roll out into thin sheet on well-floured surface and cut into squares.
2. Serve with choice of chicken broth recipe.

Chicken Barbecue
Ruth Good
Ephrata, PA

Makes 6-8 servings

10¾-oz. can tomato soup
2 Tbsp. brown sugar
2 Tbsp. margarine *or* butter
1 Tbsp. vinegar
2 tsp. dry mustard
½ tsp. celery salt
½ tsp. onion salt
½ tsp. parsley flakes
8-10 chicken legs

1. Combine all ingredients except chicken and bring to a boil. Reduce heat and simmer 10 minutes. Cool.
2. Place chicken, skin side up in shallow baking dish. Season with salt and pepper. Spoon ½ of sauce over chicken.
3. Cover and bake at 350° for 25 minutes. Spoon remaining sauce over chicken and bake, uncovered, another 30-40 minutes or until chicken is tender.

Baked Chicken with Barbecue Sauce
Naomi E. Yoder
Gordonville, PA

Makes 8 servings

2 3-lb. whole chickens
1 cup ketchup
¼ cup water
¼ cup vinegar
¼ cup butter
3 Tbsp. brown sugar
2 Tbsp. Worcestershire sauce
1 tsp. dry mustard
¼ tsp. pepper
1½ tsp. salt
Juice of ¼ lemon
1 onion, diced

1. In a saucepan combine all ingredients except chicken. Bring to a boil and simmer for 10 minutes.
2. Spoon sauce over chickens in baking dish. Add ¼ cup water.
3. Bake, uncovered, at 350° for 2 hours, basting occasionally.

Variation: Omit onion. Add ½ tsp. paprika and ¼ tsp. hickory smoke seasoning to sauce.
—*Anna Z. Martin, East Earl, PA*

Sunday Evening Supper

In my parental home we had a traditional Sunday evening supper consisting of bologna, cheese, and steamed crackers. For dessert we had warm, freshly made chocolate pudding. As the pudding cooled, a skin formed across the top. Some of us thought getting to eat that skin was a real bonus! Others preferred spooning under the skin for a serving of "cornstarch."

—*Betty Pellman, Millersville, PA*

Oven-Baked Barbecue Chicken
Jo Zimmerman, New Holland, PA
Lois Hoover, Ephrata, PA

Makes 10 servings

15 pieces chicken
2 Tbsp. butter
1 cup ketchup
3 Tbsp. vinegar
2 Tbsp. prepared mustard
¾ cup brown sugar

1. Skin chicken pieces and arrange pieces in 9" x 13" baking pan.
2. Turn oven to broil and broil chicken 15 minutes on each side.
3. Meanwhile combine all remaining ingredients and mix well.
4. Dip each piece chicken into sauce. Pour extra sauce evenly over chicken.
5. Cover and bake at 300° for 30 minutes. Uncover to brown for last 10 minutes.

Yogurt Marinated Chicken
Sandy Shaub
Lancaster, PA

Makes 4-6 servings

3-lb. whole chicken, cut up
2 Tbsp. lemon juice
1 cup plain yogurt
¼ cup fresh minced ginger
½ tsp. ground cardamom
½ tsp. chili powder
½ tsp. cinnamon

1. Combine all ingredients except chicken and mix well.
2. Marinate chicken pieces in sauce at least 8 hours or overnight.
3. Bake at 375° for 40-45 minutes, basting occasionally.

Oven-Fried Sesame Chicken
Madeline Hartzell
Lancaster, PA

Makes 4 servings

3 Tbsp. sesame seeds
2 Tbsp. all-purpose flour
¼ tsp. pepper
4 whole chicken breasts, skinned
2 Tbsp. soy sauce
2 Tbsp. margarine, melted

1. Combine sesame seeds, flour, and pepper. Dip chicken pieces into soy sauce and dredge in sesame seed mixture.
2. Arrange chicken breasts, bone side down, in large shallow baking dish. Drizzle margarine over chicken.
3. Bake at 400° for 40-45 minutes or until chicken is tender.

Cheese Cache Chicken
Deb Lied
Akron, PA

Makes 4 servings

2 whole chicken breasts
4 slices Monterey Jack cheese
2 eggs
1 tsp. grated Parmesan cheese
$\frac{1}{4}$ tsp. salt
$\frac{1}{4}$ tsp. pepper
1 Tbsp. parsley
Flour
$\frac{1}{4}$ cup cooking oil

1. Skin, halve, and bone each chicken breast. Cut pocket into each chicken piece by holding knife parallel to breast and making about a 2-inch deep slit in the side. Place a strip of cheese in each pocket.
2. In a large bowl beat together eggs, Parmesan cheese, salt, pepper, and parsley. Roll breasts in flour, then dip into egg mixture.
3. Heat cooking oil in skillet. Sauté breasts just until crisp and golden. Turn with spatula, not tongs. Transfer chicken to baking dish.
4. Bake at 375° for 8-10 minutes or until coating begins to brown.

Twila's Chicken
Susanne Brubaker
Lancaster, PA

Makes 6-8 servings

4 chicken breasts
$\frac{1}{2}$ tsp. garlic powder
4 eggs
Juice of 2 lemons
2 cups bread crumbs
$\frac{1}{2}$ cup margarine
2 cups sliced mushrooms
$\frac{1}{2}$ cup chicken broth
$\frac{1}{2}$ cup white wine
8 slices Muenster cheese

1. Bone, skin, and pound chicken breasts.
2. Combine garlic powder, eggs, and lemon juice. Pour over chicken breasts and marinate for 1 hour.
3. Roll chicken breast in bread crumbs and brown in margarine. Remove from skillet and arrange in baking dish.
4. Sauté mushrooms in same skillet.
5. Combine chicken broth and wine and pour over chicken. Sprinkle with mushrooms and lay cheese slices over top.
6. Cover and bake at 350° for 30 minutes. Uncover and bake another 10 minutes.

Columbia

*O*riginally called Wright's Ferry after John Wright, a Quaker settler who operated a ferry system on the Susquehanna River, the Lancaster County river town of Columbia was once considered as a possible site for the nation's capital. In fact, after a 1777 visit to the area by the Continental Congress, the newly-formed House of Representatives voted yes for the Wright's Ferry location. The Senate later overturned the House vote, recommending instead a place further south on the banks of the Potomac River.

One of the saddest moments in Columbia's history occurred in 1863 during the Civil War. Rapidly advancing troops prompted the Union Army to escape to the Lancaster County side and burn the massive covered bridge which connected the town with Wrightsville on the York County side of the Susquehanna. Built in 1834, the wooden structure included double tracks for the Pennsylvania Railroad Line, towpaths for canal mules, and a roadway for horses and wagons. Today, two concrete and steel bridges convey traffic across the river in Columbia—the Inter-County bridge, built in 1930, carries local Route 462 traffic and the Wright's Ferry Bridge, built in 1972, carries Route 30's superhighway traffic.

A sleepy river town, with its share of decaying neighborhoods, Columbia also sports delightfully restored homes and rows of red-brick houses with ornately carved woodwork along their roof lines. An occasional antique or craft shop stands next to a video store. And landmark restaurants such as the Rising Sun Hotel, on the corner of Cherry and Sixth Streets, and Hinkle's Pharmacy, on the corner of Locust and Third Streets, attract both a local and an out-of-town clientele.

*C*hicken Cordon Bleu
Ruth F. Hurst
Gordonville, PA

Makes 6 servings

6 chicken breasts
6 thinly sliced pieces ham
6 thinly sliced pieces Monterey Jack
    cheese
2 Tbsp. flour
¼ cup butter
¼ lb. mozzarella cheese, grated
¼ cup milk
8 medium mushrooms, sliced
¼ cup dry white wine

1. Debone and pound chicken breasts until thin. Arrange ham and cheese slices on each breast. Roll and pin edges together with toothpicks. Dust with flour.

2. Melt butter and coat each chicken breast with butter, arranging in baking dish.

3. Heat mozzarella cheese and milk together. Add mushrooms and wine and blend until smooth. Pour over chicken.

4. Bake at 350° for 35-40 minutes. Serve.

French Chicken
Denise Martin
Lancaster, PA

Makes 4-6 servings

4 chicken breasts, split
1 cup French dressing
1 cup bread crumbs
½ cup margarine, melted

1. Coat chicken breasts with French dressing. Cover and marinate overnight.
2. Roll chicken in bread crumbs and arrange in baking dish. Drizzle ¼ cup margarine over chicken.
3. Bake, uncovered, at 325° for 40 minutes. Drizzle remaining ¼ cup margarine over chicken and bake 15 minutes longer.

Chicken Wrapped in Ham
Ashley Hendrickson
Ephrata, PA

Makes 4 servings

4 skinless, boneless chicken breasts
1 Tbsp. cooking oil
4 slices baked ham
1 pint light cream
10¾-oz. can cream of celery soup

1. Brown chicken pieces on both sides in cooking oil.
2. Remove from skillet and wrap one slice of ham around each piece of chicken. Arrange, seam side down, in a baking dish.
3. Mix cream and soup together and pour over chicken.
4. Bake at 350° for 45 minutes or until done.

Lemon Chicken with Rotini
Marian E. Going
Lancaster, PA

Makes 2 servings

1 chicken breast
1 Tbsp. chopped garlic
6 lemons
Salt and pepper to taste
½ lb. rotini

1. Skin chicken breast and cut into strips.
2. Lightly grease skillet and sauté chicken with garlic until chicken is tender.
3. Meanwhile squeeze juice from lemons. Add to chicken and cook for about 5 minutes, stirring occasionally. Add salt and pepper to taste. Lower heat and allow sauce to thicken, about 7 minutes.
4. Meanwhile cook rotini according to package directions. Drain.
5. Toss rotini with lemon chicken and serve immediately.

100 Years with the Akron Fire Company

The Akron Fire Company was organized in 1893, beginning with 21 active members and a hand-drawn pumper. During 1993, we celebrated 100 years of serving the community. Today, two of Akron's early fire trucks may be seen at the Landis Valley Farm Musuem, about 4 miles south of the borough of Akron.

The Fire Company and Ladies' Auxiliary are community oriented and raise needed funds by serving banquets and weddings as well as holding annual fund raising sales.

—*Joanne Gestewitz, Akron, PA*

Glazed Chicken Strips

Jeanette Oberholtzer
Akron, PA

Makes 8 servings

6-8 chicken breasts, boned & skinned
$\frac{1}{4}$ cup all-purpose flour
1$\frac{1}{2}$ tsp. garlic salt
$\frac{1}{2}$ tsp. seasoned salt
1 tsp. paprika
$\frac{1}{2}$ tsp. dried dill weed
$\frac{1}{4}$ cup cooking oil
1 cup dry white wine
$\frac{1}{3}$ cup wine vinegar
$\frac{1}{3}$ cup brown sugar, packed
$\frac{1}{3}$ cup ketchup
1 tsp. dry mustard
1 large loaf unsliced bread

1. Cut each chicken breast into finger-sized strips.
2. Measure flour, salts, paprika, and dill into paper bag. Toss chicken strips, a few pieces at a time, in bag to coat well.
3. In a skillet brown chicken strips in heated oil. Remove browned strips to shallow baking pan and arrange in single layer.
4. In a bowl combine all remaining ingredients except bread and spoon over chicken in pan.
5. Bake at 375° for about 20 minutes.
6. To prepare bread cut off top for lid. Scoop out center, leaving $\frac{1}{2}$-inch shell. Cut bread from center into cubes and reserve. Brush inside of shell with melted butter and sprinkle with choice of seasonings or herbs.
7. Toast bread basket at 375° for 10-15 minutes until lightly browned.
8. Pile hot chicken into toasted bread basket, drizzle remaining sauce over top. Cover with lid and let stand about 10 minutes before serving.
9. Serve glazed chicken strips in bread basket with reserved bread cubes.

Chicken Soufflé

Esther Becker, Gap, PA
Patti Fisher, Mount Joy, PA
Reba I. Hillard, Narvon, PA

Makes 12 servings

12 slices bread, quartered
$\frac{1}{2}$ cup diced green pepper
1 cup diced onion
$\frac{1}{2}$ cup diced celery
4 cups cooked, diced chicken
1 cup mayonnaise
Salt and pepper to taste
3 eggs, beaten
3 cups milk
2 10$\frac{3}{4}$-oz. cans cream of mushroom soup
$\frac{1}{2}$ cup grated cheese

1. Line bottom of lightly-greased 3-quart casserole dish with $\frac{1}{2}$ of the bread.
2. In separate bowl combine green pepper, onion, celery, chicken, mayonnaise, salt, and pepper and mix well. Spoon over bread in casserole dish. Cover with remaining bread.
3. Beat eggs together with milk and add mushroom soup, mixing well. Pour over bread layer. Top with grated cheese.
4. Cover and refrigerate at least 8 hours or overnight.
5. Uncover and bake at 325° for 1 hour and 15 minutes.

Chicken and Fried Rice

Van Dien Trinh
Mount Joy, PA

Makes 6 servings

2 Tbsp. cooking oil
2 cloves garlic, diced
10-oz. chicken breast, diced
2 carrots, diced
$\frac{1}{2}$ cup green peas
1 medium onion, diced
2 eggs, beaten
4 cups cooked rice
$1\frac{1}{2}$ Tbsp. soy sauce

1. Sauté garlic in oil over medium heat until garlic turns yellow. Add chicken and cook until tender. Add carrots, peas, and onion and stir-fry until tender, about 7 minutes.

2. Stir in eggs, rice, and soy sauce and heat through. Serve.

Shrimp and Fried Rice

Dorothy Greenawald
Willow Street, PA

Makes 4-6 servings

Shrimp and Rice:
10-12 medium shrimp
1 medium onion, sliced
$\frac{1}{4}$ cup butterormargarine
1 cup uncooked rice
$1\frac{1}{2}$ tsp. salt
Dash cayenne
$\frac{1}{8}$ tsp. pepper
1 tsp. paprika
1 cup chicken broth
3 cups boiling water

Curry Sauce:
3 Tbsp. butter *or* margarine
2 Tbsp. flour
$1\frac{1}{2}$ tsp. curry powder
2 tsp. onion juice
$\frac{1}{2}$ tsp. salt
$1\frac{1}{2}$ cups water from shrimp
$\frac{1}{2}$ cup cream

1. Steam shrimp in 2 cups water. Reserve $1\frac{1}{2}$ cups water for curry sauce.

2. Cook onion in margarine until transparent. Remove onion. Add rice and sauté until golden.

3. Combine salt, cayenne, pepper, paprika, chicken broth, and water and mix well. Add to onion and rice and turn into greased casserole dish.

4. Cover and bake at 350° for 20 minutes. Remove from oven and arrange shrimp over rice. Bake another 15 minutes.

5. To prepare curry sauce melt butter in skillet. Stir in flour, curry powder, onion juice, and salt until bubbly. Gradually add shrimp water and cream and cook until thickened, stirring constantly.

6. Serve shrimp and rice dish with curry sauce.

Batter-Fried Shrimp

Van Dien Trinh
Mount Joy, PA

Makes 4 servings

1 lb. shrimp, cleaned
1 egg, beaten
3 Tbsp. flour
⅛ tsp. salt
2 green onions, diced
1 cup cooking oil

1. Combine egg, flour, salt, and green onion and mix well.
2. Heat oil in pan over medium heat.
3. Dip each shrimp into batter and drop into hot oil. Fry until shrimp turn yellow. Serve immediately.

Seafood Kabobs

Shirley Prosser
Elizabethtown, PA

Makes 6-8 servings

Kabobs:
2 lbs. seafood (scallops, shrimp, etc.)
6 cups vegetables, cut in chunks
    (zucchini, green peppers, onions, etc.)
2 cups fruit, cut in chunks
    (pineapple, tomatoes, etc.)

Marinade:
¼ cup light soy sauce
¼ cup cooking oil
¼ cup white wine
1 tsp. sugar
1 garlic clove, minced
2 dashes hot pepper sauce
1 dash black pepper
2-inch strip fresh orange peel

1. Combine marinade ingredients in small bowl and mix well. Pour over

seafood and marinate up to 8 hours, depending on the amount of flavor desired.
2. Prepare a charcoal grill.
3. Thread seafood onto skewers, alternating with fruits and vegetables. (If using wooden skewers, soak skewers in water before threading them.)
4. Grill about 10 minutes or until seafood is done, watching carefully. Serve.

Haddock Shrimp Bake

Rhoda Kilheffer
Manheim, PA

Makes 6-8 servings

2½-3 lbs. fresh *or* frozen haddock
10¾-oz. can cream of shrimp soup
½ tsp. grated onion
½ tsp. Worcestershire sauce
1½ cups crushed Ritz crackers

1. Arrange haddock fillets in lightly greased 9" x 13" baking pan. Spread soup over fillets.
2. Bake at 375° for 20 minutes.
3. Combine onion, Worcestershire sauce, and crushed crackers. Remove fish from oven and sprinkle with cracker mixture. Return to oven and bake 15 minutes longer.

Shrimp and Scallops

Ruth E. Wenger
Akron, PA

Makes 4-6 servings

¾ lb. fine noodles
2 Tbsp. butter
2 Tbsp. flour
½ tsp. salt
⅛ tsp. pepper
1 Tbsp. lemon juice
½ tsp. Worcestershire sauce
3 cups milk
¾ lb. sharp cheese, grated
1½ cups cleaned, medium shrimp
1½ cups scallops
2 cups soft bread crumbs

1. Cook noodles according to package directions. Drain and rinse.

2. In a saucepan melt butter. Stir in flour, salt, and pepper until bubbly. Slowly add lemon juice, Worcestershire sauce, milk, and ½ of cheese and cook until cheese melts and mixture thickens, stirring constantly.

3. In a greased casserole dish combine noodles, white sauce, raw shrimp, and raw scallops. Top with remaining cheese and soft bread crumbs.

4. Bake, uncovered, at 325° for 1½ hours.

Fish Bake with Almonds

Betty J. Hendricks
Lancaster, PA

Makes 4 servings

1 lb. fish fillets, fresh *or* frozen
1 Tbsp. lemon juice
½ tsp. salt (optional)
¼ tsp. pepper
3 Tbsp. margarine
2 Tbsp. chopped onion
2 Tbsp. flour
1 cup milk
½ tsp. basil
½ cup cooked, chopped broccoli
½ cup slivered almonds

1. Brush fish fillets with lemon juice. Sprinkle with salt and pepper. Arrange in greased, shallow baking dish.

2. In a saucepan melt margarine; add onion and sauté. Stir in flour until bubbly. Gradually add milk, stirring until it comes to a boil.

3. Reduce heat and stir in basil, broccoli, and almonds, reserving 2 Tbsp. almonds for top. Spoon broccoli cream sauce over fish. Sprinkle with remaining almonds.

4. Bake at 350° for 20-25 minutes until fish flakes and sauce bubbles.

Maryland Crab Cakes

Darlene Harding
Sinking Spring, PA

Makes 6 servings

1 lb. crab meat
1 cup bread cubes
1 large egg
½ tsp. parsley flakes
1 tsp. onion flakes (optional)
¼ tsp. black pepper
1 tsp. Worcestershire sauce
1 tsp. dry mustard
¼ cup mayonnaise
½ tsp. salt
Cooking oil

1. Pick through crab meat for any leftover pieces of shell.
2. Combine all ingredients except crab and oil and mix well. Gently fold in crab. Shape into crab cakes.
3. Pan fry in hot oil until both sides are evenly done.

Salmonettes

Nancy B. Wallace
New Holland, PA

Makes 4 servings

15½-oz. can salmon
1 egg, slightly beaten
½ cup flour
Pepper to taste
1 heaping tsp. baking powder
Cooking oil

1. Drain salmon and reserve ¼ cup of liquid.
2. In a bowl combine salmon, egg, flour, and pepper and mix well, breaking up salmon.
3. Stir baking powder into reserved salmon liquid and beat well with fork until foamy. Pour into salmon mixture and stir until blended.
4. Using 2 teaspoons scoop out the mixture with one of them and use the other to push the mixture off the teaspoon into a deep fryer of hot oil. Watch closely as they will brown fast. Remove and drain on a paper towel. Serve.

Salmon Roll-Up

Betty J. Hendricks
Lancaster, PA

Makes 4 servings

15½-oz. can salmon
½ tsp. salt
¼ tsp. pepper
½ cup chopped green pepper
½ cup chopped celery
1 small onion, chopped
1 Tbsp. lemon juice
2 cups biscuit mix
½ cup milk

1. Empty salmon into large mixing bowl. Season with salt and pepper. Add green pepper, celery, onion, and lemon juice and mix well.
2. Prepare biscuit mix and milk into dough. Roll out into rectangle shape. Spread salmon mixture on top. Roll up as a jelly roll. Place seam side down on a greased baking dish. Pinch ends together.
3. Bake at 400° for 25-30 minutes. Serve.

Salmon Burgers

Florence Morrison
Lancaster, PA

Makes 4-6 servings

15½-oz. can salmon
¾ cup uncooked quick oats
½ cup finely chopped onion
2 eggs, slightly beaten
2 Tbsp. minced parsley
2 Tbsp. lemon juice
1 Tbsp. Worcestershire sauce
2 Tbsp. cooking oil

1. Drain and flake salmon. Combine salmon, oats, onion, eggs, parsley, lemon juice, and Worcestershire sauce. Mix and shape into patties.
2. Heat oil in skillet and pan fry on both sides until golden brown.

Tuna Loaf

Janet Weaver
Ephrata, PA

Makes 6 servings

1½ cups uncooked macaroni
1⅓ cups milk
¾ cup water
1½ cups grated white American cheese
2½ Tbsp. butter *or* margarine
1¼ cups bread crumbs
¼ cup diced onion
7-oz. can tuna
3 eggs, lightly beaten
1 tsp. salt
Pepper to taste

1. Cook macaroni according to package directions. Drain and rinse.
2. Combine milk, water, cheese, and butter in a saucepan. Heat to boiling; simmer and stir until cheese melts. Remove from heat and mix in bread crumbs, onion, tuna, eggs, salt, pepper, and macaroni. Spoon into greased casserole dish.
3. Bake at 350° for 45 minutes to 1 hour. Serve.

Ham Loaf

Sylvia E. Stoltzfus
Gap, PA

Makes 6 servings

1½ lbs. ground, cured ham
⅔ lb. fresh pork
1 cup dry bread crumbs
¼ tsp. pepper
2 eggs, beaten
1 cup milk

Glaze:
¼ cup vinegar
⅓ cup brown sugar
1 tsp. dry mustard

1. Combine meats, crumbs, pepper, eggs, and milk and mix thoroughly. Form into loaf, making a trough through top of loaf.
2. To prepare glaze combine all ingredients and mix well. Pour glaze into trough on ham loaf.
3. Bake at 350° for 1-1½ hours. Baste occasionally with glaze.

Lititz

*I*n 1749 a small band of Moravians—a group of Christians who had once been severely persecuted in their European homeland— established a *Land Gemeine* or country congregation around the site of the present-day town of Lititz. From 1749 until 1856 only members of the Moravian Church were permitted to live in Lititz. In 1764 the Church established a country inn, called *Zum Anker* (The Sign of the Anchor). The inn became well known throughout the region for its unique feather beds, good food, and prohibition of dancing, cursing, and gossip.

Now called the General Sutter Inn, the building which housed Zum Anker still offers rooms and good food to locals and weary travelers alike. While the town has been open to non-Moravians since 1856, many current residents of Lititz either belong to the Lititz Moravian Church, the centerpiece of Moravian Square on the east side of town, or they have an ongoing love affair with the rich traditions of the congregation.

While describing the yearly Christmas services when the church offers a musical celebration, a simple love feast, and a candle lighting ceremony, Jonel Herr, who lives just outside the nearby village of Rothsville, said with a hushed tone, "When all the lights go down inside the old church and the Moravian star lights up, you know it is Christmas in Lititz."

In modern-day Lititz, basket, herb, and antique shops blend with hardware, pharmacy, and women's specialty stores along the revived Main Street between Moravian Square and General Sutter Inn. Thanks to Wilbur Chocolate Company, which moved to Lititz in 1930, the irresistible smell of melted chocolate often wafts across the town.

Baked Ham

Emma King
Gordonville, PA

Makes 8-10 servings

12 slices ham, ¼-inch thick
1 tsp. dry mustard
4 Tbsp. brown sugar
1 cup milk

1. Arrange ham in roast pan or Dutch oven. Rub with dry mustard and cover with brown sugar.
2. Add enough milk to barely cover ham.
3. Bake at 325° for 1-1¼ hours. When ham is done, milk should be absorbed.

Ham Balls

Anna Mae Weaver
Ephrata, PA

Makes 8-10 servings

Ham Balls:
1½ lbs. ground ham
1½ lbs. ground pork
1 cup milk
1 cup fine bread crumbs
2 eggs, beaten
Pinch salt and pepper

Sauce:
1 cup brown sugar
½ cup water
¼ cup vinegar
1 Tbsp. cornstarch
1 tsp. dry mustard

1. Combine all ham ball ingredients and mix well. Shape into 30 balls and arrange in baking pan.

2. In a saucepan combine all sauce ingredients and bring to a boil. Lower heat and simmer for 3 minutes until well blended. Pour sauce over ham balls.

3. Bake at 325° for 1 hour.

Pork Pudding
Betty Pellman
Millersville, PA

Makes 2-4 servings

1 lb. pork pudding
1 large onion, chopped
$\frac{3}{4}$ cup water

1. Heat pork pudding, breaking it apart. Bring to a boil, stirring occasionally. Remove all excess fat.

2. Add onion and water and cook until onion is tender. Serve.

Sausage Balls
Rhoda H. Lind
Lititz, PA

Makes 4-6 servings

Sausage Balls:
1 lb. ground sausage
1 egg, lightly beaten
$\frac{1}{3}$ cup bread crumbs
$\frac{1}{2}$ tsp. sage

Sauce:
$\frac{1}{2}$ cup ketchup
2 Tbsp. brown sugar
1 Tbsp. vinegar
1 Tbsp. soy sauce

1. Mix together all ingredients for balls. Form into medium-sized balls. In a skillet brown on all sides. Drain any excess fat.

2. Combine all sauce ingredients and pour over sausage balls. Simmer for about 30 minutes. Serve.

Pig's Stomach
Denise Martin
Lancaster, PA

Makes 6 servings

1 large pig's stomach
8 cups bread cubes
6 eggs
$10\frac{3}{4}$-oz. can cream of chicken soup
1 Tbsp. poultry seasoning
2 lbs. ground sausage
4-5 medium potatoes, diced

1. Soak pig's stomach in salt water overnight.

2. In large bowl combine bread cubes, eggs, soup, and poultry seasoning and mix until bread cubes are moist. Add sausage and potatoes and mix well.

3. Drain all water off pig's stomach and stuff with sausage mixture. Be careful not to overstuff. Close the ends.

4. Cover and bake at 250° for $2\frac{1}{2}$-3 hours or until stomach is very brown.

Note: I use extra stuffing to fix a casserole dish for those who do not enjoy pig's stomach.

Pork Egg Roll
Van Dien Trinh
Mount Joy, PA

Makes 25 egg rolls

2 lbs. ground pork
1 large onion, diced
4 green onions, diced
4 ozs. carrots, shredded
1/8 tsp. ground pepper
1 tsp. salt
1 egg, beaten
25 egg roll shells
2 cups cooking oil

1. Combine all ingredients except egg roll shells and oil in medium bowl and mix well.
2. Lay each square egg roll shell in a diamond shape. Spoon 2½ Tbsp. pork mixture slightly below the center of the diamond. Pull bottom corner and sides over mixture. Roll up to top corner.
3. Heat oil in deep pan over medium heat. Cook each egg roll until it turns yellow. Set aside to drain and serve.

Pork Chops Italiano
Colette Carrow
Akron, PA

Makes 4 servings

4 pork chops, ½" thick
1 Tbsp. cooking oil
Salt and pepper to taste
½ cup chopped onion
2-3 cloves garlic, minced
1 medium green pepper, chopped
15-oz. can tomato sauce
1 Tbsp. Parmesan cheese
1 bay leaf
1 tsp. basil

1. In a large, heavy skillet brown pork chops in oil. Remove from skillet. Season with salt and pepper.
2. In the pan drippings sauté onion, garlic, and green pepper. Return chops to skillet. Add tomato sauce, cheese, and seasonings. Cover and simmer about 45 minutes or until tender.

Szechwan Pork and Stir-Fry
Audrey Brubaker
Lancaster, PA

Makes 6 servings

1 lb. fresh lean pork tenderloin
6-8 green onions, chopped
1 red pepper, chopped
1½ cups chopped fresh broccoli
1 large onion, chopped
12 pea pods
3 Tbsp. cooking oil

Sauce:
4 cloves garlic, minced
4 slices fresh ginger, chopped
¼ tsp. crushed red pepper
4 Tbsp. water
4 tsp. sugar
¾ cup ketchup
½ cup soy sauce

1. Cut pork into narrow 1-inch strips, ¼-inch thick, and set aside.
2. In a wok or large skillet heat oil over high heat. Stir-fry pork until browned. Remove from wok and keep warm. Add more oil if necessary and stir-fry all vegetables until tender/crisp.
3. To prepare sauce combine all ingredients and mix well.
4. Stir pork and sauce into wok and cook until thickened. Serve over hot rice.

Saucy Pork Chops
Deb Ament
Silver Spring Fire Hall

Makes 4 servings

1½ lbs. pork chops
10¾-oz. can cream of chicken soup
¼ cup ketchup
2 tsp. Worcestershire sauce

1. Arrange pork chops in a crockpot.
2. Combine all other ingredients and pour over pork chops.
3. Cook on low for 10-12 hours.

Baked Lamb Chops
Beverly McCauley
Lancaster, PA

Makes 4 servings

1½ cups sliced potatoes
¾ cup sliced carrots
½ cup sliced celery
½ cup thinly sliced onion
Salt and pepper to taste
4 shoulder lamb chops
2 Tbsp. flour
1 Tbsp. cooking oil
1 cup water

1. Place alternating layers of sliced vegetables in casserole, starting with potatoes and ending with potatoes. Salt and pepper to taste.
2. Roll lamb chops in flour and brown in heavy skillet in cooking oil. When browned, arrange on top of vegetables and add water.
3. Bake, uncovered, at 350° for approximately 1 hour. If necessary, more water may be added.

Veal Birds
Beverly McCauley
Lancaster, PA

Makes 8 servings

½ cup butter
1 cup chopped celery
2 small onions, chopped
8 cups dry bread cubes
¼ tsp. salt
Dash pepper
3 eggs
1 cup milk
1 tsp. saffron
¼ cup water
2 Tbsp. cooking oil
1 cup water
8 veal steaks, ¼" thick

1. To prepare a bread filling melt butter in large, heavy pan. Gently sauté celery and onion until tender. Add bread cubes, salt, and pepper and mix well.
2. In small bowl whip eggs and add milk. Pour over bread mixture and stir gently.
3. In small saucepan scald saffron in ¼ cup water. Pour mixture over bread filling and mix well until eggs are set. Remove from heat. Let cool.
4. Lay veal steaks out flat. Spoon about 1 cup bread filling on each steak. Roll up and fasten with toothpicks.
5. In large, heavy pan melt cooking oil and place veal birds in pan to brown, turning constantly. When browned, add 1 cup water to pan and cover. Simmer for approximately two hours or until meat is tender.

Kansas-Style Beef Brisket
Janet M. Schwert
Mountville, PA

Makes 10-12 servings

5-6-lb. beef brisket
Water to cover
2 bottles Kansas City Barbecue Sauce
 (or your favorite)

1. In a roaster cover beef with water and cover tightly.
2. Bake at 350° for 3-3½ hours. Pour off liquid and reserve for future use.
3. Pour barbecue sauce over meat. Cover and bake 45 minutes longer. Slice thinly and serve with sauce.

Beef Roast
Susan H. King
Lancaster, PA

Makes 6-8 servings

4-lb. beef roast
12-oz. can Coca Cola
10¾-oz. can cream of mushroom soup
1 pkg. dry onion soup mix
Flour

1. Put beef roast in roaster.
2. Blend Coca Cola and mushroom soup and pour over roast. Sprinkle with onion soup.
3. Bake at 300° for 4½-5 hours or until nice and tender.
4. Before serving, pour off juices and heat in saucepan. Add flour to thicken to desired consistency.
5. Serve hot beef roast with gravy.

Venison Roast
Sue Steffy
Leola, PA

Makes 6-8 servings

2-3-lb. venison roast
1 pkg. steak marinade
2 tsp. Gravy Master
¼ cup chopped onion
¼ cup chopped green pepper (optional)

1. Thaw frozen venison slowly in refrigerator until ice crystals are gone.
2. Prepare steak marinade according to package directions. Add Gravy Master, onion, and green pepper. Pour over thawed venison and marinade for 2 days, turning occasionally. Keep in refrigerator.
3. Put in crockpot and cook on low for 10-12 hours.

Barbecue Roast
Louise Weaver
Denver, PA

Makes 8-10 servings

3-4-lb. beef roast
1 medium onion, diced
10¾-oz. can cream of mushroom soup
½ cup water
¼ cup brown sugar
¼ cup vinegar
1 tsp. salt
1 tsp. dry mustard
1 tsp. Worcestershire sauce

1. Place roast in roast pan.
2. Cover and bake at 450° for 2 hours.
3. Combine all remaining ingredients and beat with a whisk until smooth. Pour over roast.

4. Cover and bake at 250° for 4 more hours.

5. Cut roast into serving pieces and serve with sauce.

Texas Barbecue Spareribs
Dianna S. Ross
Akron, PA

Makes 6-8 servings

3 lbs. spareribs
2 lemons, sliced
½ cup chopped onions

Sauce:
2 Tbsp. brown sugar
½ tsp. chili powder
1 tsp. salt
2 Tbsp. Worcestershire sauce
1 tsp. cayenne pepper
¼ cup ketchup
1 cup tomato sauce
½ cup tomato juice
½ cup water
1 Tbsp. paprika
¼ cup vinegar

1. Arrange spareribs in roaster or baking pan. Place a lemon slice on each rib. Sprinkle with onions.

2. Bake at 450° for 30 minutes. Drain off excess fat.

3. Combine all sauce ingredients in a saucepan and simmer for 15 minutes until slightly thickened. Pour sauce over ribs.

4. Return to oven and bake at 350° for 1½ hours, basting frequently.

Barbecue Beef Strips
Stacey Rettew
Denver, PA

Makes 4 servings

2 lbs. steak
2 Tbsp. shortening
1½-2 cups ketchup
⅓ cup water
3 Tbsp. brown sugar
1 Tbsp. prepared mustard
1 Tbsp. Worcestershire sauce
1 onion, chopped

1. Slice steak into strips, ⅛-inch thick and about 3 inches long. In a skillet brown strips in shortening. Pour off drippings.

2. In a bowl combine all remaining ingredients and pour over beef strips and stir well.

3. Cover and cook slowly for 35-40 minutes or until beef is tender, stirring occasionally. Serve with cooked rice.

Meatloaf
Ruth F. Hurst, Goodville, PA
Sarah Evans, Akron, PA

Makes 8-10 servings

2 lbs. ground beef
1 cup tomato juice
¾ cup uncooked oats
1 egg
¼ cup chopped onion
Salt and pepper to taste
1 tsp. parsley flakes

1. Combine all ingredients and mix well. Spoon into ungreased loaf pan.

2. Bake at 350° for 1½ hours.

Poor Man's Steak
Doris Becker
Manheim, PA

Makes 6-8 servings

2 lbs. ground beef
1 cup saltine cracker crumbs
1 cup milk
1 tsp. salt
¼ tsp. pepper
½ cup chopped onion
10¾-oz. can mushroom soup
1 soup can water

1. In a bowl combine ground beef, cracker crumbs, milk, salt, pepper, and onion. Press into loaf pan and chill overnight.
2. Remove from loaf pan and slice. In large skillet brown pieces lightly on both sides. Arrange in roasting pan.
3. Mix mushroom soup and water and pour over meat.
4. Bake at 300° for 1½ hours.

Meatballs
Kerwin Getz
Denver, PA

Makes 10-12 servings

1 lb. ground beef
1 egg
¼ cup grated onion
2 Tbsp. ketchup
1 tsp. dry mustard
⅛ tsp. garlic powder
⅛ tsp. Italian seasoning
1 tsp. oregano
2 tsp. basil leaves
Salt and pepper to taste
8 ozs. mozzarella cheese, shredded

2¼ Tbsp. Parmesan cheese
6 Tbsp. bread crumbs
28-oz. jar spaghetti sauce

1. With hands combine ground beef and egg. Add onion, ketchup, mustard, and seasonings and mix well. Add cheeses and bread crumbs and mix well again.
2. Shape into balls and cook with spaghetti sauce in large skillet until done or microwave at level 6 for 6-8 minutes, turning once during cooking time.

Barbecued Meatballs
Karen Burkholder
New Holland, PA

Makes 6-8 servings

Meatballs:
1 cup bread crumbs
1 lb. lean ground beef
½ cup milk
1 tsp. salt
½ tsp. pepper

Sauce:
1 Tbsp. Worcestershire sauce
1 Tbsp. vinegar
3 Tbsp. brown sugar
1½ cups ketchup
½ cup water
½ cup chopped onion

1. To prepare meatballs combine all ingredients and shape into balls. Arrange in baking dish.
2. To prepare sauce combine all ingredients and mix well. Pour over meatballs.
3. Bake at 350° for 1 hour.

Make-Ahead Barbecued Meatballs

Edna Smucker
New Holland, PA

Makes 80 meatballs

Meatballs:
3 lbs. ground beef
12-oz. can evaporated milk
1 cup uncooked oats
1 cup cracker crumbs
2 eggs
½ cup chopped onions
½ tsp. garlic powder
2 tsp. salt *or* less
½ tsp. pepper
2 tsp. chili powder

Sauce:
2 cups ketchup
1 cup brown sugar
½ tsp. liquid smoke
½ tsp. garlic powder
¼ cup chopped onions

1. To make meatballs combine all ingredients (mixture will be soft) and shape into walnut-sized balls. Arrange meatballs in a single layer on waxed paper-lined cookie sheets. Freeze until solid. Store frozen meatballs in freezer bags until ready to cook.
2. To prepare sauce combine all ingredients and stir until sugar dissolves.
3. Place 20-30 frozen meatballs in a 9" x 13" baking pan. Pour sauce over meatballs.
4. Bake at 350° for 1 hour.

Sweet and Sour Meatballs

Patti Smith, Columbia, PA
Esta M. Ansel, Reamstown, PA

Makes 4-6 servings

Meatballs:
1 lb. sausage
2 lbs. ground beef
1½ cups bread crumbs
1-2 eggs
Pinch nutmeg
Pinch garlic salt
1 medium onion, chopped
¼ cup milk

Sauce:
½ cup sugar
½ cup vinegar
⅓ cup pineapple juice
¼ cup ketchup
1 Tbsp. soy sauce
3 Tbsp. cornstarch
3 Tbsp. water
15¼-oz. can pineapple chunks
1 medium green pepper, chopped

1. Mix all meatball ingredients and shape into balls.
2. Bake at 325° for 15 minutes.
3. In a large saucepan combine sugar, vinegar, pineapple juice, ketchup, and soy sauce and bring to a boil.
4. Combine cornstarch and water and stir into sauce. Add pineapple chunks and green pepper and heat through, stirring occasionally.
5. Add meatballs to sauce. Heat and serve.

Beef Barbecue

Anna N. Buckwalter, Ronks, PA
Valerie Voran, Ephrata, PA
Traci Kreider, Lancaster, PA
Sara Steffy, Ephrata, PA
Anna Mary Boyer, Akron, PA

Makes 6-8 servings

2 lbs. ground beef
1 medium onion, diced
½ cup ketchup
¼ cup water
Salt and pepper to taste
2 Tbsp. vinegar
2 Tbsp. brown sugar
1 tsp. dry mustard
1 tsp. Worcestershire sauce
6-8 hamburger rolls

1. Brown ground beef and onion until light brown. Drain excess fat.
2. Add all remaining ingredients and simmer 20 minutes or longer. Serve with hamburger rolls.

Sloppy Joes

Esther Gingrich, Lancaster, PA
Pam Nussbaum, Reinholds, PA

Makes 4-6 servings

1 lb. lean ground beef
1 onion, chopped
2 stalks celery, chopped
¼ cup chopped green pepper
¼ cup ketchup
3 Tbsp. brown sugar
2 Tbsp. vinegar
2 tsp. prepared mustard
1 tsp. Worcestershire sauce
1 tsp. salt

1 tsp. chili powder
6-oz. can tomato paste

1. In a skillet brown ground beef. Add onion, celery, and green pepper and heat through.
2. Add all other ingredients except tomato paste and simmer for 10-15 mintues. Add tomato paste and heat through. Serve.

Corned Beef Barbecue

Barbara Hoffert
Denver, PA

Makes 8-10 servings

½ cup chopped onion
2 Tbsp. chopped celery
2 Tbsp. green pepper
1 Tbsp. vinegar
1 cup ketchup
1 cup water
2 Tbsp. prepared mustard
1 Tbsp. sugar
2 small cans corned beef
8-10 sandwich rolls

1. Combine all ingredients except sandwich rolls in a saucepan and cook over medium heat, stirring frequently to blend ingredients.
2. When blended, simmer for 20 minutes.
3. Serve on your favorite rolls.

Rangeburgers
Elsie M. Beachy
Lancaster, PA

Makes 8 servings

1 egg
½ cup milk
½ cup dry bread crumbs
1 tsp. salt
¼ tsp. pepper
1 Tbsp. chopped onion
1½ lb. ground beef
8 hamburger rolls

1. In a bowl beat egg with fork until foamy. Add milk, bread crumbs, salt, pepper, and onion. Mix well with a fork.
2. Add ground beef and mix well by hand. Shape into 8 patties.
3. Fry in skillet for 10-12 minutes or make on the grill. Serve with hamburger rolls and choice of condiments.

Cheese Steak Sandwiches
Mary Louise Kurtz
Ephrata, PA

Makes 4 servings

1 pound raw chipped steak
1 onion, diced
Salt and pepper to taste
8-oz. jar steak sauce
8 slices white American cheese
4 steak rolls

1. In a skillet brown steak slowly. Add onions, salt, and pepper and sauté until onions are transparent.
2. In a saucepan heat steak sauce over medium-low heat.
3. Lay cheese over browned steak and cover skillet to melt cheese.

4. Fill each roll with cheese steak. Top with sauce. Serve.

Greco's Sandwiches
Ida Jane Zercher
Willow Street, PA

Makes 20 sandwiches

1½ lbs. chipped ham
½ lb. Velveeta cheese
4 hard-boiled eggs, chopped
2 small onions, chopped
1 cup mayonnaise
½ cup chili sauce
20 sandwich rolls

1. Cut through chipped ham to make fine pieces.
2. Cut Velveeta cheese into small pieces.
3. Combine all ingredients except sandwich rolls and mix well.
4. Fill each sandwich roll with mixture and wrap individually in aluminum foil. (May be refrigerated overnight.)
5. Immediately before serving, place in 400° oven for 10 minutes.

Casseroles

Turkey Crockpot Stew

Marilyn Langeman
Akron, PA

Makes 6-8 servings

2 lbs. skinless turkey thighs
1 lb. carrots
2 onions, chopped
20 small, new potatoes
2 bay leaves
2 Tbsp. Worcestershire sauce
1 tsp. salt
1/4 tsp. pepper
15-oz. can tomato sauce

1. Cut turkey thighs into chunks.
2. Peel and cut carrots into 1-inch lengths.
3. Combine all ingredients in crockpot.
4. Cook on low for 8-12 hours.

Turkey Noodle Casserole

Virginia W. Paxson
Quarryville, PA

Makes 6 servings

4 ozs. fine noodles
1 1/2 cups cubed, cooked turkey
10 3/4-oz. can cream of mushroom soup
10-oz. pkg. frozen peas, thawed
2 Tbsp. diced pimento
1/2 cup milk
1 cup shredded cheddar cheese

1. Cook noodles according to package directions. Drain and rinse.
2. Combine all ingredients except cheese. Arrange 1/2 of mixture in greased 1 1/2-quart baking dish. Sprinkle with 1/2 of cheese. Repeat layers.
3. Bake at 350° for 25-30 minutes.

Turkey Strata Casserole

Betty Kissinger
Lancaster, PA

Makes 6 servings

8 slices bread
2½ cups diced, cooked turkey
½ cup chopped celery
¼ cup chopped onion
½ cup mayonnaise
¾ tsp. salt
Dash pepper
2 eggs, slightly beaten
1 cup milk
½ cup turkey broth
10¾-oz. can cream of mushroom soup
½ cup grated American cheese

1. Trim crusts from bread. Butter 2 slices of bread, cut in ½-inch cubes and set aside.
2. Cut remaining bread into 1-inch cubes and put ½ of unbuttered cubes in bottom of 2-quart casserole dish.
3. In a bowl combine turkey, vegetables, mayonnaise, and seasonings. Spoon over bread cubes. Sprinkle remaining unbuttered cubes over turkey mixture.
4. Combine eggs, milk, and broth and pour over all. Cover and chill 1 hour or overnight.
5. Spoon mushroom soup over top of dish. Sprinkle with buttered bread cubes.
6. Bake at 325° for 40 minutes or until set and bubbly. Sprinkle grated cheese over top and bake 10 minutes longer.

Turkey Hash

Madeline Hartzell
Lancaster, PA

Makes 4 servings

1½ cups coarsely ground turkey
1 cup cubed, cooked potatoes
5-oz. can evaporated milk
¼ cup parsley
¼ cup chopped onions
1 tsp. Worcestershire sauce
½ tsp. salt
Dash pepper
¼ tsp. sage
¼ cup crushed saltine crackers
1 Tbsp. butter *or* margarine, melted

1. Stir together all ingredients except cracker crumbs and butter. Turn into lightly greased 1-quart casserole dish.
2. Toss together cracker crumbs and butter and sprinkle on top of casserole ingredients.
3. Bake, uncovered, at 350° for 30 minutes.

The Farmersville Quilting

Once a year the Ladies' Auxiliary of the Farmersville Fire Company holds a three-day quilting to prepare quilts for our annual community sale. On each of these days we prepare food for those who come out to the quilting bee. Each woman brings along a salad and dessert, and we prepare the Oven-Baked Barbecue Chicken recipe found on page 74.

Over the three-day period we usually quilt as many as twenty donated quilts which are then auctioned at our sale.

—*Sara Steffy, Ephrata, PA*

Elm and Penryn

*A*bout two-and-a-half miles southeast of Elm in northern Lancaster County, where Memorial Road meets Newport Road, a roadside monument commemorates the arrival of the region's first Bombergers. Christian and Maria Bomberger with their eight children left Baden, Germany in 1722 and settled the tract of land which surrounds the area where some of their descendants still live and work.

When superstores began to take over village groceries and gas stations, the current Bombergers decided to try to keep local business in Elm. Today Bomberger's Lawn and Garden, Bomberger's Grocery Store, and Bomberger's Hardware serve the nearby towns and rural community.

About a mile-and-a-half west of Elm, the picturesque, residential village of Penryn is quiet most of the year. According to local resident, Dorothy Galebach, the Penryn Fire Company, the Lutheran Church, and the United Church of Christ all prepare Chicken Corn Soup for fund raiser events. Galebach says, "All roads lead to Penryn when the aroma of Chicken Corn Soup floats from the fire hall or one of the churches."

Scalloped Potatoes with Turkey
Jeanette Barr
Stevens, PA

Makes 4-6 servings

10¾-oz. can cream of mushroom soup
½ cup milk
½ tsp. salt
¼ tsp. pepper
¼ cup finely chopped onion
3 cups sliced, cooked potatoes
2 cups diced, cooked turkey
1 Tbsp. butter *or* margarine

1. In large bowl blend together soup, milk, salt, pepper, and onion.
2. Alternate layers of potatoes and turkey in greased 1½-quart casserole dish. Top each layer with some of the soup mixture. Dot with butter.
3. Cover and bake at 350° for 30 minutes. Uncover and bake 10 minutes longer.

Chicken Broccoli Casserole
Margie Jones
Lancaster, PA

Makes 6-8 servings

3 chicken breasts
2 10-oz. pkgs. frozen broccoli
10¾-oz. can cream of mushroom soup
10¾-oz. can cream of celery soup
10¾-oz. can cream of chicken soup
1½ cups mayonnaise
1 tsp. lemon juice
1-1½ cups grated cheese
2 cups dry bread cubes
2 Tbsp. melted butter

1. Cook chicken breasts. Debone and dice meat.
2. Cook broccoli according to package directions. Drain and arrange in 9" x 13" baking pan. Put chicken pieces on top of broccoli.
3. In a bowl combine 3 cans of cream soups, mayonnaise, and lemon juice. Spread on top of chicken. Sprinkle with grated cheese.

4. Mix dry bread cubes with melted butter and sprinkle on top of cheese.

5. Bake at 350° for 35 minutes.

Easy Chicken Casserole

Audrey Landis
Ronks, PA

Makes 8-10 servings

2 cups diced, cooked chicken
1 cup diced, raw carrots
1 cup frozen peas
1 cup diced onion
½ tsp. salt
2 10¾-oz. cans cream of chicken soup
1 medium bag Tater Tots

1. Combine all ingredients except Tater Tots and pour into greased 9" x 13" casserole dish. Arrange Tater Tots over top of casserole ingredients.

2. Cover and bake at 350° for 1½ to 2 hours.

Chicken and Vegetable Bake

Barbara Hummel
Brownstown, PA

Makes 4-6 servings

2 chicken breasts
2 10¾-oz. cans cream of chicken soup
½ soup can milk
½ cup mayonnaise
1 box triscuits, crushed
10-oz. pkg. frozen peas
2 8-oz. jars mushrooms, drained

1. Cook chicken breasts. Cool, skin, debone, and dice meat.

2. In a bowl mix soup with milk and mayonnaise. Stir in chicken, peas, mushrooms, and ½ of triscuits. Spoon into greased, 8-inch square baking dish. Top with remaining triscuits.

3. Bake at 350° for 30 minutes.

Chicken Rice Casserole

Barbara and Leah Martin
East Earl, PA

Makes 4-5 servings

1½ cups cubed, cooked chicken
1 cup chopped celery
2 Tbsp. finely chopped onion
10¾-oz. can cream of chicken soup
1 Tbsp. lemon juice
½ tsp. salt
½ tsp. pepper
1½ cups cooked rice
¾ cup mayonnaise
½ cup water
2 cups potato chips, crushed

1. Combine all ingredients except potato chips and mix well. Spoon into greased casserole dish and top with potato chips.

2. Bake at 350° for 30 minutes.

Rice and Cheese

Jane Groff
Lancaster, PA

Makes 4 large servings

1 cup uncooked rice
1 pint tomato juice
1 small onion, chopped
5 Tbsp. brown sugar
2 tsp. salt
½ lb. grated cheese

1. Cook rice according to directions.
2. To cooked rice add tomato juice, onion, sugar, and salt and cook 5 minutes longer.
3. In a casserole dish alternate layers of rice with layers of cheese.
4. Bake at 350° for 20-25 minutes.

Baked Rice

Betty Pellman
Millersville, PA

Makes 4-5 servings

1 medium onion, chopped
2 Tbsp. butter *or* margarine
10¾-oz. can beef broth
⅔ cup water
1 cup uncooked, long-grain rice
¼ cup sliced almonds
1 tsp. butter *or* margarine

1. Sauté onion in 2 Tbsp. butter. Add beef broth and water and bring to a boil.
2. Pour uncooked rice into greased casserole dish. Pour hot broth over rice.
3. Cover and bake at 350° for 40-45 minutes.
4. Toast almonds in 1 tsp. butter. Immediately before serving, sprinkle over baked rice.

Rice, Corn, and Cheese Casserole

Miriam E. Lefever
East Petersburg, PA

Makes 6 servings

1 cup uncooked brown *or* white rice
2 cups fresh corn
½ cup finely chopped onion
2 cups grated sharp cheddar cheese
1½ cups skim milk
½ tsp. salt
½ tsp. chili powder
¼ tsp. black pepper
Paprika

1. In large mixing bowl combine all ingredients except paprika and mix well. Spoon into greased 2-quart casserole dish. Sprinkle with paprika.
2. Bake at 350° for 40-45 minutes.

Corn Patch Casserole

Fannie Ressler
Lititz, PA

Makes 4-6 servings

8-oz. pkg. noodles
2 cups canned corn, drained
10¾-oz. can cream of mushroom soup
¾ cup milk
8-oz. can spam, cubed
½ cup grated sharp cheese
½ tsp. paprika

1. Cook noodles according to package directions. Drain and spoon into casserole dish. Add corn, mushroom soup, milk, and spam and mix lightly. Top with cheese and paprika.
2. Bake at 350° for 30 minutes.

Mushroom Surprise

Mary Ella Herr
Quarryville, PA

Makes 8 servings

1½ lbs. fresh mushrooms
2 Tbsp. margarine
2 Tbsp. flour
1 cup milk
½ cup grated cheddar cheese
2 Tbsp. minced onion
¾ cup soft bread crumbs
1 tsp. salt
2 egg yolks, well beaten
2 egg whites, stiffly beaten
½ cup crushed potato chips

1. Cut mushrooms into small pieces. In a saucepan with small amount of water cook until tender.

2. In separate saucepan melt margarine. Blend in flour until bubbly. Gradually add milk, stirring constantly until smooth and thickened. Remove from heat. Blend in cheese until melted, stirring frequently.

3. Add drained mushrooms, onion, bread crumbs, salt, and egg yolks and mix lightly. Fold in beaten egg whites. Turn into greased baking dish and top with potato chips.

4. Place in pan of hot water and bake at 350° for 50 minutes or until browned and firm.

Green Dragon Market

Going to Green Dragon Farmer's Market in Ephrata was a favorite Friday-evening ritual in our family. The weekend officially began as we piled into the car and headed to "the Dragon". From French Fries soaked in vinegar to a juicy cheese steak sandwich, the market overflowed with culinary delights. We browsed through the new additions at the used book stand, cast a sideways glance at the gawdy wares peddled by out-of-towners, and savored the candy from one of the many brown bags Dad accumulated throughout the evening. A grand place for smells and sights and sounds and tastes, I never remember coming home disappointed. Each week there was something new, yet the Dragon had enough familiarity to feel as comfortable as home.

—*Gina Burkhart, Landisville, PA*

Unstuffed Cabbage

Verna Graham
Gordonville, PA

Makes 6-8 servings

1¼ lbs. ground beef
½ cup onion, chopped
2 eggs, beaten
¾ cup uncooked rice
Salt and pepper to taste
1 head cabbage
10¾-oz. can tomato soup
1½ soup cans water
1 cup spaghetti sauce

1. Combine ground beef, onion, eggs, rice, salt, and pepper and mix well. Form into balls and arrange in casserole dish.

2. Shred cabbage over and around meatballs.

3. In a bowl combine tomato soup, water, and sauce. Pour over cabbage and meat.

4. Bake at 400° for 30 minutes. Reduce oven temperature to 325° and bake 1 hour longer, stirring occasionally to keep juice on cabbage.

Eggplant Skillet

Esta M. Ansel
Reamstown, PA

Makes 4-6 servings

1 lb. ground beef
¼ cup chopped onion
¼ cup chopped celery
8-oz. can tomato sauce
½ cup water
½ tsp. oregano
½ tsp. chili powder
1 medium eggplant
Salt and pepper to taste
4 ozs. American cheese, grated
Paprika

1. In a skillet cook beef, onions, and celery until meat is browned. Drain excess fat. Stir in tomato sauce, water, oregano, and chili powder.

2. Cut eggplant in ½-inch slices. Season with salt and pepper. Arrange over meat sauce. Cover and simmer until eggplant is tender, about 15-20 minutes.

3. Spoon into serving dish. Top with grated cheese and sprinkle with paprika.

Soybean Casserole

Miriam E. Lefever
East Petersburg, PA

Makes 6 servings

1 Tbsp. cooking oil
½ cup chopped onion
1 cup chopped celery
¼ cup chopped green pepper
¼ lb. ground beef *or* turkey
1 beef bouillon cube
1 cup hot water
1 tsp. salt
⅛ tsp. pepper
½ tsp. seasoned salt
2½ cups cooked soybeans
1¼ cups tomato sauce *or* stewed tomatoes
2 cups cooked rice
¾ cup soft bread crumbs
1 Tbsp. melted butter
½ cup grated cheese

1. Sauté oil, onion, celery, green pepper, and ground meat in large, heavy skillet to brown.

2. Dissolve bouillon cube in hot water. Add remaining ingredients except bread crumbs, butter, and cheese and simmer until well mixed. Spoon into greased casserole dish.

3. Combine bread crumbs and melted butter and sprinkle over casserole ingredients.

4. Bake at 350° for 40 minutes. Remove from oven and sprinkle with cheese. Return to oven and bake 5 minutes longer.

Baked Potatoes Stuffed with Salmon

Mildred M. Ney
Columbia, PA

Makes 6-8 servings

1 lb. canned salmon
8 medium baked potatoes
½ cup milk
1 onion, chopped
Salt and pepper to taste
1 cup bread crumbs
2 Tbsp. butter

1. Flake salmon, removing all skin and bones.

2. Slice off tops of potatoes and scoop out contents. Mash thoroughly, adding milk, onion, and seasoning to taste. Fold in salmon.

3. Stuff mixture into potato shells. Cover with bread crumbs and dot with butter. Arrange in greased casserole dish, putting any extra stuffing on the side.

4. Bake at 400° for 25 minutes.

Corn and Oyster Bake
Darlene Rohrer-Meck
Lancaster, PA

Makes 8-10 servings

2 dozen medium oysters with broth
2 pints frozen corn
10¾-oz. can cream of mushroom soup
1 cup grated cheddar cheese
2 eggs, beaten
Seasoned salt to taste
2 package-sized stacks Ritz crackers, crushed
½ cup margarine

1. Cut up oysters. In a saucepan heat oysters in their broth. Remove from heat and add corn, soup, cheese, eggs, seasoning, and ½ of crackers. Pour into 9" x 13" baking dish.

2. Melt margarine and stir in remaining crackers. Sprinkle over casserole ingredients.

3. Bake at 350° for 30 minutes.

Dried Beef Casserole
Audrey Landis
Ronks, PA

Makes 4-6 servings

2 cups peas
1½ cups water
3 Tbsp. butter
3 Tbsp. flour
¾ cup milk
1 cup liquid from peas
¼ lb. shredded dried beef
¼ tsp. pepper
3 cups sliced, cooked potatoes
¼ tsp. salt
⅓ cup fine bread crumbs

1. Cook peas in 1½ cups water until just tender. Reserve 1 cup liquid.

2. In a saucepan melt butter. Blend in flour and quickly add milk and liquid from peas. Cook until thickened, stirring constantly. Stir in dried beef, peas, and pepper.

3. Arrange cooked potatoes in greased 8-inch square casserole dish. Sprinkle with salt. Pour dried beef mixture over potatoes. Arrange bread crumbs over top.

4. Bake at 375° for 20 minutes.

Luncheon Meat Skillet
Esther Becker
Gap, PA

Makes 4-6 servings

2 tsp. margarine
12-oz. can luncheon meat, cut into
    thick strips
1/2 cup coarsely chopped pecans
2 16-oz. cans yams
2 medium apples
1/2 cup raisins
1/2 tsp. ginger
1/4 cup maple-flavored syrup

1. Melt margarine in large, deep skillet.
Add luncheon meat and stir fry for 3-4
minutes. Add pecans and stir fry 1 minute
longer. Remove ingredients to a bowl.

2. Drain yams, reserving 3/4 cup liquid.

3. Core, peel, and slice apples.

4. Stir yams, 3/4 cup liquid, apples,
raisins, and ginger into skillet. Bring to a
boil. Reduce temperature, cover, and
simmer for about 8 minutes, stirring
occasionally. Gently stir in meat and pecan
mixture. Pour syrup over mixture and heat
through. Serve immediately.

Ham, Peas, and Potato Casserole
Ruth Good
Ephrata, PA

Makes 6 servings

1 cup chopped celery
1/2 tsp. salt
1 1/2 cups boiling water
1 1/2 cups cubed potatoes
Milk
1/4 cup butter *or* margarine
1/4 cup chopped onion
1/4 cup flour
2 cups cubed ham
2 Tbsp. parsley
1 cup cooked peas
1/2 cup grated cheese

1. Add chopped celery and salt to
boiling water. Cook for 10 minutes. Add
potatoes and cook 15 minutes longer. Drain
and reserve liquid.

2. Add enough milk to potato water to
make 1 1/2 cups.

3. In a large saucepan melt butter. Add
onion and cook on low heat until it turns
yellow. Add flour and blend well.
Gradually add liquid, stirring constantly
until sauce thickens. Boil for 1 minute.
Remove from heat and add ham, parsley,
celery, potatoes, and peas.

4. Spoon into greased 1 1/2-quart casserole
dish and top with grated cheese.

5. Bake, uncovered, at 325° for about 30
minutes or until hot and bubbly.

*Note: Occasionally, I mix this the day before
and refrigerate it overnight. Bake at 350° for
45 minutes if it has been refrigerated.*

Ephrata

*H*ome of Doneckers, the Ephrata Cloister, and the Mountain Springs Hotel, the north-central Lancaster County borough of Ephrata combines a fascinating blend of the old and the new.

The first Europeans arrived in 1732 when a German religious group sought refuge on the banks of the Cocalico Creek, which flows through the center of the town. Calling for celibacy and communal living, the group's leader, Conrad Beissel, established a thriving monastic order, including both sisters and brothers. Residents of the Ephrata Cloister, as it came to be called, became famous throughout the colonies for their beautiful music, inspired fraktur illumination, and the first German printing of the *Martyrs' Mirror*, a collection of profiles of early Anabaptist Christians. After Beissel's death in 1768, he was succeeded by Peter Miller, most often remembered as the person who translated the *Martyrs' Mirror* from its original Dutch to German. During the Revolutionary War, the Cloister also served as a hospital for wounded troops following the battle at Brandywine. By the late 1800s the community had been dissolved and the buildings had fallen into disrepair.

Instead much of the energy and life in Ephrata revolved around a magnificent resort built in 1848 on the opposite ridge of the Cocalico. Noted for its pure water and relaxing atmosphere, the Mountain Springs Hotel provided accommodations for people like Thaddeus Stevens and James Buchanan. The town was officially named Ephrata in 1891.

One hundred years later in 1993 the state-owned museum, called the Ephrata Cloister, recreates the stories of the brothers and sisters who lived and worked on the site in the eighteenth and nineteenth centuries. The hotel, on the other hand, stands behind an overgrowth of weeds and trees, the subject of many a haunted house tale.

Built around the point where State Street crosses Route 322, modern-day Ephrata attracts people as varied as Old Order Mennonites, who live in the surrounding rural areas, and upscale shoppers examining the latest fashions at Doneckers, an eighteen-department specialty store offering the latest designer lines. The Doneckers community also includes two guest houses, The Restaurant at Doneckers, and The Artworks at Doneckers.

Sausage Potato Fry
Alice Whitman
Lititz, PA

Makes 4-6 servings

1 lb. Italian sausage
4 medium potatoes, diced
1 large onion, chopped
1 green pepper, chopped
1 garlic clove, minced
½ tsp. paprika
Salt and pepper to taste
½ cup water

1. Brown meat in skillet. Drain excess fat.
2. Add chopped potatoes, onion, green pepper, garlic, seasonings, and water.
3. Cover and cook on low heat about 20-30 minutes or until potatoes are cooked. Stir occasionally. Serve.

Easy Potato Sausage Casserole
Ruth Ann Becker
Manheim, PA

Makes 4 servings

4-6 potatoes
1½-2 lbs. link sausage
10¾-oz. can cream of celery soup
1 soup can milk
Paprika

1. Slice potatoes thinly. Cut sausage into 1-inch pieces. In a greased casserole dish alternate layers of potatoes and sausage.

2. In a saucepan heat together soup and milk. Pour soup mixture over casserole ingredients. Sprinkle with paprika.

3. Bake at 350° about 1 hour or until potatoes are cooked.

Farm-Style Sausage Potato Swirl
Wanda Eby
Denver, PA

Makes 4 servings

4-5 large potatoes
3-4 green onions, sliced
2 cloves garlic, minced
2 Tbsp. butter *or* margarine
¾ cup hot milk
2 egg yolks
Dash black pepper
Dash nutmeg
3 Tbsp. chopped parsley
½ cup diced mozzarella cheese
1-lb. link smoked sausage, sliced
2 Tbsp. Parmesan cheese
1 tsp. dried thyme

1. Peel and cube potatoes. Cook in salt water until tender. Drain.

2. Mash potatoes. Add green onions and garlic; mix to blend. Add butter, hot milk, egg yolks, pepper, and nutmeg and whip until light and fluffy.

3. Fold in parsley, mozzarella cheese, sausage slices, and Parmesan cheese. Spoon mixture into greased casserole dish. Sprinkle with thyme.

4. Turn oven to broil and heat 5-7 minutes or until lightly browned.

Six Layer Sausage Casserole
Linda Seldomridge
Gap, PA

Makes 6-8 servings

1¼ lbs. link sausage
2 cups sliced raw potatoes
½ cup sliced onions
1¼ cups sliced carrots
1 cup uncooked rice
1 quart tomato juice
½ tsp. salt
⅛ tsp. pepper
1 Tbsp. sugar

1. Lightly brown sausage. Drain all excess fat and cut into small pieces.

2. Layer potatoes, onions, carrots, and rice into greased 2-quart casserole dish. Pour tomato juice over all and sprinkle with seasonings. Top with sausage.

3. Cover and bake at 350° for 1½ to 2 hours.

Sausage and Browned Potato Skillet

Betty Pellman
Millersville, PA

Makes 2-3 servings

1 lb. fresh link sausage
3 medium potatoes
Water
Salt and pepper to taste

1. Pierce sausage on all sides and arrange in skillet.
2. Scrub potatoes, cut into quarters, and place in skillet with sausage. Add ½ cup water.
3. Cover and cook on medium. After water has absorbed, turn sausage and potatoes. Add ½ cup water.
4. Cover again and cook on medium until water has absorbed. Repeat until sausage and potatoes are browned.
5. Immediately before serving, season potatoes to taste.

Spicy Sausage and Beans

Barbara Evans
Ephrata, PA

Makes 4-6 servings

½ lb. Italian sausage, sliced
1 cup chopped onion
1 clove garlic, minced
16-oz. can stewed tomatoes
16-oz. can kidney beans, drained
8-oz. can tomato sauce
½ tsp. chili powder

1. In a skillet cook meat, onion, and garlic until onion is tender. Drain excess fat.
2. Add tomatoes, beans, tomato sauce, and chili powder. Cook over medium heat for 15 minutes or until desired consistency.

Salsa Beef Potatoes

Tammy Foltz
Mountville, PA

Makes 4 servings

2 medium potatoes, baked
¼ lb. ground beef
½ cup salsa
2-4 Tbsp. sour cream
1 oz. cheddar cheese, shredded

1. Cut baked potatoes in half and mash inside ingredients slightly with a fork.
2. Brown ground beef in skillet. Stir in salsa and heat through. Spoon beef mixture evenly over each potato half. Top with sour cream and cheese. Serve.

Chili Burritos
Cindy Bryan
Adamstown, PA

Makes 4-6 servings

8-10 soft tortillas
½ lb. ground beef
16-oz. can baked beans
1 cup shredded cheese
Salsa

1. Warm tortillas slightly in oven or microwave.
2. Brown ground beef in skillet. Drain excess fat. Stir in baked beans and cheese and heat through.
3. Spread mixture evenly onto tortillas. Roll up and tuck ends under. Arrange in greased, shallow casserole dish.
4. Bake at 350° for 10 minutes. Serve with salsa as a dip.

Jiffy Meat and Potato Pie
Catherine Shirk
Ephrata, PA

Makes 6 servings

1 lb. ground beef
½ cup chopped onion
½ cup milk
1 egg, beaten
1 tsp. salt
¼ tsp. pepper
½ cup soft bread cubes
2 cups mashed potatoes
¾ cup grated cheese

1. Combine all ingredients except potatoes and cheese. Mix thoroughly and press into bottom of 9-inch pie pan.

2. Bake at 350° for 35 minutes. Drain all excess fat.
3. Spread mashed potatoes over meat. Sprinkle with cheese.
4. Return to oven and bake 10 minutes longer or until cheese melt.

Shepherd's Pie
Lori Ney
Columbia, PA

Makes 6 servings

1 lb. ground beef
1 small onion, chopped
12-oz. can corn
2 cups firm mashed potatoes

1. Brown ground beef and onion. Drain the excess fat. Press into bottom of shallow casserole dish.
2. Layer corn and potatoes over meat mixture.
3. Bake at 350° for 30 minutes.

Hamburger Cheese Bake
Anna Mae Conley
Mount Joy, PA

Makes 8-10 servings

1 lb. ground beef
½ cup chopped onion
2 8-oz. cans tomato sauce
1 Tbsp. sugar
¾ tsp. garlic salt
¼ tsp. pepper
4 cups uncooked noodles
1 cup cottage cheese
8-oz. pkg. cream cheese
¼ cup sour cream
⅓ cup sliced green onions

¼ cup chopped green pepper
¼ cup Parmesan cheese

1. Brown ground beef and onion. Drain excess fat.
2. Add tomato sauce, sugar, garlic salt, and pepper and simmer, stirring occasionally.
3. Cook noodles according to package directions. Drain and add cottage cheese, cream cheese, and sour cream. Fold in green onions and peppers. Spread ½ of noodle mixture into 9" x 13" baking dish. Spread ½ meat mixture. Add remaining noodles and remaining meat. Top with Parmesan cheese.
4. Bake at 350° for 30 minutes.

𝒱egetable Beef Casserole
Ida E. Winters
Lititz, PA

Makes 6 servings

½ lb. ground beef
½ cup chopped onions
1 clove garlic, crushed
½ cup sliced carrots
16-oz. can pinto beans, drained
16-oz. can tomatoes
1¾ cups beef broth
1 cup water
1 bay leaf
½ tsp. basil
¼ tsp. pepper
1 tsp. salt
½ cup uncooked elbow macaroni
10-oz. pkg. frozen green beans

1. Brown ground beef, onions, and garlic. Drain excess fat. Add carrots, pinto

beans, tomatoes, broth, water, and seasonings.
2. Simmer for 20 minutes, stirring occasionally.
3. Add macaroni and cook 10 minutes longer. Add green beans and cook 10 more minutes. Remove bay leaf and serve.

𝓑rown Beef Stew
Loretta Lapp
Kinzer, PA

Makes 6 servings

1 lb. beef cubes
3 Tbsp. chopped onions
Salt and pepper to taste
2 Tbsp. margarine
1½ cups boiling water
4 potatoes, cut into quarters
1½ cups canned tomatoes *or* tomato
    juice
4 large carrots, sliced lengthwise
2 medium onions, quartered
1½ cups green beans
Pinch basil

1. In a skillet brown beef cubes, 3 Tbsp. chopped onions, salt, and pepper in margarine. Add boiling water and potatoes and cook until potatoes soften.
2. Add tomatoes and simmer for 1 hour. Add all remaining ingredients, bring to a boil, and simmer for 30 minutes or until vegetables are soft.

Biscuit and Beef Casserole
Debra Hoover
Paradise, PA

Makes 6 servings

1½ lbs. ground beef
1 Tbsp. minced onion
1 cup barbecue sauce
1 Tbsp. brown sugar
16-oz. can baked beans
10-oz. can refrigerated biscuits
½ cup shredded cheddar cheese

1. Brown ground beef and onion together. Drain excess fat. Stir in barbecue sauce, sugar, and baked beans and heat until bubbly. Pour into 2½-quart casserole dish.
2. Separate dough into 10 biscuits. Cut each in half crosswise. Arrange biscuits, cut side down, over hot meat mixture in a spoke fashion. Sprinkle with cheese.
3. Bake at 375° for 25-30 minutes or until biscuits are golden brown.

Pizza
Tina Snyder
Manheim, PA

Makes 4-6 servings

½ lb. ground beef
1 pkg. yeast
1 tsp. sugar
1 cup warm water
2 Tbsp. cooking oil
2½ cups flour
1 tsp. salt
15-oz. can tomato sauce
½ cup chopped onion
½ tsp. salt
½ tsp. garlic salt

2 tsp. oregano
½ lb. pepperoni, sliced
1 cup sliced mushrooms
2 green peppers, sliced
½ cup Parmesan cheese
8 ozs. mozzarella cheese, sliced

1. Brown ground beef. Drain excess fat and set aside.
2. Dissolve yeast and sugar in warm water. Add oil.
3. Combine flour and 1 tsp. salt. Pour yeast mixture over dry ingredients and mix thoroughly. Let rest 5 minutes.
4. Roll dough out onto greased pizza pan or cookie sheet, forming edges. Pour tomato sauce over crust. Add remaining ingredients in order listed.
5. Bake at 425° for 20-25 minutes. Serve.

Pizza Cups
Julia S. Horst
Gordonville, PA

Makes 10 pizza cups

¾ lb. ground beef
6-oz. can tomato paste
1 Tbsp. minced onion
1 tsp. Italian seasoning
½ tsp. salt
10-oz. can refrigerated biscuits
½ cup shredded mozzarella cheese

1. Brown and drain ground beef. Stir in tomato paste, onion, seasoning, and salt and cook over low heat for 5 minutes, stirring frequently.
2. Place biscuits in greased muffin tins, pressing each one to cover bottoms and sides.
3. Spoon about ¼ cup meat mixture into biscuit-lined cups. Sprinkle evenly with cheese.

4. Bake at 400° for 12 minutes or until golden brown.

Variation: Substitute 6 English muffins, sliced in half, for biscuits. Arrange muffins on baking sheet and divide meat mixture evenly over each muffin half. Sprinkle with cheese. Broil 2-4 minutes or until cheese has melted.
—*Arlene Martin, Stevens, PA*

Upside-Down Pizza
Anne H. Strickler
Lititz, PA

Makes 8-10 servings

1½ lbs. ground beef
1 medium onion, chopped
15½-oz. jar pizza sauce
½ tsp. garlic powder
¼ tsp. oregano
8 ozs. mozzarella cheese, grated
2 eggs
1 cup milk
1 Tbsp. cooking oil
1 cup flour
½ cup grated Parmesan cheese

1. In a skillet brown ground beef and onion. Drain all excess fat. Blend in pizza sauce, garlic powder, and oregano. Pour into greased 9" x 13" baking pan. Sprinkle with mozzarella cheese.
2. In a small bowl combine eggs, milk, oil, and flour and mix well. Spoon over meat mixture. Sprinkle with Parmesan cheese.
3. Bake at 350° for 30 minutes.

Note: Your choice of additional pizza ingredients may be added to meat mixture, if desired.

Wakefield

A few miles north of the Maryland border in the southern tip of Lancaster County, the farming village of Wakefield stretches thinly along the Robert Fulton Highway. In fact, numerous places in Fulton Township, which surrounds Wakefield, preserve the larger-than-life story of Robert Fulton, the nineteenth century inventor credited with developing the steamboat. The Robert Fulton Birthplace occasionally opens its doors for tours. The Robert Fulton Inn, nextdoor to the birthplace, is widely regarded as the best restaurant in southern Lancaster County. The Robert Fulton Fire Company and Fulton Elementary School offer community services to residents of the southern end. And the Fulton Grange serves the surrounding farm population.

Wakefield further has a strong Quaker influence. The Penn Hill Friends Meeting, established in 1758, still gathers each Sunday in its sturdy red-brick meetinghouse, just south of the point where Route 272 meets Route 222. Legend maintains Jeremiah Brown, husband of the congregation's leader, Mercy Brown, built the structure for $2000 in the 1820s when the building being used at the time became to small to hold the congregation.

Several old-fashioned garages, a food store, and a hardware store make up the tiny core of the village at the corner of Peach Bottom Road and Robert Fulton Highway.

Pizza Casserole
Linda Jean Martin
Reinholds, PA

Makes 4 servings

1 lb. lean ground beef
⅓ cup minced onion
½ tsp. garlic salt
¾ tsp. oregano
10¾-oz. can tomato soup
⅓ cup water
2 cups cooked noodles
½ cup grated mozzarella cheese

1. Brown ground beef with onion, garlic salt, and oregano. Drain any excess fat. Stir in all remaining ingredients except cheese. Spoon into casserole dish and sprinkle with cheese.
2. Bake at 350° for 30 minutes.

French Bread Stromboli
Elizabeth Anderson
Lancaster, PA

Makes 6 servings

2 Tbsp. sugar
1 tsp. salt
2 Tbsp. margarine
2 cups boiling water
2 pkgs. yeast
½ cup warm water
1 Tbsp. sugar
6 cups flour
½ lb. bulk sausage
½ lb. ground beef
½ lb. pepperoni, sliced
15-oz. can tomato sauce
½ lb. provolone cheese, grated
½ lb. mozzarella cheese, grated

1. In a large bowl combine 2 Tbsp. sugar, salt, margarine, and boiling water. Set aside to cool.
2. In small bowl combine yeast, warm water, and 1 Tbsp. sugar.
3. Combine boiling water mixture and yeast mixture. Gradually stir in flour, working with a spoon. Work by hands to form soft dough and place in warm place to rise.
4. Work down dough every 10 minutes for 50 minutes. Divide into 2 pieces and let rest 10 minutes. Roll each piece out to ¼"-thick round.
5. While dough is rising, brown sausage and ground beef in skillet. Drain all excess fat.
6. Arrange sausage, ground beef, pepperoni, tomato sauce, and cheeses evenly on each round of dough. Fold over and seal edges. Place on greased cookie sheet. Let rise until doubled.
7. Bake at 350° for 25-30 minutes.

Yummasetti
Lydia Shirk
Talmage, PA

Makes 12-15 servings

½ loaf bread
2 10¾-oz. cans mushroom soup
4 soup cans water
10¾-oz. can cream of chicken soup
2 soup cans water
1 cup sour cream
3 lbs. ground beef
1 large onion, diced
1 large pkg. noodles
1 pint peas

1. Toast and butter ½ loaf of bread.
2. In a large bowl combine mushroom soup, cream of chicken soup, waters, and sour cream and mix well.

3. Brown ground beef with onion. Drain all excess fat.

4. In a saucepan cook noodles according to package directions. Drain and rinse.

5. Combine all ingredients in large bowl and mix well. Pour into a roastpan.

6. Bake at 350° for 1 hour.

Lasagna Casserole
Gladys Stoesz
Akron, PA

Makes 8 servings

Meat Mixture:
2 lbs. ground beef
2 onions, chopped
16-oz. can tomatoes
6-oz. can tomato paste
1 tsp. salt
¼ tsp. pepper
½ tsp. oregano
¼ tsp. basil
1 clove garlic, minced
4-oz. jar sliced mushrooms

Cheese Mixture:
½ lb. rotini
10¾-oz. can cheddar cheese soup
1 cup cottage cheese
½ cup sour cream

1. In a skillet brown ground beef. Drain excess fat. Add all remaining meat mixture ingredients and simmer to blend flavors.

2. Cook rotini according to directions. Drain and rinse. Stir soup, cottage cheese, and sour cream into noodles.

3. In a 9" x 13" baking dish alternate layers of rotini mixture with meat mixture.

4. Bake at 350° for 30 minutes.

Lasagna
Jennifer Martin
Stevens, PA

Makes 15-20 servings

Meat Sauce:
½ lb. ground beef
½ lb. ground pork
1 cup chopped onion
1 garlic clove, minced
2 Tbsp. sugar
2 cups tomato juice
2 12-oz. cans tomato paste
1 cup water
2½ tsp. salt
1 tsp. black pepper
½ tsp. oregano

Other Ingredients:
1 lb. broad lasagna noodles
4 quarts boiling water
2 tsp. salt
2 lbs. cottage cheese
1 lb. mozzarella cheese, shredded
1 cup grated Parmesan cheese

1. To prepare meat sauce brown ground beef and pork in a skillet. Add onion and garlic and brown until golden. Stir in all remaining ingredients.

2. Cook meat sauce over low heat for 45 minutes to 1 hour.

3. Drop lasagna noodles into boiling salted water and cook 15 minutes. Rinse; handle carefully. Drain.

4. Place layer of noodles in bottom of two greased 9" x 13" baking pans. Top with layer of meat sauce. Sprinkle with cheeses. Repeat each layer two more times in each pan.

5. Bake at 375° for 30 minutes. Let set 10-15 minutes before serving. (Freeze one pan if not needed immediately.)

Meatless Lasagna
Colette Carrow
Akron, PA

Makes 15-20 servings

1-lb. pkg. lasagna noodles
46 ozs. ricotta cheese, grated
16 ozs. mozzarella cheese, grated
¼ tsp. oregano
2 eggs
¼ cup Parmesan cheese
Parsley flakes
Salt and pepper to taste
28-oz. jar spaghetti sauce

1. Cook noodles according to package directions. Drain noodles, place them on paper towels and pat dry.
2. Mix all remaining ingredients except spaghetti sauce in a large bowl.
3. Pour very thin layer of sauce into each of two greased 9" x 13" baking pans. Add layer of noodles and a thick layer of cheese mixture. Repeat layers 2 more times in each pan, adding small amount of sauce each time. Pour thin layer of sauce over top.
4. Bake at 350° for 1 hour. Let stand 10-15 minutes before serving. Serve with spaghetti sauce for those who desire more sauce.

Baked Spaghetti
Tammy Groff
Quarryville, PA

Makes 12-15 servings

2 lbs. ground beef
½ lb. bulk sausage
1½ cups chopped onion
2 large cloves garlic, minced
1 pkg. Italian seasoning mix
2 28-oz. jars spaghetti sauce
1 lb. spaghetti
8-10 slices American cheese

1. In large heavy pan brown beef, sausage, chopped onion, garlic, and Italian seasoning, stirring occasionally. Add spaghetti sauce and heat through.
2. Cook spaghetti according to package directions. Drain and rinse.
3. Fold spaghetti into meat mixture and spoon into large, shallow baking dish. Layer with slices of American cheese.
4. Bake at 400° for 20 minutes or until cheese is melted.

Spaghetti Pie
Margie Jones
Lancaster, PA

Makes 10-12 servings

1 lb. spaghetti
2 eggs
5-oz. can evaporated milk
12 ozs. mozzarella cheese, grated
1 lb. ground beef
28-oz. jar spaghetti sauce

1. Cook spaghetti according to package directions. Drain and rinse. Arrange over bottom of greased 9" x 13" baking pan.
2. In small bowl combine eggs and evaporated milk. Pour over spaghetti. Sprinkle with mozzarella cheese.
3. Brown ground beef in skillet. Drain all excess fat. Add spaghetti sauce and heat through. Pour over spaghetti mixture.
4. Bake at 350° for 45 minutes.

Macaroni Casserole
Julia C. Herman
Leola, PA

Makes 4 servings

4 ozs. elbow macaroni
1 lb. lean ground beef
1 small onion, diced
10¾-oz. can cream of mushroom soup
½ tsp. salt
Dash pepper
¾ cup grated cheese
2 slices bread, cubed
1 Tbsp. butter, melted

1. Cook macaroni according to directions. Drain, rinse, and set aside.

2. Brown ground beef and onion lightly in skillet. Drain any excess fat. Add soup, salt, and pepper and mix well. Add macaroni and stir lightly. Pour into 1-quart casserole dish. Sprinkle with cheese.

3. Combine bread cubes and melted butter and spread over casserole ingredients.

4. Bake at 350° for 15-20 minutes or until browned.

Creamy Macaroni and Cheese
Anne Nolt
Reinholds, PA

Makes 6 servings

8 ozs. elbow macaroni
¼ cup butter
¼ cup flour
1 tsp. dry mustard
Salt and pepper to taste
2 cups milk
2 cups grated cheddar cheese
1 tomato, sliced
½ cup croutons

1. Cook macaroni as directed. Rinse, drain, and set aside.

2. In a saucepan melt butter. Remove pan from heat and stir in flour, mustard, salt, and pepper. Cook until bubbly, stirring frequently. Gradually stir in milk and bring to a boil, stirring constantly. Lower heat and simmer for 1 minute. Stir in 1½ cups cheese and cooked macaroni.

3. Spoon mixture into 1½-quart casserole dish. Sprinkle with remaining ½ cup cheese. Top with sliced tomato and croutons.

4. Bake at 375° for 15 minutes or until golden brown and bubbly.

Baked Macaroni and Cheese
Ginny Lausch
Akron, PA

Makes 6 servings

1 lb. shells *or* regular macaroni
1/2 lb. sharp cheddar cheese, cubed
1/2 lb. Velveeta cheese, cubed
1/4 cup butter *or* margarine
Salt and pepper to taste
1 1/2 cups milk
1/2 cup bread crumbs

1. Cook macaroni according to directions; drain and rinse with cold water.
2. Spoon 1/2 of macaroni into greased casserole dish. Add 1/2 of cheddar cheese and 1/2 of Velveeta cheese. Dot with butter. Salt and pepper to taste. Repeat layers. Pour milk over all, moving layers so milk also reaches bottom of casserole.
3. Cover and bake at 325° for 30 minutes, stirring occasionally. Remove from oven, spread bread crumbs over top, and bake, uncovered, another 15 minutes.

Stuffed Giant Shells
Julie Weaver, Reinholds, PA
Karen Burkholder, New Holland, PA

Makes 6-8 servings

18 giant pasta shells
1 lb. ground beef
1/2 cup finely chopped onion
1 clove garlic, chopped
1/2 cup shredded mozzarella cheese
1/2 cup bread crumbs
1/2 tsp. oregano
1/2 tsp. salt
1/8 tsp. pepper
2 eggs, lightly beaten

28-oz. jar spaghetti sauce
1/2 cup Parmesan cheese (optional)

1. Cook shells in boiling, salted water for about 10 minutes. Drain and spread on waxed paper to keep shells from sticking together.
2. In a skillet brown ground beef, onion, and garlic. Drain excess fat and set aside to cool.
3. When slightly cooled, stir in mozzarella cheese, bread crumbs, oregano, salt, pepper, and eggs. Fill each shell with meat mixture.
4. Spoon a thin layer of spaghetti sauce on the bottom of a 9" x 13" baking pan. Place shells, open side down, into pan in single layer. Cover with remaining sauce and sprinkle with Parmesan cheese, if desired.
5. Cover and bake at 375° for 1 hour.

Thanksgiving Filling
Ruth E. Wenger
Akron, PA

Makes 12 servings

2 loaves stale bread
1 1/2 cups herb-seasoned stuffing
4 eggs, beaten
1 quart milk
Pinch saffron
1 1/2 cups chopped celery
1 bunch parsley, chopped
2 large onions, chopped
16 Tbsp. margarine

1. Cut or tear bread into bite-sized pieces. Add herb-seasoned stuffing and mix together.
2. Beat eggs and milk together. Stir in saffron and pour over bread. Mix well. (If

it is too dry, add more milk.) Add all remaining ingredients except margarine and mix thoroughly.

3. In a saucepan melt margarine until it begins to brown. Pour over bread mixture and mix well. Spoon bread filling into large roaster.

4. Bake at 350° for 20-25 minutes.

Bread Filling
Karen Burkholder
New Holland, PA

Makes 6 servings

4 eggs
2 cups milk
2 quarts soft bread cubes
4 Tbsp. butter, melted
1 Tbsp. chopped parsley
1 tsp. salt
1 tsp. sage

1. Beat eggs and add milk. Pour over bread cubes and mix well by hand.

2. Combine melted butter and seasonings. Add to bread cube mixture and mix well. Spoon into greased casserole dish.

3. Bake at 350° for 45 minutes.

Note: This recipe may also be used as stuffing for fowl.

Potato Filling
Rhoda Kilheffer, Manheim, PA
Erma J. Frey, Leola, PA
Norma I. Martin, Lititz, PA

Makes 10 servings

1 cup celery, diced
1 medium onion, diced
6 Tbsp. butter
1 large loaf bread
2 pinches saffron
1 cup boiling water
1 quart mashed potatoes
1 tsp. pepper
3 tsp. salt
1 quart milk or more
6 eggs, beaten

1. In a skillet sauté celery and onion in butter.

2. Tear bread into bite-sized pieces. Pour sautéed vegetables and butter over bread.

3. Dissolve saffron in boiling water. Pour over bread. Add all other ingredients and mix well. Spoon into greased 9" x 13" baking pan.

4. Bake at 350° for 45 minutes.

Note: Make sure mixture is moist. Add more milk if necessary.

Meat and Potato Quiche

Nora Eberly, New Holland, PA
Debra Stoltzfus, Kinzers, PA

Makes 1 9" quiche

½ lb. ground sausage
3 Tbsp. cooking oil
3 cups coarsely grated raw potatoes
1 cup grated Swiss *or* cheddar cheese
12-oz. can evaporated milk
2 eggs
½ tsp. salt
⅛ tsp. pepper
1 Tbsp. parsley flakes

1. Brown sausage and drain all excess fat. Set aside.
2. Combine cooking oil and grated potatoes and press into 9-inch pie pan.
3. Bake potato crust at 425° for 15-20 minutes or until just beginning to brown. Remove from oven.
4. Layer sausage and cheese over potato crust.
5. In a small bowl combine milk, eggs, salt, and pepper and mix well. Pour over sausage and cheese. Sprinkle with parsley flakes.
6. Return to oven and bake another 30 minutes until lightly browned and knife inserted in center comes out clean.
7. Cool 5 minutes and serve.

Microwave Bacon Quiche

Julia S. Horst
Gordonville, PA

Makes 4-6 servings

½ lb. bacon
1 cup shredded Swiss cheese
¼ cup minced onion
4 eggs
12-oz. can evaporated milk
½ tsp. salt
⅛ tsp. pepper
1 Tbsp. sugar

1. Fry, drain, and crumble bacon. Arrange in glass pie plate. Top with shredded cheese.
2. In a bowl combine all remaining ingredients and mix well. Pour over bacon and cheese.
3. Microwave at 80% power for 10-12 minutes or until toothpick inserted in center comes out clean.
4. Let stand 1-2 minutes before cutting. Serve.

Garden Vegetable Quiche

Deb Ament
Silver Spring Fire Company

Makes 8 servings

10-oz. pkg. frozen broccoli and
    cauliflower
½ cup chopped onion
1 cup shredded cheddar cheese
1½ cups milk
3 eggs
¾ cup biscuit mix
1 tsp. salt
1 tsp. pepper

1. Thaw and drain broccoli and cauliflower mix. Lightly grease 10-inch pie plate. Mix broccoli and cauliflower, onion, and cheese in pie plate.

2. Combine all remaining ingredients and beat until smooth. Pour over other ingredients in pie plate.

3. Bake at 400° for 35-40 minutes until golden brown and knife inserted in center comes out clean. Let stand 5 minutes before cutting to serve.

Spinach Ricotta Pie
Dorothy Greenawald
Willow Street, PA

Makes 6-8 servings

Crust:
1 cup flour
1/4 cup whole wheat flour, scant
1/3 cup cold butter
3 Tbsp. cold buttermilk *or* water

Filling:
1/2 lb. spinach, chopped
1 small onion, minced
3 Tbsp. flour
3 Tbsp. butter
1/2 tsp. salt
Dash pepper
1 lb. ricotta cheese
3 eggs, beaten
1/2 cup grated sharp cheese
Dash nutmeg
1 cup sour cream
Paprika

1. To prepare crust cut butter into flours. Add buttermilk or water and work to form stiff dough. Form into ball and chill for 1 hour.

2. Meanwhile sauté spinach, onion, and flour in butter, stirring constantly. Stir in salt and pepper.

3. Remove from heat and add ricotta cheese, eggs, sharp cheese, and nutmeg and mix well.

4. Remove pie dough from refrigerator and roll out to 9-inch pastry shell. Spread into pie plate. Spoon spinach mixture into pie shell. Top with sour cream, spreading to edge of crust. Sprinkle with paprika.

5. Bake at 375° for 40-45 minutes.

Pineapple Casserole
Janet M. Schwert, Mountville, PA
Ashley Hendrickson, Ephrata, PA
June Hassel, Quarryville, PA

Makes 6-8 servings

1/2 cup butter *or* margarine
1 cup white sugar
4 eggs, beaten
8-oz. can crushed pineapple, drained
8-oz. can chunk pineapple, drained
8 slices bread, cubed

1. Cream together butter and sugar. Add eggs and mix well. Stir pineapple and bread cubes into mixture. Spoon into greased casserole dish.

2. Bake, uncovered, at 350° for 45 minutes or until brown. Serve with baked ham.

Pies

Pear Apple Crumb Pie

Tina Snyder
Manheim, PA

Makes 1 9" pie

Filling:
3½ cups sliced pears
4 small tart apples, sliced
½ cup sugar
2 Tbsp. flour
¼ tsp. salt
½ tsp. cinnamon
1 Tbsp. lemon juice
½ tsp. grated lemon peel
½ cup raisins
2 Tbsp. butter
1 9" unbaked pie shell

Crumb Topping:
¼ cup flour
½ cup brown sugar
¼ tsp. salt
3-oz. pkg. cream cheese
¼ cup chopped walnuts

1. Combine pears and apples.
2. Combine sugar, flour, salt, and cinnamon. Stir into fruit mixture and add lemon juice, lemon peel, and raisins. Pile into pie shell. Dot with butter.
3. To prepare topping combine flour, brown sugar, and salt. Cut in cream cheese until crumbly. Add walnuts and toss. Sprinkle over pie filling.
4. Bake at 375° for 45 minutes.

Wild Raspberry Picking

When I was a girl, I looked forward to raspberry season. My mother and I would scour the woods for wild raspberries. I'd return home scratched and stained, but with several quarts of raspberries to pedal to the neighbors or to take to the local farmer's market.

— *Dawn J. Ranck*

Impossible French Apple Pie
Retta J. Kline, Columbia, PA
Carolyn Espigh, Terre Hill, PA

Makes 8-10 servings

6 cups sliced apples
1¼ tsp. ground cinnamon
1 tsp. ground nutmeg
1 cup sugar
¾ cup milk
½ cup biscuit mix
2 eggs
2 Tbsp. margarine *or* butter

Topping:
1 cup biscuit mix
½ cup chopped nuts
⅓ cup brown sugar
3 Tbsp. margarine *or* butter

1. Mix apples, cinnamon, and nutmeg and turn into 10-inch deep-dish pie plate or 8-inch square baking dish.
2. Beat together sugar, milk, biscuit mix, eggs, and margarine until smooth. Pour into plate.
3. To prepare topping combine all ingredients until crumbly. Sprinkle over apple ingredients.
4. Bake at 325° for 55-60 minutes.

Crustless Apple Pie
Marilyn E. Weaver, New Holland, PA
Esther W. Sensenig, New Holland, PA

Makes 1 9" pie

1 egg, lightly beaten
½ cup sugar
2 cups diced apples
½ cup chopped pecans (optional)
¾ cup flour
1 tsp. baking powder
½ tsp. salt
½ tsp. cinnamon

1. Mix egg, sugar, apples, and pecans together. Add flour, baking powder, salt, and cinnamon. Spoon into greased 9-inch pie plate.
2. Bake at 350° for 30 minutes.

Apple Pie Filling
Emma R. King
Gordonville, PA

Makes 6 quarts pie filling

5-6 lbs. apples
4½ cups sugar
1 cup cornstarch
2 tsp. ground cinnamon
¼ tsp. nutmeg
1 tsp. salt
10 cups water
3 Tbsp. lemon juice

1. Peel, core, and slice apples. Keep in fresh water until time to drain and put into jars.
2. In large saucepan combine sugar, cornstarch, cinnamon, nutmeg, and salt and mix well. Stir in water and cook until thickened, stirring frequently. Add lemon juice and mix well.
3. Sterilize quart jars in hot water. Put 2 inches syrup in each hot jar and fill jar ⅔ full of apples. Add more syrup and apples to within ½ inch of top of each jar. Cover each jar with a canning lid.
4. Process in boiling water bath for 20 minutes. Remove from water and set aside to seal. Use as needed.

Smoketown

$\mathcal{B}$eginning where the roadway crosses Mill Creek as far west as Witmer Road, the village of Smoketown stretches along Route 340. Today a thriving seed company, a greenhouse and gardening center, a barber shop, and a struggling local restaurant form the heart of the village. Elegant red-brick homes as well as more modest middle-income frame dwellings line both sides of the busy highway which runs through the center of the town. A working feed mill, an airport with a grass runway, and a popular flea market give the village its sense of energy and life.

Fresh Blueberry Pie

Fannie Ressler
Lititz, PA

Makes 1 9" pie

½ cup water
¾ cup sugar
¼ cup clear gel
¼ cup water
¼-½ cup water
3 cups blueberries
1 9" baked pie shell

1. In a saucepan combine ½ cup water and sugar and bring to a boil. Remove from heat and stir in clear gel and ¼ cup water.
2. Return to heat and cook until clear, stirring occasionally. Add ¼-½ cup water if needed. Cool mixture slightly and fold in blueberries.
3. Pour mixture into baked pie shell. Chill and serve.

Rhubarb Meringue Pie

Naomi E. Yoder
Gordonville, PA

Makes 1 9" pie

3 cups diced rhubarb
1¼ cups sugar
¼ tsp. salt
2 Tbsp. water
1½ Tbsp. cornstarch
3 Tbsp. cold water
1 Tbsp. lemon juice
4 eggs, separated
1 9" baked pie shell

1. Combine rhubarb, 1 cup sugar, salt, and 2 Tbsp. water in a saucepan. Bring to a boil over low heat.
2. Dissolve cornstarch in 3 Tbsp. cold water and add to rhubarb mixture. Cook, stirring constantly, until clear and thickened. Add lemon juice and slightly beaten egg yolks. Remove from heat.
3. Beat 2 egg whites until stiff but not dry. Fold into rhubarb mixture. Pour into pie shell.
4. Beat remaining egg whites until soft peaks form. Gradually add remaining ¼ cup sugar and beat well. Spoon meringue over rhubarb mixture.
5. Bake at 350° for about 15 minutes or until meringue is lightly browned.

Rhubarb Pie

Rachel Pellman
Lancaster, PA

Makes 2 8" pies

Filling:
2 cups sugar
3 Tbsp. flour
2 eggs, beaten
5½ cups coarsely chopped rhubarb
2 8" unbaked pie shells

Crumbs:
1 cup flour
½ cup brown sugar
¼ cup shortening
½ tsp. baking soda
½ tsp. baking powder

1. To prepare filling combine sugar, flour and eggs. Stir to form a thick paste. Fold in rhubarb pieces.

2. Spoon into 2 unbaked pie shells.

3. To prepare crumbs combine all ingredients and mix well. Sprinkle evenly over rhubarb mixture.

4. Bake at 400° for 10 minutes. Reduce oven temperature to 350° and bake 40-50 minutes longer.

Strawberry Cream Pie

Mary C. Sage
Pequea, PA

Makes 1 9" pie

½ cup powdered sugar
3-oz. pkg. cream cheese, softened
½ tsp. vanilla
1 heaping cup whipped topping
1 quart fresh strawberries
½ cup white sugar
1 tsp. fresh lemon juice
1 Tbsp. cornstarch
1 tsp. margarine
2 drops red food coloring (optional)
1 9" baked pie shell

1. Beat together powdered sugar, cream cheese, and vanilla. Fold in whipped topping and spoon over baked pie shell. Refrigerate and chill.

2. Mix strawberries with sugar. Let stand about one hour. Drain and reserve juice, adding enough water to make one cup juice. Stir lemon juice into liquid.

3. Pour juice into saucepan. Add cornstarch and margarine and cook until thickened and clear, stirring constantly. Add red food coloring if desired.

4. Arrange berries over chilled cream cheese mixture. Spoon glaze over berries. Chill and serve.

Strawberry Pie

Jo Zimmerman
New Holland, PA

Makes 1 9" pie

1 quart fresh strawberries
1½ cups water
¾ cup sugar
2 Tbsp. clear gel *or* cornstarch
3-oz. pkg. strawberry gelatin
1 cup whipped topping
1 9" baked pie shell

1. Wash and slice strawberries horizontally into baked pie shell.
2. Combine all remaining ingredients except whipped topping in a saucepan and bring to a boil, stirring constantly until thickened.
3. Pour sauce over berries. Chill until firm. Top with whipped topping and serve.

Green Tomato Pie

Anna N. Buckwalter
Ronks, PA

Makes 1 9" pie

3 cups thinly sliced green tomatoes
½ cup sugar
3 Tbsp. molasses
4 Tbsp. water
2 Tbsp. flour
1 tsp. cinnamon
2 9" unbaked pie shells

1. Cover tomatoes with boiling water and boil a few minutes. Drain well. Arrange in unbaked pie shell.
2. Combine sugar, molasses, water, and flour and mix well. Pour over green tomatoes. Sprinkle cinnamon over top. Cover with top crust.

3. Bake at 425° for 15 minutes. Reduce oven temperature to 375° and bake 30 minutes longer.

Green Tomato Mincemeat

Doris Nissley
Bainbridge, PA

Makes 12 quarts mincemeat

4 quarts green tomatoes
6 quarts tart apples
6 tsp. cinnamon
1 tsp. salt
1 tsp. allspice
1 tsp. ground cloves
8 cups sugar
1 cup brown sugar
1 cup vinegar
4 lbs. raisins

1. In a blender or food processor grind tomatoes. Drain well. Grind apples.
2. Combine all ingredients in a saucepan. Bring to a boil and cook about 20 minutes.
3. Fill one 9-inch unbaked pie shell with mincemeat. Freeze remaining mixture for future use.
4. Bake at 350° for 45 minutes.

Sweet Potato Pie

Martha L. Stoner
Leola, PA

Makes 1 9" pie

Filling:
1¼ cups sugar
½ tsp. ground cinnamon
½ tsp. ground nutmeg
2 eggs
12-oz. can evaporated milk
1 tsp. vanilla
1½ cups mashed, cooked sweet potatoes
1 9" unbaked pie shell

Topping:
⅓ cup margarine
⅓ cup all-purpose flour
½ cup brown sugar
½ cup shredded coconut
½ cup chopped pecans
1 cup whipped topping

1. To prepare filling blend together sugar, cinnamon, and nutmeg in mixing bowl.

2. In separate bowl beat eggs; add milk and vanilla. Combine with sugar mixture. Stir in potatoes and beat until smooth. Pour into unbaked pie shell.

3. Bake at 425° for 15 minutes. Reduce oven temperature to 350° and bake for an additional 30 minutes.

4. To prepare topping combine all ingredients and mix well. Remove pie from the oven and sprinkle with topping. Bake 10-15 minutes longer or until topping is golden brown. Cool on wire rack.

5. Chill in refrigerator and top with whipped topping before serving.

Easy Peach Pie

Lois Nafziger
Lancaster, PA

Makes 1 9" pie

4-5 cups sliced peaches
1 cup sugar
2 rounded Tbsp. cornstarch
1 tsp. lemon juice
1 cup water
1 9" baked pie shell

1. Spoon peaches into baked pie shell.

2. Combine sugar, cornstarch, lemon juice, and water in a glass quart measure and stir until smooth.

3. Microwave on high for 1½ minutes. Stir. Repeat this procedure until mixture is thickened and glossy.

4. Pour over sliced peaches. Chill and serve.

Variation: Substitute choice of fruit with this filling—cherries, blueberries, rhubarb, strawberries, or apples.

Pumpkin Pie
Anna Mary Boyer
Akron, PA

Makes 1 9" pie

2 cups cooked pumpkin
1½ cups sugar
14-oz. can condensed milk
3 eggs, separated
2 Tbsp. flour
½ cup butter, melted
¼ tsp. ginger
¼ tsp. cloves
¼ tsp. nutmeg
¼ tsp. cinnamon
1 tsp. salt
1 tsp. pumpkin spice
1 9" unbaked pie shell

1. Combine all ingredients except egg whites and pie shell and mix well.
2. Beat egg whites until stiffened and fold into pumpkin mixture.
3. Pour into 9-inch pie shell.
4. Bake at 425° for 10 minutes. Reduce oven temperature to 350° and bake 30 minutes longer.

Pumpkin Custard Pie
Deb Herr
Mountville, PA

Makes 4 9" pies

3 cups cooked pumpkin
1 cup flour
8 eggs
2 quarts milk
2 cups sugar
4-6 tsp. cinnamon
4 9" unbaked pie shells

1. Mix flour into pumpkin.
2. Beat eggs with whisk and add to pumpkin, mixing well. Add milk and sugar and beat until smooth and well mixed. Pour evenly into 4 unbaked pie shells. Generously sprinkle top of each pie with cinnamon.
3. Bake at 400° on bottom rack of oven for 30-35 minutes. Move to middle rack and bake an additional 10-15 minutes.

Coconut Pie
Elsie Kauffman
Stevens, PA

Makes 6 servings

4 eggs
¾ cup sugar
½ cup margarine *or* less
½ cup biscuit mix
2 cups milk
1 tsp. vanilla
¾ cup coconut

1. Combine all ingredients except coconut and beat until well mixed. Pour into lightly greased 9-inch pie plate. Sprinkle coconut evenly over top.
2. Bake at 350° for 45 minutes.

Kentucky Pecan Pie
Nancy Beiler
Leola, PA

Makes 1 9" pie

1 cup light corn syrup
½ cup brown sugar
⅓ cup butter, melted
1 tsp. vanilla

3 eggs, slightly beaten
$\frac{1}{3}$ tsp. salt
1 cup chopped pecans
1 9" unbaked pie shell

1. Combine all ingredients except pecans and pie shell and beat until thoroughly mixed. Fold in pecans. Spoon into unbaked pie shell.
2. Bake at 350° for 40-45 minutes or until mixture sets.

Christmas Pie
Mary Ella Herr
Quarryville, PA

Makes 10-12 servings

1$\frac{1}{2}$ cups ground Brazil nuts
3 Tbsp. sugar
1 envelope unflavored gelatin
$\frac{1}{4}$ cup cold water
1$\frac{1}{2}$ cups milk
$\frac{1}{2}$ cup sugar
$\frac{1}{2}$ tsp. salt
4 Tbsp. flour
3 egg whites
$\frac{1}{2}$ cup sugar
$\frac{1}{4}$ tsp. cream of tartar
$\frac{1}{2}$ cup chopped maraschino cherries

1. Prepare a crust by mixing Brazil nuts and 3 Tbsp. sugar. Press into bottom and sides of 9-inch deep-dish pie pan.
2. To prepare filling dissolve gelatin in cold water. Set aside.
3. In a medium saucepan combine milk, $\frac{1}{2}$ cup sugar, salt, and flour. Cook over medium heat until thickened, stirring frequently. Stir in gelatin mix and set aside to cool.

4. Beat egg whites until stiffened. Slowly add $\frac{1}{2}$ cup sugar and cream of tartar, beating until dissolved.
5. Fold egg whites and cherries into filling mixture. Spoon over Brazil nut crust and chill at least 1 hour before serving.
6. Slice into small pieces and serve.

Vanilla Pie
Jean R. Ressel, Quarryville, PA
Amanda S. Stoltzfus, Gap, PA
Erma Wenger, Lancaster, PA
Lydia Shirk, Talmage, PA
Irene Shirk, Akron, PA
Emily Linton Reath, Kirkwood, PA

Makes 1 10" pie

Vanilla Filling:
1 cup sugar
1 cup molasses
2 cups water
3 Tbsp. flour
1 egg
1 tsp. vanilla
1 10" unbaked pie shell

Crumb Topping:
2 cups flour
1 cup sugar
$\frac{1}{2}$ cup margarine
1 tsp. cream of tartar

1. Combine all filling ingredients except vanilla and pie shell in saucepan and bring to a boil. Cook until thickened, stirring frequently. Remove from heat and add vanilla. Pour into pie shell.
2. Mix together topping ingredients until crumbly. Spread crumbs evenly and thickly over top of filling.
3. Bake at 375° for 40-45 minutes.

Elizabethtown

In Lancaster County's far northwestern corner, just off busy Route 283, lies Elizabethtown. Home of Elizabethtown College, a four-year liberal arts school operated by the Church of the Brethren, the stately, tree-shaded homes along High Street and College Avenue gently blend with the school's understated red-brick architecture and manicured lawns.

In a bow to its student population, strip malls and fast food restaurants surround Elizabethtown's outer edges. The busy town center includes enterprises as different from each other as Water Street Rescue Mission Thrift Store and Wolgemuth's Bed and Breakfast. Rows of neatly-kept, well-trimmed lawns crisscross this quiet, residential Lancaster County town.

On the southwest edge of town along the road to Bainbridge stands Masonic Homes, owned and operated by the Masons of Pennsylvania. On the northwest side of town is the University Hospital and Rehabilitation Center for Children and Adults.

Shoofly Pie

Sara Steffy, Ephrata, PA
Retta J. Kline, Columbia, PA
Janet Weaver, Ephrata, PA
Mildred M. Ney, Columbia, PA

Makes 1 9" pie

1 cup flour
⅔ cup brown sugar
1 Tbsp. shortening
1 tsp. baking soda
¾ cup hot water
1 cup molasses
1 egg, beaten
1 9" unbaked pie shell

1. Combine flour and brown sugar. Cut shortening into flour mixture until crumbly. Reserve ½ cup crumbs.
2. Dissolve baking soda in hot (but not boiling) water.
3. In a small bowl combine molasses, egg, and baking soda water and beat well. Pour into unbaked pie shell. Sprinkle reserved crumbs over top.
4. Bake at 375° for 35 minutes.

Molasses Pie

Anne Nolt, Reinholds, PA
Millie Eisemann, Ephrata, PA

Makes 2 9" pies

Filling:
2 cups sugar
2 eggs
1 cup molasses
1 tsp. baking soda
1 tsp. cinnamon
4 Tbsp. flour
2 cups thick milk
1 cup sour cream
2 9" unbaked pie shells

Sweet Dough:
½ cup sugar
½ tsp. baking soda
1¼ cups flour
½ cup sour cream

1. To prepare filling mix together sugar, eggs, and molasses.
2. Combine dry ingredients and add to molasses mixture, stirring well. Add thick milk and sour cream and mix well. Pour into unbaked pie shells.

3. To prepare sweet dough combine sugar, baking soda, and flour. Cut in sour cream and mix with hands until smooth lump of dough forms. Roll out and cut into inch-wide strips. Arrange in trellis-fashion over pies.

4. Bake at 375° for 35-45 minutes.

Honey Crumb Pie
Joyce E. Zercher
Holtwood, PA

Makes 1 9" deep-dish pie

Filling:
½ cup brown sugar
½ cup honey
3-6 Tbsp. corn syrup
1 egg, slightly beaten
½ tsp. baking soda
½ cup prepared strong black coffee
½ cup butter, melted
¾ cup flour
½ tsp. salt
½ tsp. cinnamon
¼ tsp. ground cloves
Pinch nutmeg
1 9" unbaked pie shell

Crumb Topping:
⅔ cup flour
½ cup brown sugar
¼ cup butter

1. Mix together brown sugar, honey, syrup, and egg.

2. Dissolve baking soda in black coffee.

3. To brown sugar mixture add butter, coffee, and dry ingredients and mix well. Spoon into unbaked pie shell.

4. Prepare crumb mixture by combining all ingredients until crumbly. Sprinkle crumbs over top.

5. Bake at 400° for 15 minutes. Reduce oven temperature to 350° and bake another 35-40 minutes.

6. Cut into small pieces and serve.

Buttermilk Pie
Jeanette Oberholtzer
Akron, PA

Makes 1 9" pie

¾ cup granulated sugar
2 Tbsp. flour
¼ tsp. salt
2 eggs, beaten
1 Tbsp. melted butter *or* margarine
2 cups buttermilk
1 tsp. lemon flavoring
1 9" unbaked pie shell

1. Combine sugar, flour, and salt. Add the remaining ingredients and blend well. Pour into unbaked pie shell.

2. Bake at 350° for 50-60 minutes or until knife inserted in center comes out clean.

Frozen Pumpkin Pie
Shirley Hoover
Lancaster, PA

Makes 1 9" pie

1 quart vanilla ice cream, softened
1 cup cooked pumpkin
⅓ cup sugar
½ tsp. salt
1 tsp. cinnamon
½ tsp. nutmeg
¼ cup graham cracker crumbs
1 9-inch graham cracker crust

1. Beat together all ingredients except graham cracker crumbs and crust and mix until well blended. Pour into graham cracker crust. Sprinkle with graham cracker crumbs.
2. Freeze until firm and serve frozen.

Chocolate Funny Cake Pie
Sandra L. Biondo
Reinholds, PA

Makes 1 9" pie

1 cup sugar
¼ cup butter
½ cup milk
1 egg, beaten
1 cup flour
1 tsp. baking powder
½ tsp. vanilla
4 Tbsp. cocoa
½ cup sugar
6 Tbsp. water
½ tsp. vanilla
1 9" inch unbaked pie shell

1. Cream together 1 cup sugar and butter.

2. Beat together milk and egg. Pour into creamed mixture, alternating with flour and baking powder. Add the vanilla. Spoon into unbaked pie shell.
3. Mix the cocoa and ½ cup sugar. Gradually, stir in water and vanilla. Pour over batter in pie shell.
4. Bake at 350° for 40-45 minutes or until firm.

Butterscotch Pie
Pauline M. Gayman
Lancaster, PA

Makes 1 9" pie

5 Tbsp. flour
2 cups milk
1 cup brown sugar, scant
2 Tbsp. white sugar
2 eggs, separated
¼ tsp. salt
2 Tbsp. butter
1 9" baked pie shell

1. Mix flour with ¼ cup milk. Set aside.
2. In a saucepan scald remaining milk. Stir in flour and milk mixture and cook for about 5 minutes, stirring constantly. Add sugars, egg yolks, and salt to boiling milk mixture and bring to a boil again, stirring frequently. Remove from heat.
3. Beat egg whites until soft. Add a bit of egg white and butter to filling and mix well. Pour filling into baked pie shell and top with balance of beaten egg whites for the meringue.
4. Brown meringue at 350° for 5-10 minutes.

Peanut Butter Pie

Helen E. Keener
Rheems, PA

Makes 1 8" pie

½ cup peanut butter
4-ozs. cream cheese, softened
1 cup powdered sugar
½ cup milk
8-oz. carton whipped topping
1 8" prepared graham cracker crust

1. Cream together peanut butter and cream cheese. Add sugar and milk and mix well. Fold in whipped topping. Spoon into graham cracker crust.
2. Place in freezer until firm. Serve.

Peanut Butter Cheesecake Pie

Mary Ella Herr
Quarryville, PA

Makes 1 9" pie

8-oz. pkg. cream cheese, softened
14-oz. can condensed milk
¼ cup lemon juice
1 cup peanut butter
12-oz. carton whipped topping
½ cup chopped peanuts
1 9" prepared graham cracker crust

1. Beat cream cheese until smooth. Add condensed milk and lemon juice and beat until well mixed. Add peanut butter and mix well. Fold in whipped topping. Spoon into graham cracker crust. Sprinkle chopped peanuts over top.
2. Chill at least 1 hour before serving.

Cream Cheese Pie

Debbie Landis
Denver, PA

Makes 1 9" pie

8-oz. pkg. cream cheese
14-oz. can condensed milk
⅓ cup lemon juice
1 tsp. vanilla
21-oz. can pie filling, any flavor
1 9" prepared graham cracker crust

1. In large bowl beat cream cheese until fluffy. Gradually beat in condensed milk until smooth. Stir in lemon juice and vanilla. Pour into graham cracker crust.
2. Chill 3 hours or until set. Top with pie filling. Keep refrigerated until ready to serve.

Pineapple Millionaire Pie

Dorothy Greenawald
Willow Street, PA

Makes 1 8" pie

2 cups powdered sugar
8 Tbsp. margarine, softened
¼ tsp. salt
1 egg
¼ tsp. vanilla
1 cup whipped topping
1 cup drained, crushed pineapple
½ cup chopped nuts
1 8" baked pie shell

1. Cream together sugar, margarine, salt, egg, and vanilla. Beat until fluffy. Spoon into baked pie shell and chill for 30 minutes.
2. Blend together whipped topping, pineapple, and nuts. Spoon onto filling mixture in pie shell. Chill thoroughly and serve.

*H*ershey Pie

Laura Mae Voran
New Holland, PA

Makes 1 9" pie

18 large marshmallows
1½-oz. Hershey chocolate bar
½ cup milk
1 cup heavy cream
1 9" baked pie shell

1. Heat marshmallows, Hershey bar, and milk in double boiler until melted, stirring frequently. Cool.
2. Whip cream until stiffened. Fold into chocolate mixture. Pour into baked pie shell.
3. Refrigerate several hours or until ready to serve.

Variation: Add a handful of miniature semi-sweet chocolate chips in step 2.

*C*rumbs for Fruit Pie

Retta J. Kline
Columbia, PA

Makes topping for 6 pies

6 cups flour
3 cups sugar
3 tsp. baking soda
3 tsp. cream of tartar
1½ cups shortening

1. Combine all dry ingredients. Cut in shortening until crumbly.
2. Use 1 cup crumbs per pie. Freeze for future use.

*P*ie Dough

Barbara Martin, East Earl, PA
Marcene Becker, Manheim, PA
Diane K. Gehman, Stevens, PA

Makes 4 9" pie shells

¾-1 cup shortening
4 cups unsifted flour
1 Tbsp. sugar
2 tsp. salt *or* less
1 tsp. vinegar
½ cup cold water
1 egg, beaten

1. Cut shortening into flour, sugar, and salt and mix well. Add vinegar, cold water, and egg and mix to form a soft dough.
2. Chill at least 1 hour.
3. Divide into four parts and roll out for 9-inch pies.

Cakes

Chocolate Chip Cake
Lydia Shirk
Talmage, PA

Makes 16-20 servings

Cake:
2 cups sifted flour
1½ tsp. baking powder
1 tsp. baking soda
½ cup butter
1 cup sugar
2 eggs
1 cup sour cream
1 tsp. vanilla

Topping:
½ cup sugar
1 tsp. cinnamon
6 ozs. chocolate chips

1. Mix flour, baking powder, and baking soda and set aside.
2. Cream together butter and sugar and add eggs. Mix well. Add flour mixture to creamed mixture, alternating with sour cream. Add vanilla and mix well.
3. To prepare topping combine sugar and cinnamon and set aside.
4. Spoon ½ of cake batter into a greased 9" x 13" baking pan. Sprinkle with ½ of topping and ½ of chocolate chips. Top with remaining batter. Sprinkle with remaining topping and chocolate chips.
5. Bake at 350° for 35 minutes.

Chocolate Coffee Cake with Peanut Butter Icing

Arlene Eaves, Strasburg, PA
Mary E. Kunkel, Lancaster, PA
Ginny Lausch, Akron, PA
Tamara Lausch, Akron, PA
Betty Eberly, Denver, PA
Helen E. Keener, Rheems, PA

Makes 16-20 servings

Cake:
¾ cup cooking oil
2 cups sugar
2 eggs
2 cups flour
⅛ tsp. salt
1 tsp. baking powder
2 tsp. baking soda
¾ cup cocoa powder
1 cup milk
1 tsp. vanilla
1 cup prepared hot black coffee

Peanut Butter Icing:
¼ cup peanut butter
1 lb. powdered sugar
¼ tsp. vanilla
4-5 Tbsp. milk

1. To prepare cake combine all ingredients in the order given and mix well. Pour into greased and floured 9" x 13" baking pan.
2. Bake at 375° for 45 minutes or until toothpick inserted in center comes out clean. Let cool for 1 hour.
3. Meanwhile prepare frosting by combining all ingredients and beating until smooth and creamy. Frost cake and serve.

Moist Chocolate Cake

Dawn J. Ranck
Strasburg, PA

Makes 16-20 servings

4 eggs, beaten
1⅔ cups sugar
1 tsp. vanilla
1 cup mayonnaise
2 cups flour
⅓ cup cocoa
½ tsp. baking powder
1½ tsp. baking soda
½ tsp. salt
1¼ cups water

1. Combine eggs, sugar, and vanilla and beat until fluffy. Blend in mayonnaise and beat well.
2. Sift together flour, cocoa, baking powder, baking soda, and salt. Add to creamed ingredients, alternating with water. Pour into 2 greased and floured 9-inch layer pans.
3. Bake at 350° for 30-35 minutes. Cool and frost with favorite chocolate frosting.

Texas Sheet Cake

Wanda Eby
Denver, PA

Makes 48 servings

Cake:
2 cups all-purpose flour
2 cups white sugar
½ cup butter *or* margarine
½ cup shortening
1 cup strong, brewed coffee
¼ cup unsweetened cocoa
½ cup buttermilk
2 eggs

1 tsp. baking soda
1 tsp. vanilla

Icing:
½ cup butter *or* margarine
2 Tbsp. cocoa
¼ cup milk
3½ cups powdered sugar
1 tsp. vanilla

1. In large mixing bowl combine the flour and sugar.

2. In heavy saucepan combine butter, shortening, coffee, and cocoa. Stir and heat to boiling. Pour boiling mixture over flour and sugar mixture. Add buttermilk, eggs, baking soda, and vanilla. Mix well, using a wooden spoon or high speed on mixer.

3. Pour into a well-greased 11" x 17" jelly roll pan.

4. Bake at 400° for 20 minutes or until toothpick inserted in center comes out clean.

5. Meanwhile prepare icing by combining butter, cocoa, and milk in a saucepan. Stir and heat to boiling. Remove from heat and add powdered sugar and vanilla and beat until frosting is smooth.

6. Pour warm frosting over sheet cake as soon as it is removed from oven. Cool. Cut and serve.

Chocolate Cake with Caramel Icing

Miriam E. Lefever, East Petersburg, PA
Helen Stoltzfus, Gap, PA

Makes 16-20 servings

Cake:
3 cups flour
½ cup cocoa
2 cups sugar
2 tsp. baking soda
1 tsp. salt
⅔ cup cooking oil
2 Tbsp. vinegar
1 Tbsp. vanilla
2 cups cold water

Caramel Icing:
½ cup butter
1 cup brown sugar
¼ cup milk
1½ cups powdered sugar

1. To prepare cake combine all ingredients in large bowl. Beat only to blend. Pour into 9" x 13" baking pan.

2. Bake at 350° for 40-45 minutes.

3. To prepare icing melt butter and add brown sugar. Cook over low heat for 2 minutes. Add milk and cook, stirring until mixture comes to a boil. Remove from heat and cool. Add powdered sugar and beat until smooth. After cake cools, apply icing to top. Serve.

Easy Chocolate Cake
Barbara Hummel
Brownstown, PA

Makes 16-20 servings

½ cup shortening
1¾ cups sugar
1 egg
1 tsp. vanilla
2½ cups flour
2 tsp. baking soda
½ tsp. salt
6 Tbsp. cocoa
2 cups sour milk

1. Cream together shortening and sugar. Beat in egg and vanilla.
2. Combine flour, baking soda, salt, and cocoa. Add dry ingredients to creamed ingredients, alternating with sour milk. Pour into greased 9" x 13" baking pan.
3. Bake at 350° for 30-40 minutes or until knife inserted in center comes out clean. If desired, frost cake with favorite icing. Serve.

French Butter Cream Icing
Ashley Hendrickson
Ephrata, PA

Makes 2 cups icing

⅔ cup white sugar
¼ cup flour
¼ tsp. salt
¾ cup milk
1 cup cold butter
1 tsp. vanilla

1. Place sugar, flour, and salt in saucepan and mix thoroughly. Stir in milk. Cook over medium heat until thickened,

stirring constantly. Remove from heat and spoon into medium mixing bowl. Cool to room temperature.
2. Cut butter into several pieces. Add to icing mixture, 1 piece at a time, and beat at medium high speed until smooth. Add vanilla and beat well.
3. Chill icing for a few minutes before frosting cake. Refrigerate cake until ready to serve.

Chocolate Angel Food Cake
Betty Kissinger
Lancaster, PA

Makes 12-16 servings

¾ cup cake flour
¼ cup cocoa
¼ tsp. salt
2 cups egg whites
1 tsp. cream of tartar
1 tsp. vanilla
1½ cups sugar

1. Sift together flour, cocoa, and salt.
2. Add cream of tartar to egg whites and beat until they will hold peaks. Add vanilla. Gradually add sugar until well blended. Fold egg white mixture into flour mixture. Pour into ungreased tube pan.
3. Bake at 350° for 40-45 minutes. Remove from oven and invert to cool.

Millersville

A university town with a swelling student population, the borough of Millersville anchors Manor Township just to the west of Lancaster. High-rise student housing sprawls around the edges of the George Street campus. A few blocks south and east along Creek Drive, one of the long gentle bends of the Conestoga Creek reaches north to stroke the edge of the borough. On the west side of Millersville some of Lancaster County's most beautiful farmland fans north and west toward the Susquehanna River.

Betty Pellman, a longtime resident, recently reminisced about Millersville during the 1920s and 1930s. "We shopped at Herr's Store on Manor Avenue or at Rettews on Frederick Street. However, Millersville was basically residential and numerous merchants offered door-to-door service to our town." Pellman remembered regular visits to her family's Ferdinand Street (now an extension of Walnut Hill Road) home by a bread and baked goods truck, a local butcher, and Rettew's Store-at-Your-Door. "Mother didn't drive so she welcomed such services."

Today, the growing Millersville University attracts visitors with rows of green "Commit to Opportunity" banners along the George Street entrance. First called Lancaster County Normal School, the site has been home to a school for higher education since 1855. In 1983 it became part of the state university system of Pennsylvania.

Cherry Chocolate Cake

Mary C. Sage, Pequea, PA
Sandra Kautz, Mount Joy, PA

Makes 12-16 servings

Cake:
2 cups flour
2 cups sugar
2 tsp. baking soda
1 rounded tsp. baking powder
¾ cup cocoa
4 eggs
¼ cup milk
½ cup cooking oil
1½ tsp. vanilla
½ tsp. almond extract
21-oz. can cherry pie filling

Chocolate Icing:
5 Tbsp. margarine
1 cup sugar
6-oz. pkg. chocolate chips
⅓ cup milk

1. Sift together flour, sugar, baking soda, baking powder, and cocoa. Add eggs, milk, oil, vanilla, and almond extract and mix well. Fold in cherry pie filling. Pour into two greased and floured 9-inch cake pans.

2. Bake at 350° for 45-50 minutes.

3. To prepare icing combine margarine, sugar, and chocolate chips in saucepan. Stir until melted over medium heat. Add milk and stir until shiny.

4. Spread warm icing over cooled cake.

The Story of Henry's Bakery

Back in 1922 Mary Graybill tended curb market in the city of Lancaster for her parents, selling butter, eggs, and produce that had been grown on the family farm near Bird-in-Hand, Pennsylvania.

Being the go-getter that Mary was, she begged her mother to bake a few cakes to sell on market. Her mother finally said, "OK, you bake them, but they won't sell." Mary made a chocolate and an angel food cake and took them with her to market. A gentleman stopped by her curbside stand and asked, "Did you bake that chocolate cake?" When Mary said yes, he bought the cake. Mary was so excited she decided to bake a few more cakes the next week. She sold all of them, and her business was on its way.

Mary married Clayton S. Henry, and he began helping her with the weekly baking. They were soon able to rent a small stall inside the Central Market building where Mary could keep her cakes dry and protect them from bad weather. The Henrys' business grew, even surviving the Great Depression when they expanded and began tending markets in Chester and Philadelphia. In 1943 they purchased a larger Central Market stall and discontinued the Chester and Philadelphia markets. In 1951 they started a bakery route, going door to door in Lancaster City. Many weeks they sold as many as 1000 homemade pies and 250 homemade cakes. After supplying Lancaster with fresh baked goods for almost 50 years, Mary Graybill Henry and her husband retired in 1969.

—*Ruth E. Wenger, Akron, PA*

Fat-Free Chocolate Cake

Sandra Kautz
Mount Joy, PA

Makes 8-10 servings

1¼ **cups flour**
1 **cup sugar**
½ **cup cocoa**
¼ **cup cornstarch**
½ **tsp. baking soda**
½ **tsp. salt**
4 **egg whites**
1 **cup water**
½ **cup light corn syrup**

1. In a large bowl combine all dry ingredients and mix well.
2. In medium bowl whisk together egg whites, water, and corn syrup. Stir into dry ingredients and mix well until smooth. Pour into 9-inch square baking pan which has been sprayed with non-stick cooking spray.
3. Bake at 350° for 20-30 minutes.

Turtle Cake

Betty Pellman
Millersville, PA

Makes 16-20 servings

1 **German chocolate cake mix**
10-oz. **pkg. caramel candies**
¾ **cup butter** *or* **margarine**
½ **cup milk**
1½ **cups chopped walnuts**
6-oz. **pkg. miniature chocolate chips**
¼ **cup powdered sugar**

1. Prepare cake mix according to package directions. Pour ½ of cake batter into greased and floured 9" x 13" baking pan.

2. Bake at 375° for 15 minutes.

3. Meanwhile combine caramel candies, butter, and milk in double boiler and cook until melted. Remove cake from oven and pour caramel mixture over cake. Sprinkle with walnuts and chocolate chips. Pour remaining cake batter over all.

4. Return to oven and bake 30 minutes longer or until done. Let cake cool completely.

5. Sprinkle with powdered sugar and serve.

ℛed Velvet Cake

Mary E. Kunkel
Lancaster, PA

Makes 16-20 servings

½ cup shortening
1½ cups sugar
2 eggs
2 ozs. red food coloring
2 Tbsp. cocoa
1 tsp. salt
1 tsp. vanilla
1 cup buttermilk
2¼ cups cake flour
1½ tsp. baking soda
1 Tbsp. vinegar

Ivory Butter Icing:
1 cup milk
5 Tbsp. flour
1 cup butter *or* margarine
1 cup sugar
1 tsp. vanilla

1. Cream together shortening, sugar, and eggs.

2. Make a paste of red food coloring and cocoa. Stir into creamed mixture. Add salt,

vanilla, and buttermilk and mix well. Blend in flour.

3. Combine baking soda and vinegar and beat into cake batter. Spoon into greased 9" x 13" baking pan.

4. Bake at 350° for 30-40 minutes.

5. To prepare icing combine milk and flour in a double boiler to make a smooth paste. Cook, stirring frequently, until mixture is thick like custard, 5-7 minutes. Remove from heat and immediately cover with plastic wrap to prevent a top film from forming. Set aside to cool.

6. Cream together butter, sugar, and vanilla. Combine creamed mixture with cooled custard, beating until good spreading consistency. Frost cooled cake and serve.

𝒜pple Pie Cake

Sara Newswanger
Narvon, PA

Makes 8-10 servings

12 Tbsp. margarine
2 cups sugar
2 eggs
2 tsp. cinnamon
1 tsp. baking soda
¼ tsp. salt
2 cups flour
4 cups chopped raw apples
1 cup chopped nuts

1. Cream together margarine, sugar, eggs, cinnamon, baking soda, and salt. Add flour and mix well.

2. Fold in apples and nuts. Pour into lightly greased 9-inch square pan.

3. Bake at 350° for 30-40 minutes. Serve warm with milk or ice cream.

German Raw Apple Cake

Elsie Houser, Lampeter, PA
Carmen Watson, Lititz, PA

Makes 16-20 servings

Cake:
2¼ cups cake flour
¼ tsp. salt
2 tsp. cinnamon
½ cup shortening
½ cup brown sugar
1 cup white sugar
2 eggs
2 tsp. baking soda
1 cup sour milk *or* buttermilk
2 cups diced apples

Topping:
¼ cup white sugar
½ cup brown sugar
½ cup chopped nuts
½ tsp. cinnamon

1. Sift together flour, salt, and cinnamon.
2. Cream together shortening, sugars, and eggs.
3. Stir baking soda into sour milk. Add milk and dry ingredients alternately to creamed mixture. Fold in apples. Spread into greased 9" x 13" baking pan.
4. To prepare topping combine all ingredients and sprinkle over cake batter.
5. Bake at 350° for 30-40 minutes or until done.

Jewish Apple Cake

Carrie M. Ney
Columbia, PA

Makes 12-16 servings

Cake:
3 cups flour
2 cups sugar
3 tsp. vanilla
½ cup orange juice
4 eggs
1 cup cooking oil
3 tsp. baking powder
5-6 apples, sliced

Topping:
2 Tbsp. cinnamon
5 Tbsp. sugar

1. Combine all cake ingredients except apples and mix well. Pour ½ of batter into greased and floured tube pan. Spread ½ of apples over batter. Sprinkle ½ of cinnamon sugar topping over apples. Repeat layers with remaining ingredients.
2. Bake at 350° for 1 hour or until done.

Pineapple Cream Cake

Verna Douts, Quarryville, PA
Debra A. Stoltzfus, Kinzers, PA
Donella King, Cochranville, PA

Makes 12-16 servings

Cake:
2 cups sugar
2 cups flour
2 eggs
2 tsp. baking soda
1 tsp. vanilla
20-oz. can crushed pineapple, undrained

Icing:
8 Tbsp. margarine
8-oz. pkg. cream cheese
1⅓ cups powdered sugar
1 tsp. vanilla

1. Combine all cake ingredients and beat well to blend. Pour into 9" x 13" baking pan.
2. Bake at 350° for 30 minutes.
3. Combine all icing ingredients and mix well. Spread over warm cake. Chill and serve.

𝓑anana Cake

Carrie M. Ney, Columbia, PA
Arlene Eaves, Strasburg, PA

Makes 16-20 servings

½ cup shortening
1¼ cups sugar
2 eggs
2½ cups flour
2½ tsp. baking powder
½ tsp. baking soda
1½ cups mashed bananas
1 tsp. vanilla
1 cup chopped nuts

1. Cream together shortening, sugar, and eggs.
2. Combine flour, baking powder, and baking soda. Add dry ingredients along with ½ of bananas to creamed ingredients and mix well. Add vanilla, remaining bananas, and nuts and stir until mixed. Pour into greased 9" x 13" baking pan.
3. Bake at 350° for 30 minutes or until done.

𝓟umpkin Cake with Cream Cheese Icing

Rosie Yeakel
Ephrata, PA

Makes 16-20 servings

2 cups sugar
2 cups cooked pumpkin
1½ cups cooking oil
4 eggs
2 cups flour
1 tsp. salt
2 tsp. baking soda
2 tsp. baking powder
2 tsp. cinnamon
½ cup chopped nuts
½ cup coconut

Cream Cheese Icing:
2 3-oz. pkgs. cream cheese, softened
4 Tbsp. butter *or* margarine
½ tsp. vanilla
1 cup powdered sugar

1. Mix sugar, pumpkin, and oil together. Add eggs one at a time, beating after each addition.
2. Sift together dry ingredients. Add to pumpkin mixture and mix well. Fold in nuts and coconut. Pour into greased 9" x 13" baking pan.
3. Bake at 350° for 45 minutes.
4. Combine all icing ingredients and beat well. Spread icing over cooled cake.

Pumpkin Cake Deluxe

Greta Smith
Ephrata, PA

Makes 16-20 servings

Cake:
½ cup shortening
1¼ cups sugar
2 eggs
1 cup cooked, mashed pumpkin
2¼ cups flour
2½ tsp. baking powder
1½ tsp. baking soda
1 tsp. salt
½ tsp. ginger
½ tsp. nutmeg
¾ cup milk

Icing:
1 cup brown sugar
½ cup white sugar
2 Tbsp. flour
1 cup milk
2 eggs
1 cup chopped walnuts
1 cup raisins
1 cup coconut
1 tsp. vanilla
2 Tbsp. butter

1. Cream together shortening, sugar, and eggs. Add pumpkin and mix well.
2. Stir together flour, baking powder, baking soda, salt, ginger, and nutmeg. Add dry ingredients to creamed ingredients, alternating with milk. Mix well. Spoon into greased 9" x 13" baking pan.
3. Bake at 350° for 35-40 minutes or until done. Cool.
4. To prepare frosting combine sugars, flour, milk, and eggs in double boiler. Bring to a boil and cook for 20 minutes, stirring frequently. Fold in all remaining ingredients and cook 5 minutes longer. Spread frosting over cooled cake and serve.

Pumpkin Pie Cake

Joyce Eby
Denver, PA

Makes 12-16 servings

1 box yellow cake mix
5⅓ Tbsp. margarine
2 cups cooked pumpkin
⅔ cup milk
½ cup brown sugar
¼ cup white sugar
1½ tsp. cinnamon
½ cup white sugar
½ cup chopped nuts
2⅔ Tbsp. margarine, melted
1½ cups whipped topping

1. Reserve 1 cup yellow cake mix and set aside.
2. Cut 5⅓ Tbsp. margarine into remaining cake mix. Pat into bottom of 9" x 13" baking pan.
3. In a bowl combine pumpkin, milk, brown sugar, ¼ cup white sugar, and cinnamon and mix well. Pour mixture over cake mix crust.
4. Combine 1 cup reserved cake mix with ½ cup white sugar, nuts, and 2⅔ Tbsp. margarine and mix until crumbly. Sprinkle over pumpkin mixture.
5. Bake at 350° for 45-50 minutes. Cool.
6. Top with whipped topping and serve.

Best Ever Rhubarb Cake

Gladys Stoesz, Akron, PA
Loretta Lapp, Kinzers, PA

Makes 16-20 servings

1½ cups brown sugar
½ cup shortening
1 cup buttermilk *or* sour milk
1 egg
1 tsp. vanilla
2 cups flour
1 tsp. baking soda
1½ cups finely diced rhubarb
¼ cup white sugar
1½ tsp. cinnamon

1. Cream together brown sugar and shortening. Add buttermilk, egg, and vanilla and mix well. Add flour and baking soda and mix well. Fold in rhubarb. Spoon into greased 9" x 13" baking pan.
2. Combine white sugar and cinnamon and sprinkle evenly over batter.
3. Bake at 350° for 40 minutes.

Rhubarb Upside-Down Cake

Laura Mae Voran
New Holland, PA

Makes 12-16 servings

6 cups chopped rhubarb
2 cups miniature marshmallows
2 cups sugar *or* less
2 Tbsp. butter
1 yellow cake mix
3 eggs
1 cup milk
¼ cup cooking oil

1. Lightly toss together rhubarb, marshmallows, and sugar. Spoon into greased 9" x 13" baking pan. Dot with butter.
2. Combine dry cake mix, eggs, milk, and oil and mix well. Pour over rhubarb.
3. Bake at 325° for 50-60 minutes or until toothpick inserted in center comes out clean. Cool and invert onto serving plate.

Peach Upside-Down Cake

Gladys Kautz
Columbia, PA

Makes 10-12 servings

¾ cup brown sugar, packed
16 Tbsp. butter
29-oz. can peach slices, drained
2¼ cups flour
1 Tbsp. baking powder
2 tsp. cinnamon
1½ cups sugar
3 large eggs, separated
¾ cup milk
1½ tsp. vanilla

1. In a saucepan combine brown sugar and 4 Tbsp. butter. Melt over medium heat, stirring well. Spread into bottom of 9-inch square baking pan. Arrange peach slices over sauce.
2. In a small bowl combine flour, baking powder, and cinnamon.
3. In a large bowl beat remaining butter with sugar until creamy. Beat in egg yolks, dry ingredients, milk, and vanilla until well blended.
4. In small bowl beat egg whites until soft peaks form. Fold into batter. Spread batter over peaches.
5. Bake at 350° for 55-60 minutes. Cool and turn over onto serving plate.

Marietta

At the point where Route 23 meets the Susquehanna River, residents of Marietta take great pride in the ongoing restoration of their once-declining river town. From the churches and homes lining East Market Street to the classic 1820s Railroad House and 1860s Railroad Station along the river front, Marietta's old buildings generally are treated with great care.

In the 1800s the Pennsylvania Main Line Canal ran directly in front of the hotel, and the Railroad House provided accommodations, food, and drink for the river and canal traffic. While it flourished into the 1930s, the Railroad House was effectively put out of business by the Depression and the flood of 1936. The building stood vacant for about thirty years before it was carefully restored. Today it offers "a respectable fine dining experience" along with twelve bed and breakfast rooms.

Raisin Spice Cake
Alice Whitman
Lititz, PA

Makes 16-20 servings

Cake:
2 cups flour
1 tsp. baking soda
1 tsp. cinnamon
½ tsp. nutmeg
¼ tsp. salt
1 cup raisins
2 cups water
1 egg
½ cup shortening
1 cup sugar
½ cup chopped pecans *or* walnuts

Orange *or* Lemon Frosting:
2 cups powdered sugar
2 Tbsp. orange *or* lemon juice
1 Tbsp. butter

1. Sift together flour, baking soda, cinnamon, nutmeg, and salt. Set aside.

2. In uncovered saucepan boil raisins rapidly in water for 10 minutes. Transfer raisins with liquid to large mixing bowl. Cool to lukewarm. Stir in egg, shortening, and sugar. Add dry ingredients and mix well. Fold in pecans. Turn into greased 9" x 13" baking pan.

3. Bake at 350° for 25 minutes or until toothpick inserted in center comes out clean. Cool completely in baking pan.

4. To prepare frosting beat together powdered sugar, juice, and butter until smooth and spreadable. Frost cooled cake and serve.

Boiled Raisin Cake
Dorothy H. Johnson
Quarryville, PA

Makes 12-16 servings

Cake:
2 cups sugar
2 cups raisins
2 cups cold water
1 cup shortening
1 Tbsp. cinnamon
1 tsp. nutmeg
½ tsp. ground cloves
3 cups flour
2 tsp. baking soda
½ tsp. salt
1 tsp. vanilla

Caramel Icing:
½ cup butter
1 cup brown sugar
¼ cup evaporated milk
Pinch salt
1¾-2 cups powdered sugar

1. To prepare cake combine sugar, raisins, cold water, shortening, cinnamon, nutmeg, and ground cloves in a 3-quart saucepan and bring to a boil. Boil for 3 minutes. Cool to lukewarm.

2. In a sifter combine flour, baking soda, and salt. Sift into raisin mixture in thirds, beating well after each addition. Add vanilla and mix well.

3. Divide batter evenly into two greased and floured loaf pans.

4. Bake at 350° for 45 minutes. Cool.

5. To prepare icing melt butter in saucepan. Add all remaining ingredients except powdered sugar and bring to a boil over low heat for 2 minutes. Remove from heat and cool to lukewarm. Gradually beat in powdered sugar, beating until icing is thick enough to spread. Spread icing over cooled cakes and serve.

Date Cake

Dorothy H. Johnson
Quarryville, PA

Makes 10-12 servings

1 cup chopped dates
1 cup boiling water
1 cup white sugar
1 Tbsp. butter
1 egg, beaten
1½ cups flour
1 cup chopped English walnuts
¼ cup powdered sugar

1. Pour boiling water over dates and set aside to cool. When cooled, add sugar, butter, egg, and flour and mix well. Then add English walnuts. Pour into greased, floured loaf pan.

2. Bake at 350° for 45 minutes. Cool.

3. Sprinkle with powdered sugar and serve.

Black Walnut Cake

Anna Mary Boyer
Akron, PA

Makes 12-16 servings

Cake:
2 cups flour
1⅓ cups sugar
½ cup shortening
1 tsp. salt
⅔ cup milk
3 tsp. baking powder
2 eggs
⅓ cup milk
1 tsp. vanilla
½ cup black walnuts, chopped

Butter Frosting:
⅓ cup butter, softened
3 cups powdered sugar, sifted
1½ tsp. vanilla
3 Tbsp. cream

1. To prepare cake combine flour, sugar, shortening, salt, and ⅔ cup milk and mix well. Add baking powder, eggs, ⅓ cup milk, and vanilla. Beat. Fold in walnuts. Pour into 2 8-inch round cake pans.

2. Bake at 350° for 30-35 minutes. Cool.

3. To prepare frosting blend butter, powdered sugar, and vanilla. Add cream and beat mixture until creamy, adding more cream if needed.

Walnut Chiffon Cake
Catherine Shirk
Ephrata, PA

Makes 16-20 servings

2 cups cake flour
3 scant tsp. baking powder
1 tsp. salt
1½ cups sugar
½ cup cooking oil
7 egg yolks
¾ cup cold water
2 tsp. vanilla
1 cup finely chopped nuts
7 egg whites
½ tsp. cream of tartar

1. Measure and sift together in large bowl flour, baking powder, and salt. Add sugar and make a well. Add oil, unbeaten egg yolks, water, and vanilla and beat until smooth. Fold in nuts.

2. In separate bowl beat egg whites and cream of tartar until very stiff peaks form. Gently fold batter into egg whites until just blended. Spoon into 10-inch tube pan.

3. Bake at 300° for 10 minutes, increasing temperature slowly to 350° and baking 1 hour longer.

Walnut Wonder Cake
Esta M. Ansel
Reamstown, PA

Makes 16-20 servings

Cake:
¾ cup margarine
2 cups white sugar
1 tsp. salt
3 cups cake flour
4 tsp. baking powder

1¼ cups lukewarm water
2 tsp. vanilla
4 egg whites

Walnut Filling:
1 cup chopped nuts
½ cup light cream
⅔ cup white sugar
¼ tsp. salt
2 egg yolks, beaten
2 tsp. butter

Icing:
½ cup shortening
1 Tbsp. butter
½ tsp. salt
1 egg white
2 cups powdered sugar
2 tsp. vanilla
2 Tbsp. milk

1. To prepare cake cream together margarine, sugar, and salt. Stir in flour and baking powder, alternating with water and beginning and ending with flour. Beat thoroughly and add vanilla.

2. Beat egg whites until stiffened. Fold into cake batter. Pour into two well-greased round cake pans.

3. Bake at 350° for 25-30 minutes.

4. To prepare walnut filling combine nuts, cream, sugar, salt, and egg yolks in a saucepan and cook over low heat, stirring constantly until thickened. Stir in butter until melted. Remove from heat and cool.

5. Spread cooled walnut filling between two layers of cooled cake.

6. To prepare icing combine all ingredients and beat until smooth and spreadable. Spread icing over layer cake. Serve.

Deluxe Black Walnut Cake

Anne Nolt
Reinholds, PA

Makes 12-16 servings

1 cup coconut
1/3 cup black walnuts
1/4 cup chopped black walnuts
2 cups sifted flour
1 tsp. baking powder
1 tsp. baking soda
1/2 tsp. salt
1 1/2 cups sugar
1/2 cup shortening
1/2 tsp. vanilla
1/2 tsp. black walnut extract
2 eggs
1 cup buttermilk
1/3 cup hot, strong black coffee

1. Grind together coconut and 1/3 cup black walnuts. Add 1/4 cup chopped black walnuts and set aside.
2. Sift together flour, baking powder, baking soda, and salt.
3. Cream together sugar and shortening. Add flavorings and eggs, one at a time, beating well after each addition. Add dry ingredients alternately with buttermilk, beating well each time. Blend in coffee.
4. Reserve 2 Tbsp. coconut and walnut mixture. Fold remaining walnut mixture into batter. Spoon into 2 greased and floured 8-inch round cake pans.
5. Bake at 375° for 30-35 minutes. Remove from pans and cool on rack. Frost with favorite white icing and put layers together. Sprinkle reserved walnut mixture on top of cake. Serve.

Oatmeal Cake

Jane L. Creamer
Lancaster, PA

Makes 16-20 servings

Cake:
1 cup quick oats
1 1/4 cups boiling water
1/2 cup shortening
1 cup brown sugar
1 cup white sugar
2 eggs
1 1/2 cups sifted flour
1 tsp. cinnamon
1 tsp. baking soda
1/2 tsp. salt

Topping:
6 Tbsp. butter
1/2 cup brown sugar
1/4 cup milk
1 cup coconut
1/2 tsp. vanilla
1/2 cup chopped nuts (optional)

1. Soak oats in boiling water. Set aside to cool.
2. Cream together shortening, sugars, and eggs. Add cooled oatmeal and mix well. Stir in flour, cinnamon, baking soda, and salt and mix well. Spoon into greased 9" x 13" baking pan.
3. Bake at 350° for 30-40 minutes.
4. To prepare topping combine all ingredients except vanilla and nuts in a saucepan. Bring to a boil and cook until thickened, stirring frequently. Remove from heat immediately and fold in nuts and vanilla.
5. Spread topping over warm cake. Broil at 500° for 3-5 minutes.

Mocha Oatmeal Cake

Leah Martin
East Earl, PA

Makes 10-12 servings

Cake:
2 Tbsp. instant coffee powder
1⅓ cups boiling water
1 cup uncooked oats
½ cup butter *or* margarine, softened
1 cup white sugar
1 cup firmly packed brown sugar
1 tsp. vanilla
2 eggs
1½ cups sifted all-purpose flour
1 tsp. baking soda
½ tsp. salt
2 Tbsp. cocoa

Mocha Icing:
3 Tbsp. butter *or* margarine, softened
2 cups powdered sugar, sifted
Dash salt
1 tsp. vanilla
2 Tbsp. prepared coffee

1. Combine instant coffee powder and boiling water. Reserve 2 Tbsp. coffee for the icing. Pour remaining coffee over the oats and stir to combine. Cover and let stand for 20 minutes.
2. Beat butter until creamy. Gradually add sugars, beating until fluffy. Blend in vanilla and eggs. Add oat mixture and blend well.
3. Sift together flour, baking soda, salt, and cocoa and mix well. Pour batter into greased and floured 9-inch baking pan.
4. Bake at 350° for 50-55 minutes.
5. To prepare icing beat butter until creamy. Add sugar, salt, vanilla, and coffee. Beat until smooth and spreadable. Frost the cooled cake. If desired, decorate with chocolate curls.

Shoofly Cake

Elaine W. Good, Lititz, PA
Joyce E. Imhoff, Akron, PA
Anne Nolt, Reinholds, PA

Makes 16-20 servings

4 cups flour
2 cups brown sugar
1 cup butter *or* margarine
2 cups boiling water
1 cup molasses
2 tsp. baking soda

1. Combine flour, brown sugar, and butter until crumbly. Reserve 1½ cups crumbs for topping.
2. Combine boiling water, molasses, and baking soda. Stir into remaining crumbs and mix well. Pour into floured 9" x 13" baking pan. Sprinkle with 1½ cups reserved crumbs.
3. Bake at 350° for 35-40 minutes or until toothpick inserted in center comes out clean.

Velvet Pound Cake

Alice Whitman
Lititz, PA

Makes 12-16 servings

16 Tbsp. butter *or* margarine
½ cup shortening
3 cups sugar
6 eggs
3 cups flour
1 tsp. baking powder
¼ tsp. salt
1 cup milk
1 tsp. vanilla
1 tsp. lemon extract

1. Cream together butter, shortening, and sugar. Add one egg at a time, beating after each addition.

2. Sift together flour, baking powder, and salt. Add dry ingredients to creamed ingredients, alternating with milk. Stir in vanilla and lemon extract. Spoon into greased and floured bundt pan.

3. Bake at 325° for 1½ hours or until done.

Sour Cream Pound Cake
Janet Pickel
Lancaster, PA

Makes 12-16 servings

16 Tbsp. butter
3 cups sugar
6 eggs
3 cups flour
¼ tsp. baking soda
1 tsp. vanilla *or* lemon extract
1 cup sour cream

1. Cream together butter and sugar. Add eggs, one at a time, mixing well after each addition.

2. Sift together flour and baking soda. Add to creamed ingredients, alternating with sour cream and vanilla and mix well. Pour into greased tube pan.

3. Bake at 300° for 1 hour.

Toasted Nut Spice Cake
Dottie Donnelly
Willow Street, PA

Makes 16-20 servings

Cake:
⅔ cup shortening
2 cups brown sugar
2 egg yolks
1 tsp. baking soda
1¼ cups sour milk
2⅓ cups flour
1 tsp. baking powder
1 tsp. cinnamon
½ tsp. nutmeg
½ tsp. ground cloves
¾ tsp. salt
1 tsp. vanilla

Meringue:
2 egg whites
1 cup brown sugar
½ cup chopped nuts

1. Cream together shortening and brown sugar. Add egg yolks and mix well.

2. Dissolve baking soda in sour milk and set aside.

3. Combine all remaining dry ingredients. Add sour milk and dry ingredients alternately to creamed mixture. Add vanilla and mix until smooth. Spread into greased 9" x 13" baking pan.

4. To prepare meringue beat egg whites until stiff. Slowly add brown sugar and continue beating until smooth. Spread over cake batter and sprinkle with chopped nuts.

5. Bake at 350° for about 50 minutes.

Watergate Cake

Dorothy Rynier
Gordonville, PA

Makes 16-20 servings

Cake:
1 pkg. yellow cake mix
½ cup chopped English walnuts
2 small pkgs. instant pistachio pudding
    mix
½ cup coconut
1 scant cup cooking oil
4 eggs
1 cup ginger ale

Cream Cheese Icing:
2 Tbsp. margarine
8-oz. pkg. cream cheese
1½-2 cups powdered sugar
1 tsp. vanilla
½ cup coconut
½ cup chopped English walnuts

1. To prepare cake batter, mix together all ingredients. Pour into greased 9" x 13" cake pan.

2. Bake at 350° for 40-45 minutes. Cool.

3. To prepare frosting cream together margarine and cream cheese, beating until light and fluffy. Gradually add powdered sugar and vanilla and beat until smooth.

4. Spread over cooled cake. Sprinkle with coconut and chopped walnuts.

Peanut Butter Meltaway Cake

Lois Nafziger
Lancaster, PA

Makes 16-20 servings

Cake:
1 cup margarine
¼ cup cocoa
½ cup buttermilk
2 eggs
1 cup water
2 cups sugar
2 cups flour
1 tsp. baking soda
1 tsp. vanilla
1-2 cups peanut butter, room
    temperature

Topping:
½ cup margarine
¼ cup cocoa
1 lb. powdered sugar
1 tsp. vanilla
6 Tbsp. buttermilk

1. To prepare cake melt margarine and cocoa in a saucepan. Add buttermilk, eggs, and water. Cook on medium until bubbly, but not quite boiling. Stir in sugar, flour, baking soda, and vanilla and mix until smooth. Pour into greased 9" x 13" baking pan.

2. Bake at 350° for 25 minutes. Cool slightly. Spread peanut butter on top of cake and refrigerate.

3. To prepare topping combine margarine and cocoa and heat until bubbly, stirring constantly. Remove from heat and stir in sugar, vanilla, and buttermilk. Beat until smooth. Spread evenly over cake and refrigerate.

Note: To spread peanut butter more easily, spoon lumps of peanut butter onto still warm cake. Spread peanut butter after it softens slightly.

Coconut Mist Cake
Marian E. Kurtz
Kinzers, PA

Makes 16-20 servings

1-lb. box powdered sugar
1 cup butter
4 eggs, separated
1 tsp. vanilla
3 cups cake flour
2 tsp. baking powder
1 cup milk
1 cup coconut

1. Mix together powdered sugar, butter, egg yolks, and vanilla.
2. Combine flour and baking powder. Add dry ingredients to creamed mixture, alternating with milk and mix well. Fold in coconut.
3. Beat egg whites until stiff and fold into batter. Pour into greased 9" x 13" baking pan.
4. Bake at 350° for 30 minutes. Frost with favorite cream cheese icing.

Italian Cream Cake
Carrie M. Ney
Columbia, PA

Makes 16-20 servings

Cake:
8 Tbsp. margarine
½ cup cooking oil
2 cups sugar
5 eggs, separated
1 cup buttermilk
1 tsp. baking soda
2 cups flour
1 tsp. vanilla
1 cup flaked coconut
1 cup chopped nuts

Cream Cheese Icing:
8-oz. pkg. cream cheese
2 Tbsp. margarine
1-lb. pkg. powdered sugar
1 tsp. vanilla
½ cup coconut
½ cup chopped nuts

1. Cream margarine, oil, and sugar together. Add egg yolks, one at a time and mix well.
2. Dissolve baking soda in buttermilk.
3. Add flour to creamed ingredients, alternating with buttermilk. Fold in vanilla.
4. Beat egg whites until stiff. Fold into batter. Add coconut and nuts and mix lightly. Pour into greased 9" x 13" baking pan.
5. Bake at 350° for 45-50 minutes.
6. To prepare icing cream together all ingredients except coconut and nuts until fluffy. Spread over cooled cake. Sprinkle with coconut and nuts and serve.

Dump Cake
Sue Steffy
Leola, PA

Makes 12-16 servings

20-oz. can fruit cocktail, undrained
21-oz. can pie filling, any flavor
1 yellow *or* white cake mix
4 Tbsp. butter

1. Dump fruit and pie filling into greased 9" x 13" baking pan. Sprinkle dry cake mix over top.
2. Melt butter in saucepan and drizzle over top of cake mix.
3. Bake at 350° for 30-40 minutes.

Fruit Cocktail Cake
Jennifer Trimble
Denver, PA

Makes 10-12 servings

Cake:
2 cups flour
3 tsp. baking soda
16-oz. can fruit cocktail, drained
1½ cups sugar
2 eggs

Topping:
8 Tbsp. butter
¾ cup sugar
½ cup evaporated milk
1 cup chopped nuts
½ cup coconut

1. Combine all cake ingredients and beat well for about 2 minutes. Pour into greased loaf pan.
2. Bake at 350° for 35 minutes.

3. To prepare topping combine all ingredients in a saucepan. Bring to a boil and boil for 1 minute, stirring occasionally.
4. Spread warm topping over hot cake. Serve.

Old-Fashioned Strawberry Shortcake
Ruth E. Wenger, Akron, PA
Tamara Lausch, Akron, PA
Jean Barnes, Peach Bottom, PA
Nancy Law, East Earl, PA

Makes 4-6 servings

½ cup butter
1 cup sugar
2 eggs
1 cup milk
2 cups flour
3 tsp. baking powder
1 quart fresh strawberries, sliced

1. Cream together butter and sugar until well blended. Add eggs and mix until creamy. Add milk, flour, and baking powder and beat until well blended. Pour into greased 9-inch square baking pan.
2. Bake at 350° for 40 minutes.
3. Serve with fresh strawberries and milk.

Cinnamon Cake

Nancy B. Wallace
New Holland, PA

Makes 12-16 servings

Cake:
3 Tbsp. shortening
1½ cups sugar
2 eggs
3 cups flour
4 tsp. baking powder
½ tsp. salt
1 cup milk
1 tsp. vanilla

Topping:
6 Tbsp. margarine
1 cup sugar
2 Tbsp. cinnamon

1. To prepare cake cream together shortening, sugar, and eggs.
2. Combine all dry ingredients. Add to creamed ingredients, alternating with milk. Add vanilla and mix well. Pour into greased 9" x 13" baking pan.
3. To prepare topping melt margarine in saucepan and spread evenly over cake batter.
4. Mix sugar and cinnamon and sprinkle over cake batter.
5. Bake at 350° about 40 minutes or until toothpick inserted in center comes out clean.

Cinnamon Nut Cake

Dawn Ranck
Strasburg, PA

Makes 12-16 servings

Cake:
1 box vanilla cake mix
1 cup water
1 large pkg. instant vanilla pudding
4 eggs
½ cup cooking oil

Topping:
1 Tbsp. cinnamon
1 cup sugar
1 cup crushed black walnuts

1. To prepare cake combine all ingredients and mix well. Spoon ½ of batter into greased 9" x 13" baking pan.
2. To prepare topping combine all ingredients. Spread ½ of topping over cake batter. Add remaining batter and remaining topping.
3. Bake at 350° for 30-35 minutes. Cool and serve.

Cherry Coffee Cake
Marlene Weaver
Ephrata, PA

Makes 12-16 servings

2 cups flour
2 tsp. baking powder
½ tsp. salt
1 cup sugar
8 Tbsp. butter
2 eggs, beaten
½ cup milk
2 21-oz. cans cherry pie filling

1. Combine flour, baking powder, salt, and sugar. Cut in butter and mix until crumbly. Reserve ½ of crumbs.

2. Combine eggs and milk. Add ½ of crumbs and mix well. Spread into greased 9" x 13" baking pan. Spoon cherry pie filling over crust. Sprinkle reserved crumbs over top.

3. Bake at 325° for 50-55 minutes.

Coffee Cake
Linda Seldomridge
Gap, PA

Makes 12-16 servings

½ cup chopped nuts
2 tsp. cinnamon
¾ cup brown sugar, packed
8 Tbsp. butter
2 eggs
1 cup white sugar
1 tsp. vanilla
2 cups sifted flour
2 tsp. baking powder
1 tsp. baking soda
½ pint sour cream

1. Combine nuts, cinnamon, and brown sugar and set aside.

2. Cream together butter, eggs, white sugar, and vanilla. Add flour, baking powder, and baking soda and blend well. Add sour cream and blend well.

3. Spoon ½ of batter into greased and floured tube pan. Sprinkle ½ of nut mixture over batter. Add remaining batter and nut mixture.

4. Bake at 375° for 45 minutes.

Crumb Cake
Barbara Galebach
Ephrata, PA

Makes 12-16 servings

¾ cup butter
2 cups sugar
4 cups flour
1 tsp. cream of tartar
1 tsp. baking soda
2 eggs
1 cup buttermilk
1 tsp. vanilla
Pinch salt

1. Cream together butter and sugar.
2. Mix together flour, cream of tartar, and baking soda.
3. Stir eggs into buttermilk. Stir dry ingredients into creamed mixture, alternating with buttermilk. Add vanilla and salt and mix well.
4. Bake at 350° for 40-45 minutes or until toothpick inserted in center comes out clean.

Easy Dutch Cake
Deb Herr
Mountville, PA

Makes 10-12 servings

2 cups flour
1 cup sugar
2 tsp. baking powder
1 cup milk
1 egg
1½ Tbsp. butter, melted
1 Tbsp. sugar
1 Tbsp. cinnamon

1. Sift together flour, 1 cup sugar, and baking powder. Add milk and egg and mix well. Add ½ of butter and mix well. Pour into greased 8-inch square baking pan. Drizzle with remaining butter.
2. Mix 1 Tbsp. sugar with cinnamon and sprinkle on top of cake.
3. Bake at 350° for 35 minutes. Serve warm with butter.

Funnel Cakes

Shirley Prosser, Elizabethtown, PA
Diana Russell, Holtwood, PA
Emily Linton Reath, Kirkwood, PA

Makes 10-12 funnel cakes

2 eggs
1½ cups milk
2 cups flour
1 tsp. baking powder
½ tsp. salt
Cooking oil
Powdered sugar

1. Mix eggs, milk, flour, baking powder, and salt.

2. Heat oil in deep fryer or 2 inches deep in skillet. Pour batter into a funnel, holding the hole closed with your finger. Release finger to pour batter from funnel hole into hot oil. Make a circular motion, then crisscross. (These cook very quickly.)

3. When lightly browned, remove from oil, being careful not to break cake. Drain on paper towels.

4. Sprinkle with powdered sugar and serve immediately.

Coffee Chocolate Cupcakes

Deloris J. Miller
Manheim, PA

Makes 36 cupcakes

Cupcakes:
2 cups flour
2 cups sugar
2 tsp. baking soda
1 tsp. baking powder
½ tsp. salt
¾ cup cocoa
½ cup cooking oil
1 cup prepared hot coffee
1 cup milk
2 eggs
1 tsp. vanilla

Chocolate Icing:
6-oz. pkg. chocolate chips
2 Tbsp. butter
1 cup powdered sugar
¼ cup milk

1. To prepare cupcakes combine all dry ingredients in large bowl. Add oil, coffee, milk, eggs, and vanilla and mix well.

2. Fill cupcake liners ½ full with batter.

3. Bake at 350° for 15 minutes.

4. To prepare icing melt chocolate chips and butter in double boiler. Remove from heat and add sugar and milk. Beat until smooth and creamy. Spread over cooled cupcakes and serve.

Variation: Garnish each cupcake with chopped nuts.

Black Bottom Cupcakes

Barbara Hoffert, Denver, PA
Emily Fleck, Elizabethtown, PA

Makes 30 cupcakes

Cupcakes:
2 cups sugar
1/2 tsp. salt
2 tsp. baking soda
3 cups flour
1/2 cup cocoa
2 cups water
2 tsp. vinegar
2/3 cup cooking oil
2 tsp. vanilla

Filling:
1/3 cup sugar
1 egg
8-oz. pkg. cream cheese
Dash salt
6-oz. pkg. miniature chocolate chips

1. To prepare cupcakes combine all dry ingredients. Add water, vinegar, oil, and vanilla and mix well. Pour into greased cupcake tins, filling each tin 1/2 full.

2. To prepare filling beat together sugar and egg. Add cream cheese and salt and mix well. When smooth, fold in chocolate chips. Drop one heaping teaspoon of filling mixture on top of batter in each cupcake tin.

3. Bake at 350° for 20 minutes.

Chocolate Chip Cupcakes

Elsie M. Beachy
Lancaster, PA

Makes 16 cupcakes

Cupcakes:
1/2 cup soft butter
6 Tbsp. white sugar
6 Tbsp. light brown sugar
1/2 tsp. vanilla
1 egg
1 cup + 2 Tbsp. flour
1/2 tsp. baking soda
1/2 tsp. salt

Topping:
1/2 cup brown sugar, packed
1 egg
1/8 tsp. salt
6-oz. pkg. chocolate chips
1/2 cup chopped walnuts
1/2 tsp. vanilla

1. Cream together butter, sugars, and vanilla. Beat in egg. Add flour, baking soda, and salt and mix well. Spoon by rounded tablespoonsful into 16 paper-lined cupcake tins.

2. Bake at 375° for 10-12 minutes or until center starts to drop.

3. Meanwhile prepare topping by combining sugar, egg, and salt and beating until very thick. Stir in chocolate chips, walnuts, and vanilla.

4. Remove cupcakes from oven and quickly add 1 Tbsp. topping to center of each cupcake.

5. Return to oven and bake 15 minutes longer. Cool and serve.

Chocolate Mayonnaise Cupcakes

Janice Horning
Mohnton, PA

Makes 18 cupcakes

Cupcakes:
2 cups flour
1½ cups sugar
⅓ cup cocoa
1¾ tsp. baking soda
¾ cup mayonnaise
1 cup water
2 tsp. vanilla

Icing:
⅓ cup shortening
¼ cup margarine
1 cup powdered sugar
3 Tbsp. flour
¼ cup milk
1 tsp. vanilla

1. Sift together flour, sugar, cocoa, and baking soda. Add mayonnaise, water, and vanilla and mix well. Pour into greased cupcake tins, filling ⅔ full.

2. Bake at 350° for 20-25 minutes.

3. To prepare icing cream together shortening, margarine, and powdered sugar. Add flour, milk, and vanilla and mix well.

4. To frost cut a little circle out of the top of each cupcake, put icing in the hole, and put top back on. Serve.

Chocolate Zucchini Cupcakes

Joy Layton
Quarryville, PA

Makes 36 cupcakes

3 eggs
1 cup cooking oil
8 Tbsp. cocoa
1 tsp. vanilla
2 cups grated zucchini
3 cups flour
1 tsp. salt
1 tsp. baking soda
¼ tsp. baking powder
1 cup chopped nuts
2 cups sugar

1. Combine eggs, oil, cocoa, vanilla, and zucchini and mix well. Add remaining ingredients and beat until well mixed. Pour into greased and floured cupcake tins, filling ½ full.

2. Bake at 350° for 15-20 minutes. If desired, frost with favorite icing.

Cookies and Bars

Chocolate Chip Pudding Cookies

Rosita Beiler, Paradise, PA
Arlene Martin, Stevens, PA

Makes about 6 dozen cookies

1½ cups softened margarine
1 cup brown sugar
½ cup white sugar
1½ cups instant vanilla pudding mix
1½ tsp. vanilla
3 eggs
3½ cups flour
1½ tsp. baking soda
2 cups chocolate chips

1. Cream together margarine, sugars, pudding mix, and vanilla. Add eggs and mix well. Gradually stir in flour and baking soda, mixing well. Fold in chocolate chips.
2. Drop by teaspoonsful onto greased cookie sheet.
3. Bake at 350° for 10-12 minutes.

Chocolate Chip Cookies

Debbie Landis
Denver, PA

Makes 6 dozen cookies

1 cup margarine
1 cup peanut butter
1 cup white sugar
1 cup brown sugar
2 eggs
2 cups flour
1 tsp. baking soda
6-oz. pkg. chocolate chips

1. Cream together margarine and peanut butter until smooth. Gradually add sugars and beat until smooth. Add eggs, one at a time, and beat after each addition. Add flour and baking soda and mix well. Fold in chocolate chips.
2. Drop by teaspoonsful onto greased baking sheet. Flatten slightly with back of teaspoon.
3. Bake at 325° for 15 minutes or until done.

Deluxe Chocolate Chip Cookies
Jeanette Barr
Stevens, PA

Makes 9 dozen cookies

2 cups margarine
2 cups white sugar
2 cups brown sugar
4 eggs
2 tsp. vanilla
5 cups uncooked oats
4 cups flour
1 tsp. salt
2 tsp. baking soda
2 tsp. baking powder
24-oz. pkg. chocolate chips
8-oz. plain chocolate bar, grated
3 cups chopped nuts

1. Cream together margarine and sugars. Add eggs and vanilla.
2. Put oats through blender to powderize them.
3. In separate bowl combine powderized oats, flour, salt, baking soda, and baking powder. Add dry ingredients to creamed ingredients and mix well. Fold in chocolate chips, grated chocolate bar, and nuts.
4. Drop by golf ball-sized spoonsful onto greased cookie sheet, about 2 inches apart.
5. Bake at 350° for 8-10 minutes.

Chocolate Crinkles
Rose Scantling
Ephrata, PA

Makes 4 dozen cookies

4 squares unsweetened chocolate
1½ cups white sugar
½ cup cooking oil
2 tsp. vanilla
3 eggs
2 cups all-purpose flour
2 tsp. baking powder
2 cups powdered sugar, sifted

1. Melt chocolate in double boiler or microwave. Set aside to cool slightly.
2. In mixing bowl combine sugar, oil, melted chocolate, and vanilla. Beat in eggs.
3. Stir together flour and baking powder. Stir into chocolate mixture. Cover and chill.
4. Using 1 Tbsp. dough for each, shape into balls. Roll each ball in powdered sugar and arrange on greased cookie sheet.
5. Bake at 375° for 10-12 minutes. While still warm, roll each cookie in powdered sugar again.

Chocolate Drop Cookies
Betty Kissinger
Lancaster, PA

Makes 3 dozen cookies

Cookies:
1 cup brown sugar
½ cup butter
1 egg
2 squares chocolate
1½ cups flour
¼ tsp. baking soda
¼ tsp. baking powder
½ cup buttermilk

Icing:
1¾ cups powdered sugar
1 square chocolate, melted
1 Tbsp. cream
1 tsp. vanilla
1 cup crushed nuts

On Route 472 between Quarryville and the Chester County line, the crossroads village of Kirkwood consists of Steens Country Store and Sandwich Shop, Shaub's Garage, a collection of homes, a gleaming white-stuccoed Presbyterian church, and a miniature frame post office with a hitching post to accommodate the surrounding Amish population.

Since the late 1940s when Amish families first began buying land in the southern end of Lancaster County, Kirkwood has become a synonym for the most conservative arm of the County's Amish population. On the backroads around the village it is possible to get lost and occasionally even to meet more Amish buggies than cars. Locally owned stores such as Steens of Kirkwood, Bartville Store and Locker, and Kendigs of Ninepoints cater to both the non-Amish residents as well as the Amish community.

1. Cream together sugar, butter, and egg.

2. Melt chocolate in double boiler or microwave. Stir into creamed ingredients and add all remaining cookie ingredients, mixing well.

3. Drop by teaspoonsful onto lightly greased cookie sheet.

4. Bake at 350° for 10 minutes.

5. To prepare icing combine all ingredients except nuts and beat until smooth. Frost each cookie and dip top of cookie into crushed nuts.

Chocolate Marshmallow Cookies
Anna Mae Weaver
Ephrata, PA

Makes 2 dozen cookies

Cookies:
1½ cups sifted flour
½ cup cocoa
½ tsp. salt
1 tsp. baking soda
½ cup shortening
1 cup brown sugar
½ cup milk
2 eggs

1 tsp. vanilla
12 large marshmallows, halved

Frosting:
12-oz. pkg. chocolate chips
½ cup evaporated milk
½ cup margarine
½ lb. powdered sugar

1. Sift together flour, cocoa, salt, and baking soda.

2. Cream together shortening and sugar. Add milk, eggs, and vanilla. Add dry ingredients and mix well. Drop by teaspoonsful onto greased cookie sheet.

3. Bake at 350° for 8 minutes. Remove from oven and immediately top each cookie with ½ marshmallow. Press lightly and return to oven for 2 minutes.

4. To prepare frosting combine chocolate chips, milk, and margarine in double boiler and stir constantly until melted. Boil for 2 minutes. Remove from heat and add powdered sugar and beat until spreading consistency.

5. After cookies have cooled, frost each one. Store in cool place.

Choco-Taffy Chewies
Mabel E. Weaver
New Holland, PA

Makes 4 dozen cookies

Cookies:
2 cups all-purpose flour
1 tsp. baking soda
1 tsp. salt
8 Tbsp. margarine
1 cup sugar
$\frac{1}{2}$ cup light molasses
1 egg
1 tsp. vanilla
6-oz. pkg. chocolate chips
1 cup uncooked oats
1 cup flaked coconut

Glaze:
$\frac{3}{4}$ cup sugar
$\frac{1}{2}$ cup cream
6-oz. pkg. chocolate chips

1. Sift together flour, baking soda, and salt.
2. Cream together margarine and sugar. Add molasses, egg, and vanilla and beat until fluffy. Blend in dry ingredients and mix well. Fold in chocolate chips, oats, and coconut.
3. Drop by teaspoonsful onto greased baking sheet.
4. Bake at 375° for 10-12 minutes. Cool.
5. To prepare glaze combine sugar and cream in a saucepan and bring to a rolling boil. Remove from heat and pour over chocolate chips. Beat at high speed until chocolate is melted and glaze is of spreading consistency.
6. Glaze each cookie and serve.

Chocolate-Covered Cherry Cookies
Gina Burkhart
Landisville, PA

Makes 3 dozen cookies

$1\frac{1}{2}$ cups flour
$\frac{1}{2}$ cup cocoa
$\frac{1}{4}$ tsp. salt
$\frac{1}{4}$ tsp. baking powder
$\frac{1}{4}$ tsp. baking soda
$\frac{1}{2}$ cup margarine
1 cup sugar
1 egg
1 tsp. vanilla
10-oz. jar maraschino cherries
$\frac{1}{2}$ cup condensed milk
6-oz. pkg. chocolate chips

1. Combine flour, cocoa, salt, baking powder, and baking soda.
2. Cream together margarine and sugar. Add egg and vanilla and mix well. Stir in dry ingredients. Shape dough into 1-inch balls and arrange on ungreased cookie sheet. Press center of each ball with thumb and place cherry in indentation of each cookie.
3. In a saucepan combine milk and chocolate chips and stir until melted. Stir in 1 tsp. cherry juice. Spread topping on each cookie, completely covering cherry.
4. Bake at 350° for 10 minutes.

Peanut Butter Cookies
Sarah Evans
Akron, PA

Makes 3 dozen cookies

¾ **cup shortening**
¾ **cup peanut butter**
2 eggs
1 cup white sugar
1 cup brown sugar
½ **tsp. salt**
1 tsp. vanilla
3 cups flour
2 tsp. baking soda

1. Cream together shortening and peanut butter. Add eggs, sugars, salt, and vanilla. Sift flour and baking soda into cookie batter and mix well.

2. Drop by large, rounded teaspoonful onto greased baking sheets. Flatten with fork.

3. Bake at 375° for 10-12 minutes.

Chocolate Peanut Butter Chip Cookies
Mary Z. Stoltzfus
Gordonville, PA

Makes about 5 dozen cookies

1 cup butter *or* margarine, softened
1½ **cups sugar**
3 eggs
2 cups flour
⅔ **cup cocoa**
¾ **tsp. baking soda**
½ **tsp. salt**
2 tsp. vanilla
2 cups peanut butter chips

1. Cream together margarine, sugar, and eggs.

2. Sift flour and add cocoa and baking soda. Add these ingredients to creamed ingredients and mix well. Add salt and vanilla and mix well. Fold in peanut butter chips.

3. Drop by teaspoonsful onto greased cookie sheet.

4. Bake at 350° for 10 minutes.

Quick and Easy Peanut Butter Cookies
Yvonne Sensenig
Akron, PA

Makes about 3 dozen cookies

1 box yellow cake mix
⅓ **cup light brown sugar**
1½ **cups peanut butter**
½ **cup cooking oil**
¼ **cup water**
1 egg

1. Combine all ingredients and beat with beater until stiff. Finish mixing with a spoon.

2. Drop by rounded teaspoonsful onto greased baking sheet.

3. Bake at 375° for 10 minutes or until done. Let cool slightly before removing from baking sheet.

Peanut Butter Roundup Cookies

Christina L. Rohrer
East Petersburg, PA

Makes 6 dozen cookies

1 cup soft shortening
1 cup brown sugar, packed
¾ cup white sugar
2 eggs
1 cup creamy peanut butter
2 cups all-purpose flour
2 tsp. baking soda
½ tsp. salt
1 tsp. vanilla
1 cup uncooked oats

1. Cream together shortening and sugars. Add eggs and peanut butter; beat well.
2. Sift together flour, baking soda, and salt and add to creamed mixture, mixing well. Stir in vanilla and oats.
3. Shape cookies into 1-inch balls. Place on ungreased cookie sheets. Flatten slightly with a fork.
4. Bake at 350° for 8 minutes.

Peanut Blossom Cookies

Rosie Yeakel
Ephrata, PA

Makes about 3½ dozen cookies

1¾ cups flour
1 tsp. baking soda
½ tsp. salt
½ cup shortening
½ cup peanut butter
½ cup white sugar
½ cup brown sugar
1 egg

2 tsp. milk
1 tsp. vanilla
9-oz. pkg. Hershey Kisses
½ cup white sugar

1. Combine flour, baking soda, and salt in a bowl; set aside.
2. In large bowl cream together shortening and peanut butter. Gradually add ½ cup white and ½ cup brown sugar and stir until fluffy. Add egg, milk, and vanilla and beat well. Gradually add dry ingredients to creamed mixture, blending thoroughly.
3. Shape into 1-inch balls and roll in white sugar. Place on ungreased cookie sheet at least 1 inch apart.
4. Bake at 375° for 10-12 minutes. Remove from oven. Press a Hershey Kiss (unwrapped) in the center of each cookie. Let cool before placing in storage container.

Peanut Butter Treats

Verna Graham, Gordonville, PA
Karen Burkholder, New Holland, PA

Makes 4 dozen cookies

½ cup butter *or* margarine
½ cup brown sugar, packed
½ cup white sugar
½ cup peanut butter
½ tsp. vanilla
1 egg
1¼ cups flour
¾ tsp. baking soda
½ tsp. salt
48 miniature peanut butter cups

1. Combine butter, sugars, peanut butter, vanilla, and egg and beat until smooth.

2. Combine flour, baking soda, and salt and add to creamed ingredients, mixing well.

3. Divide dough into 4 portions. Make 12 balls from each portion and place into greased or paper-lined miniature muffin tins. Press thumb print into each ball.

4. Bake at 375° for 8-10 minutes. Remove from oven and press peanut butter cup into each cookie immediately. Cool on rack.

Old-Fashioned Iced Sugar Cookies

Anne Nolt
Reinholds, PA

Makes 6 dozen cookies

Cookies:
½ **cup butter** *or* **margarine**
1 **cup white sugar**
1 **egg**
1 **tsp. vanilla**
½ **cup milk**
3 **cups sifted flour**
3 **tsp. baking powder**

Icing:
3 **cups powdered sugar**
⅓ **cup shortening** *or* **margarine,**
   softened
1 **tsp. vanilla**
Milk

1. To prepare cookie dough cream together butter and sugar. Add egg, vanilla, and milk and mix well.

2. Sift together dry ingredients. Add gradually to creamed mixture and mix dough well. Chill overnight.

3. Roll out well-chilled dough. Cut with cookie cutter and arrange on greased cookie sheets.

4. Bake at 350° for about 8 minutes or until cookies appear done when touched.

5. To prepare icing combine powdered sugar, shortening, and vanilla. Add milk in very small amounts and stir until sugar is dissolved. Beat until fluffy.

6. Spread icing on each cookie and let dry. Store in tight container for a few weeks to help soften cookies.

Drop Sugar Cookies

Diana Russell, Holtwood, PA
Yvonne Sensenig, Akron, PA

Makes 4 dozen cookies

2 **cups sugar**
3 **eggs**
¾ **cup shortening**
Dash salt
2 **Tbsp. vanilla**
4 **cups flour**
2 **tsp. baking soda**
2 **tsp. cream of tartar**
1 **cup sour milk** *or* **buttermilk**
Cinnamon
Colored sugar

1. Cream together sugar, eggs, shortening, salt, and vanilla. Add flour and mix well.

2. Stir baking soda and cream of tartar into sour milk until it becomes bubbly. Add to batter and beat thoroughly.

3. Drop by spoonsful onto greased cookie sheet. Sprinkle with cinnamon and sugar.

4. Bake at 350° for 10-15 minutes.

Amish Sugar Cookies
Rosie Stoltzfus
Ronks, PA

Makes 12-13 dozen cookies

3 lbs. brown sugar
1¼ lbs. lard
4 lbs. flour
2 Tbsp. baking soda
1 Tbsp. nutmeg
1 Tbsp. cream of tartar
1 quart buttermilk
1 Tbsp. lemon extract
6 eggs, beaten
½ cup white sugar
½ cup brown sugar

1. Cream together 3 lbs. brown sugar and lard in very large mixing bowl.

2. Sift together flour, baking soda, nutmeg, and cream of tartar. Stir dry ingredients into creamed mixture, alternating with buttermilk. Stir in lemon extract and eggs and mix well.

4. Combine ½ cup white sugar and ½ cup brown sugar. Set aside.

5. Drop by tablespoonsful onto greased and floured cookie sheet. Sprinkle each cookie with the sugar mixture.

6. Bake at 350° for 8-10 minutes.

Note: My mother-in-law always made these delicious cookies at Christmas time. The secret to this recipe is to use lard rather than a commercial shortening.

Cut-Out Sugar Cookies
Darlene Redcay
Goodville, PA

Makes 6 dozen cookies

1 cup shortening
2 cups light brown sugar
2 eggs
1 tsp. vanilla
5 cups flour
1 tsp. salt
1 tsp. baking soda
1½ tsp. baking powder
¼ cup milk

1. Cream together shortening and sugar. Add eggs and vanilla and beat until fluffy.

2. Sift flour. Measure and add salt, baking soda, and baking powder. Sift again. Add sifted dry ingredients to creamed ingredients, alternating with milk. Stir until dough is smooth. Chill in refrigerator for several hours.

3. Roll out to ¼-inch thickness and cut into fancy shapes with various cookie cutters. Arrange 1 inch apart on greased cookie sheet.

4. Bake at 400° for 8-10 minutes.

Grandma's Soft Sugar Cookies
Sharon Weaver
Reinholds, PA

Makes 2 dozen cookies

¾ cup shortening
1 cup sugar
2 eggs
1 tsp. vanilla
¼ tsp. lemon extract (optional)
2¼ cups flour
1 tsp. baking powder
Dash salt

1. Cream together shortening and sugar. Beat in eggs, vanilla, and lemon extract, if desired.

2. Combine dry ingredients and add to creamed ingredients, mixing well.

3. Drop by teaspoonful onto greased cookie sheet. Sprinkle lightly with sugar.

4. Bake at 350° for 8-10 minutes.

Walnut Frosties

Jean R. Ressel
Quarryville, PA

Makes about 2 dozen cookies

Cookies:
½ **cup butter** *or* **margarine**
1 **cup brown sugar**
1 **egg, well beaten**
1 **tsp. vanilla**
2¼ **cups flour**
1 **tsp. baking soda**
¼ **tsp. salt**

Filling:
1 **cup finely chopped walnuts**
½ **cup brown sugar**
¼ **cup sour cream**

1. To prepare cookies cream together butter and sugar until light and fluffy. Blend in egg and vanilla. Add flour, baking soda, and salt and mix well.

2. Drop by teaspoonful onto lightly greased cookie sheet. Make a well in center of each cookie.

3. To prepare filling combine all ingredients and stir until well mixed. Spoon 1 tsp. filling into well of each cookie.

4. Bake at 350° for 10-12 minutes or until golden brown.

Rock Cookies

Debra McComsey
Christiana, PA

Makes 7-8 dozen cookies

2 **cups flour** *or* **more**
½ **tsp. cinnamon**
½ **tsp. salt**
1 **tsp. baking soda**
1 **lb. raisins**
1 **lb. chopped dates**
1 **cup chopped walnuts**
½ **cup butter, softened**
1½ **cups brown sugar**
2 **eggs**
¼ **cup water**
1 **tsp. vanilla**

1. Mix together dry ingredients; add raisins, dates, and walnuts. Set aside.

2. Cream together butter, brown sugar, eggs, water, and vanilla. Add dry ingredients to creamed ingredients and mix well.

3. Drop by rounded teaspoonful onto ungreased cookie sheet.

4. Bake at 350° for about 8 minutes.

Filled Jumbo Drops
Naomi E. Yoder
Gordonville, PA

Makes 5 dozen cookies

Cookies:
1 cup shortening
2 cups brown sugar
2 eggs
½ cup hot water
1 tsp. vanilla
3½ cups flour, sifted
1 tsp. baking soda
½ tsp. cinnamon
½ tsp. salt

Filling:
2 cups dates *or* raisins, chopped
½ cup chopped nuts
¾ cup sugar
¾ cup water

1. Cream together shortening, sugar, and eggs. Stir in hot water and vanilla. Add flour, baking soda, cinnamon, and salt and mix well.
2. To prepare filling combine all ingredients in saucepan and bring to a boil. Cook until thickened, stirring frequently. Let cool.
3. Drop cookie dough by teaspoonful onto ungreased cookie sheet. Place ½ tsp. filling on each cookie. Cover with ½ tsp. cookie dough.
4. Bake at 350° for 10-12 minutes.

Date and Nut Cookies
Katie Beiler
Leola, PA

Makes about 3 dozen cookies

2 cups brown sugar *or* less
4 eggs
½ cup cooking oil
1 Tbsp. vanilla
2 tsp. baking soda
4 cups flour
2 cups chopped nuts
4 cups chopped dates

1. Cream together sugar and eggs. Add oil, vanilla, baking soda, and flour and mix well. Fold in nuts and dates.
2. Drop by rounded teaspoonful onto ungreased cookie sheet.
3. Bake at 350° for 8-10 minutes or until light brown.

Jewel Cookies
Retta J. Kline
Columbia, PA

Makes 6 dozen cookies

1 cup shortening
1 cup brown sugar
1 cup white sugar
3 eggs, beaten
4½ cups flour
1 tsp. salt
2 tsp. baking soda
1 tsp. cinnamon
½ tsp. allspice
½ tsp. ground cloves
2 cups diced gumdrops
1 cup chopped walnuts
1 cup chopped dates

1. Cream together shortening and sugars. Add eggs and beat well.

2. Combine flour, salt, baking soda, cinnamon, allspice, and ground cloves. Add dry ingredients to creamed ingredients and mix well. Fold in gumdrops, walnuts, and dates.

3. Shape into rolls and wrap in waxed paper. Refrigerate and chill several hours or overnight.

4. Cut into ¼-inch slices and arrange on greased cookie sheet.

5. Bake at 350° about 7-10 minutes.

Date Balls
Esta M. Ansel
Reamstown, PA

Makes 4-5 dozen balls

1 cup butter
1½ cups white sugar
2 Tbsp. milk
1 tsp. salt
2 cups chopped dates
4½ cups Rice Krispies
1 cup chopped pecans
2 tsp. vanilla
2 cups finely grated coconut

1. In a saucepan combine butter, sugar, milk, salt, and dates and bring to a boil. Boil for 2 minutes. Remove from heat and cool slightly.

2. Stir in Rice Krispies, pecans, and vanilla. Shape into balls and roll into finely grated coconut. Arrange on ungreased cookie sheets.

3. Bake at 325° for 6-8 minutes, just until coconut starts to turn brown.

Fig Bar Cookies
Marian Kurtz
Kinzers, PA

Makes about 4 dozen cookies

1½ cups light brown sugar
1 cup shortening
½ cup molasses
3 eggs
1 tsp. vanilla
1 tsp. baking soda
¼ cup hot water
8-9 cups flour
1 lb. figs
4 Tbsp. warm water

1. Beat together sugar, shortening, molasses, and eggs. Beat well and add vanilla.

2. Dissolve baking soda in ¼ cup hot water. Add to creamed mixture and mix well. Gradually add flour, mixing until dough is stiff and ready to roll.

3. Grind figs with 4 Tbsp. water in food processor or blender.

4. Roll out dough and spread figs evenly over ½ of rolled out dough. Lay other ½ of dough over top. Cut into fig bar squares. Arrange on greased cookie sheets.

5. Bake at 325° for 10 minutes or until done.

Diabetic Cookies
Sadie S. Nolt
East Earl, PA

Makes about 2 dozen cookies

1 cup raisins
1/3 cup chopped dates
1/2 cup chopped apples
1 cup water
1/2 cup shortening
1 cup flour
1 tsp. baking soda
3 tsp. liquid sweetener
3/4 cup chopped nuts
1 tsp. vanilla

1. In a saucepan bring raisins, dates, apples, and water to a boil. Boil for 3 minutes. Add shortening and mix well. Remove from heat and cool.
2. Add all remaining ingredients and mix well. Refrigerate until thoroughly chilled.
3. Drop by teaspoonsful onto ungreased cookie sheet.
4. Bake at 350° for 10-12 minutes. Store in airtight container.

Raisin Drop Cookies
Barbara Evans
Ephrata, PA

Makes 4 dozen cookies

2 cups raisins
1 cup water
1 cup margarine
1 3/4 cups sugar
2 eggs
1 tsp. vanilla
4 cups flour
1 tsp. baking powder
1 tsp. baking soda

1/2 tsp. cinnamon
1/2 tsp. nutmeg

1. In a saucepan bring raisins and water to a boil. Boil until raisins are plump, about 3 minutes. Cool.
2. Cream together margarine and sugar until light and fluffy. Add eggs and vanilla and mix well.
3. Mix together flour, baking powder, baking soda, and all spices. Add dry ingredients to creamed ingredients and mix well. Add raisins with their water and mix well.
4. Drop by tablespoonsful onto ungreased baking sheet, about 1 inch apart.
5. Bake at 375° for 12-15 minutes.

Mother's Favorite Oatmeal Raisin Cookies
Ethel M. Brendle, Lititz, PA
Kathryn M. Horst, New Holland, PA

Makes about 6 dozen cookies

1 cup shortening
1 cup white sugar
1 tsp. vanilla
1/4 tsp. salt
2 eggs
2 cups boiling water
1 cup raisins
1 tsp. baking soda
1/4 cup sour milk
2 cups all-purpose flour
2 1/2 cups uncooked oats

1. Cream together shortening and sugar. Add vanilla and salt. Add eggs, one at a time, beating thoroughly after each one.
2. Pour boiling water over raisins and let stand several minutes. Drain. Add raisins to creamed mixture and mix well.

3. Dissolve baking soda in milk. Add flour to creamed ingredients, alternating with milk. Add oatmeal and blend together thoroughly.

4. Drop by teaspoonsful onto lightly greased cookie sheet.

5. Bake at 375° for 12-15 minutes.

Oatmeal Pudding Cookies
Esther Becker
Gap, PA

Makes 5 dozen cookies

1¼ **cups flour**
1 **tsp. baking soda**
1 **cup butter** *or* **margarine**
¼ **cup white sugar**
¾ **cup brown sugar**
1 **small pkg. instant vanilla pudding**
2 **eggs**
3½ **cups uncooked oats**
1 **cup raisins**
½ **cup chopped nuts**

1. Combine flour and baking soda in small bowl.

2. Combine butter, sugars, and pudding mix in a large bowl. Beat until smooth and creamy. Add eggs and beat well.

3. Gradually add flour mixture to creamed mixture, stirring constantly. Fold in oats, raisins, and nuts. (This batter will be quite stiff.)

4. Drop by teaspoonsful onto greased cookie sheet, about 2 inches apart.

5. Bake at 375° for 10-12 minutes.

Chewy Oatmeal Fruit Cookies
Elsie Nolt
New Holland, PA

Makes 3-4 dozen cookies

1 **cup butter, softened**
1 **cup brown sugar**
1 **cup white sugar**
2 **large eggs, beaten**
1 **tsp. vanilla**
1 **cup flour**
½ **tsp. salt**
1 **tsp. baking soda**
4 **cups uncooked oats**
1 **cup raisins**
1 **cup dates**
1 **cup chopped nuts**
1 **cup coconut**

1. Cream together butter, sugars, eggs, and vanilla.

2. Sift together flour, salt, and baking soda. Combine with creamed mixture. Add oats and mix well.

3. Grind together raisins, dates, nuts, and coconut. Add to batter and mix thoroughly.

4. Drop by teaspoonsful onto ungreased cookie sheet.

5. Bake at 325° for 10-15 minutes. It is normal for these cookies to fall when removed from oven. This is what makes them chewy.

Rural Lancaster County

Contrary to what some people may think, there is still lots of open farmland in Lancaster County. Each weekday morning I drive from Akron to Leola on my way to work. Some mornings I meet no more than two or three cars as I make my way along back country roads. During the school year, I often pass groups of Old Order Amish or Old Order Mennonite children walking to one of the four one-room schools I drive by each day. I watch farmers work their fields with horses and think about how much I enjoy living in Lancaster County.

—*Jeanette Oberholtzer, Akron, PA*

Chewy Oat Bran Cookies
Vera Nolt
Leola, PA

Makes 5-6 dozen cookies

1½ cups margarine
1 cup brown sugar
1 cup white sugar
2 eggs
2 tsp. vanilla
½ tsp. salt
1 tsp. baking soda
1 tsp. cream of tartar
2½ cups uncooked oats
1 cup oat bran
2¼ cups flour
2 cups cornflakes

1. Cream together margarine, sugars, eggs, and vanilla. Add remaining ingredients in order listed and mix well.
2. Drop by teaspoonful onto greased cookie sheet.
3. Bake at 350° for 10 minutes.

Crisp Bran Cookies
Florence Morrison
Lancaster, PA

Makes 3 dozen cookies

½ cup butter *or* margarine
½ cup sugar
½ cup brown sugar, packed
1 egg
1 tsp. vanilla
1⅓ cups all-purpose flour
1 tsp. baking soda
¼ tsp. salt
1 cup bran cereal

1. Cream together butter and sugars. Mix in egg and vanilla until smooth and creamy.
2. Stir together flour, baking soda, and salt. Add to creamed mixture and blend thoroughly. Fold in bran cereal.
3. Drop by level tablespoonful onto lightly greased baking sheet, about 2 inches apart.
4. Bake at 350° for 10-12 minutes or until golden brown. Remove from oven and let set for 1 minute before removing from baking sheet.

Ranger Best Cookies
Amanda S. Stoltzfus, Gap, PA
Sandy Huber, Holtwood, PA

Makes 4 dozen cookies

1 cup butter
1 cup white sugar
1 cup brown sugar
1 egg
1 cup cooking oil
1 cup uncooked oats
1 cup crushed cornflakes

½ cup shredded coconut
3½ cups flour
1 tsp. salt
1 tsp. baking soda
½ cup chopped pecans
½ cup chopped walnuts

1. Cream together butter, sugars, egg, and oil. Mix until light and fluffy. Add oats, cornflakes, and coconut and mix well.

2. Combine flour, salt, and baking soda and stir into creamed ingredients. Fold in pecans and walnuts.

3. Form into walnut-sized balls and arrange on ungreased cookie sheet. Flatten with fork.

4. Bake at 325° for 12 minutes.

Variation: Immediately after flattening each cookie with a fork, press ½ maraschino cherry on top of cookie. Proceed with step 4.
—Sandy Huber, Holtwood, PA

*M*olasses Cookies
Traci Kreider
Lancaster, PA

Makes 4 dozen cookies

1½ cups shortening
2 eggs
1 cup sugar
2 cups molasses
½ cup hot water
1 tsp. baking soda
4½ cups flour

1. Cream together shortening, eggs, and sugar. Add all remaining ingredients and mix well. Let set until cool.

2. Drop by teaspoonful onto ungreased cookie sheet.

3. Bake at 350° for about 10-12 minutes.

*S*nicker Doodles
Jennifer Martin
Stevens, PA

Makes 5-6 dozen cookies

Cookies:
2 cups shortening
3 cups sugar
4 eggs
5½ cups flour
4 tsp. cream of tartar
2 tsp. baking soda
½ tsp. salt

Topping:
2 Tbsp. sugar
2 Tbsp. cinnamon

1. Cream together shortening, sugar, and eggs.

2. Sift together flour, cream of tartar, baking soda, and salt. Add dry ingredients to creamed ingredients and mix well.

3. Roll into walnut-sized balls.

4. Combine topping ingredients. Roll each ball in topping. Place 2 inches apart on ungreased cookie sheet.

5. Bake at 375° for 8-10 minutes.

Ginger Snaps
Ruth H. Shank
Lititz, PA

Makes 5 dozen cookies

¾ cup shortening
1 cup white sugar
1 egg
¼ cup molasses
2 cups flour
¼ tsp. salt
2 tsp. baking soda
1 tsp. cinnamon
1 tsp. ginger
½ tsp. ground cloves

1. Cream together shortening, sugar, egg, and molasses. Stir in 1 cup flour, salt, baking soda, and spices and mix well. Add remaining cup flour and stir until well blended.
2. Drop by teaspoonful onto greased cookie sheet.
3. Bake at 350° for 8-10 minutes or until golden brown.

Note: These cookies will rise and crack. Take them out of oven as soon as they turn golden brown. Do not let them turn dark.

Hermits
Dottie Donnelly
Willow Street, PA

Makes 6-8 dozen cookies

1 cup shortening
2 cups brown sugar
2 eggs
½ cup cold, prepared coffee
3½ cups flour
1 tsp. baking soda
1 tsp. salt

1 tsp. nutmeg
1 tsp. cinnamon
2½ cups raisins
1¼ cups broken nuts

1. Cream together shortening, sugar, and eggs. Add cold coffee and mix well.
2. In separate bowl combine flour, baking soda, salt, nutmeg, and cinnamon. Stir dry ingredients into creamed ingredients and mix well. Fold in raisins and nuts.
3. Drop by teaspoonful onto greased cookie sheet.
4. Bake at 400° for 8-10 minutes.

Root Beer Cookies
Shirley Hoover
Lancaster, PA

Makes 3 dozen cookies

Cookies:
¾ cup brown sugar
½ cup margarine
1 egg
1¾ cups flour
½ tsp. baking powder
½ tsp. salt
¼ cup water
1 tsp. root beer extract

Root Beer Icing:
1½ tsp. root beer extract
2 cups powdered sugar
½ cup margarine
2 Tbsp. hot water

1. Cream together sugar, margarine, and egg, blending well.
2. Combine flour, baking powder, and salt.
3. Stir root beer extract into water.

4. Add dry ingredients to creamed mixture, alternating with root beer water.

5. Drop by tablespoonful onto greased cookie sheets.

6. Bake at 350° for 8-10 minutes.

7. To prepare icing combine all ingredients and beat until spreadable. Frost cookies after they have cooled.

Cut-Out Cookies
Elsie Kauffman
Stevens, PA

Makes about 12 dozen cookies

8 eggs
4 cups sugar
2 cups butter *or* margarine
1½ tsp. vanilla
2 tsp. baking soda
10 cups flour

1. Cream together eggs, sugar, and butter. Add vanilla and mix well.

2. Combine baking soda and flour. Add flour until batter is stiff and can be rolled out.

3. Roll out dough and cut with cookie cutters. Arrange on greased cookie sheet.

4. Bake at 350° for about 12-15 minutes.

Sandtarts
Marilyn Kay Martin, Manheim, PA
Darlene Redcay, Goodville, PA

Makes 4-6 dozen cookies

Sandtarts:
1 cup butter
2 cups white sugar
3 eggs
1 tsp. vanilla
3½-4 cups flour
1 tsp. salt
2 tsp. baking powder

Topping:
1 egg, beaten
Cinnamon
Chopped nuts
Colored sugars

1. Cream together butter, sugar, and eggs. Add vanilla and beat until fluffy.

2. Sift together flour, salt, and baking powder. Add to creamed ingredients and stir until a medium-soft dough forms. Refrigerate and chill at least 2 hours or overnight.

3. Roll out dough to ¼-inch thickness. Using cookie cutters, cut into various fancy shapes. Arrange 1 inch apart on greased cookie sheet. Brush tops with beaten egg. Sprinkle with any combination of cinnamon, chopped nuts, or colored sugars.

4. Bake at 350° for 8-10 minutes.

Chewy Chocolate Pan Cookies

Emily Fleck
Elizabethtown, PA

Makes about 36 bars

1¼ cups butter *or* margarine, softened
2 cups sugar
2 eggs
2 tsp. vanilla
2 cups flour
¾ cup cocoa
1 tsp. baking soda
½ tsp. salt
12-oz. pkg. peanut butter chips

1. In large bowl cream together butter and sugar until light and fluffy. Add eggs and vanilla; beat well.

2. Combine flour, cocoa, baking soda, and salt. Gradually blend into creamed mixture. Fold in peanut butter chips.

3. Press into greased 10" x 15" jelly roll pan.

4. Bake at 350° for 20 minutes or until set. Cool completely; cut into bars.

Whoopie Pies

Katie Beiler, Leola, PA
Linda Jean Martin, Reinholds, PA
Diana Russell, Holtwood, PA
Edna Smucker, New Holland, PA

Makes about 4 dozen sandwich cookies

Cookies:
2 cups sugar
2 eggs
2 tsp. vanilla
1 cup cooking oil
1 cup sour milk
4 cups flour
2 tsp. baking soda
½ tsp. salt

1 cup cocoa
1 tsp. instant coffee powder
1 cup hot water

Filling:
2 egg whites
2 tsp. vanilla
3½ cups powdered sugar
4 Tbsp. flour
2 Tbsp. milk
1½ cups shortening

1. Cream together sugar and eggs. Add vanilla, cooking oil, and sour milk and mix well.

2. Combine flour, baking soda, salt, and cocoa.

3. Dissolve instant coffee in hot water and let cool.

4. Add dry ingredients to creamed ingredients, alternating with coffee water.

5. Drop by rounded teaspoonsful onto greased cookie sheet.

6. Bake at 400° for 8-10 minutes or until done.

7. Meanwhile prepare filling by beating egg whites until soft peaks form. Add vanilla and beat a few minutes longer. Gradually add all remaining ingredients and beat until smooth and spreadable.

8. Make a cookie sandwich with two baked cookies and filling.

Oatmeal Whoopie Pies

Karen Burkholder
New Holland, PA

Makes about 2 dozen sandwich cookies

Cookies:
2 cups brown sugar
¾ cup butter *or* margarine
2 eggs
2¼ cups flour
½ tsp. salt
1 tsp. baking powder
1 tsp. cinnamon
2 cups uncooked oats
2 tsp. baking soda
3 Tbsp. boiling water

Filling:
2 cups powdered sugar
4 Tbsp. flour
4 Tbsp. milk
2 egg whites
2 tsp. vanilla
1 cup shortening

1. To prepare cookies cream together brown sugar, butter, and eggs.
2. Sift together flour, salt, and baking powder. Combine dry ingredients with creamed ingredients and mix well. Add cinnamon and oats and mix well.
3. Dissolve baking soda in boiling water. Add to batter and mix well.
4. Drop by large teaspoonful onto greased cookie sheet.
5. Bake at 350° for 10-15 minutes.
6. Meanwhile prepare filling by combining all ingredients. Beat until smooth and creamy.
7. Make cookie sandwiches by putting together two cookies with filling in center.

Chocolate Oatmeal Bars

Ruby Bontrager
Kinzers, PA

Makes about 36 bars

Bars:
1 cup margarine
2 cups brown sugar
2 eggs
2 tsp. vanilla
2½ cups flour
1 tsp. salt
3 cups uncooked oats

Chocolate Filling:
12-oz. pkg. chocolate chips
14-oz. can condensed milk
2 Tbsp. butter
¼ tsp. salt

1. Cream together margarine and brown sugar. Add eggs, vanilla, flour, salt, and oats and beat until well mixed.
2. Pour ⅔ of batter into bottom of greased 10" x 15" jelly roll pan.
3. To prepare chocolate filling combine all ingredients in saucepan and melt over low heat, stirring occasionally.
4. Pour chocolate filling over batter. Dot with remaining batter.
5. Bake at 350° for 25-30 minutes.
6. Cool and cut into bars.

Mount Joy

*W*ith fifteen eating establishments between its eastern end and its rural western side near Elizabethtown, Mount Joy is a town of restaurants. The Mennonite-owned Country Table Restaurant attracts people from far and wide. Historic A. Bube's Brewery offers patrons the chance to relax and dine in the catacomb-like recesses of the former brewery. Watering Trough Food and Spirits along Main Street has outdoor tables and a karaoke night. Grandma's Family Restaurant, Keystone Family Restaurant, and Mount Joy Family Restaurant live up to their names, offering family fare for the casual diner. Den's Pizza House, 2 Cousins Pizza, and Brothers Pizza compete for the local Italian tastebuds. The bright yellow Subway Shop sign beckons sandwich lovers. Burger King and Mount Joy Twin Kiss dispense ice cream and fast food. Mosby's Pub, near the center of the village, and Hennigans, on the rural western edge, welcome the weekend twenty- and thirty-something crowd. And the Han Palace provides a small sit-down restaurant as well as a drive-through for Chinese take-out.

Fudge Nut Bars

Susan Stoltzfus

Gap, PA

Makes 24-36 bars

Layer 1:
1 cup butter
2 cups brown sugar
2 eggs
2 tsp. vanilla
2½ cups flour
1 tsp. baking soda
1 tsp. salt
3 cups uncooked oats

Layer 2:
2 Tbsp. vanilla
14-oz. can condensed milk
½ tsp. salt
2 Tbsp. butter
12-oz. pkg. chocolate chips
1 cup chopped nuts

1. To prepare layer 1 cream together butter, brown sugar, eggs, and vanilla.
2. Combine flour, baking soda, and salt. Stir dry ingredients into creamed mixture. Fold in oats and mix well. Spread onto greased 10" x 15" jelly roll pan.
3. To prepare layer 2 combine all ingredients except nuts in double boiler and cook until smooth and creamy, stirring frequently. Remove from heat and fold in nuts. Spoon over layer 1 and smooth out.
4. Bake at 350° for 25-30 minutes.
5. Cool and cut into bars.

Magic Cookie Bars

Annetta Frackman

Paradise, PA

Makes 24-36 bars

½ cup margarine *or* butter
1½ cups graham cracker crumbs
14-oz. can condensed milk
1 cup semi-sweet chocolate chips
½ cup flaked coconut
1 cup chopped nuts

1. Melt margarine in bottom of 9" x 13" baking pan. Spoon graham cracker crumbs into margarine and mix well. Flatten crumbs to form crust. Pour condensed milk evenly over crumbs. Top with

chocolate chips, coconut, and nuts and press down firmly.

2. Bake at 350° for 25-30 minutes or until lightly browned. Cool and cut into bars. Store, loosely covered, at room temperature.

Creme de Menthe Bars
Anna Mae Conley
Mount Joy, PA

Makes 24-36 bars

Layer 1:
1 cup sugar
½ cup butter
4 eggs
1 cup flour
1 tsp. vanilla
½ tsp. salt
16-oz. can chocolate syrup
½ cup chopped nuts

Layer 2:
2 cups powdered sugar
1 Tbsp. Creme de Menthe
½ cup butter

Layer 3:
1 cup chocolate chips
6 Tbsp. butter

1. To prepare layer 1 cream together sugar, butter, and eggs. Stir in flour, vanilla, and salt and mix well. Add chocolate syrup and nuts and mix well. Spread into greased 9" x 13" baking pan.

2. Bake at 350° for 30 minutes. Cool.

3. To prepare layer 2 sift powdered sugar. Add Creme de Menthe and butter and mix well. Spread over cooled cake.

4. In a saucepan melt chocolate chips and butter, stirring constantly. Let cool

slightly and spread over cake. Chill, cut into small bars, and store in refrigerator.

Peanut Butter Swirl Bars
Esther Becker
Gap, PA

Makes 24-36 bars

½ cup crunchy peanut butter
⅓ cup margarine, softened
¾ cup brown sugar, firmly packed
¾ cup white sugar
2 eggs
2 tsp. vanilla
1 cup flour
1 tsp. baking powder
¼ tsp. salt
12-oz. pkg. chocolate chips

1. Preheat oven to 350°.

2. In a large bowl combine peanut butter, margarine, brown sugar, and white sugar and beat until creamy. Gradually beat in eggs and vanilla.

3. In a small bowl combine flour, baking powder, and salt. Blend dry ingredients into batter. Spread into greased 9" x 13" baking pan. Sprinkle chocolate chips over top.

4. Place in preheated oven for 5 minutes. Remove from oven and run knife through ingredients to marbleize.

5. Return to oven and bake for 25 minutes.

6. Cool and cut into bars.

Peanut Butter Kandy Kakes

Janet Weaver, Ephrata, PA
Sallie Getz, Denver, PA
Gladys Kautz, Columbia, PA
Annetta Frackman, Paradise, PA

Makes 36 cakes

Cake:
2 cups white sugar
2 Tbsp. cooking oil
Dash salt
1 tsp. vanilla
4 eggs
½ tsp. baking powder
2 cups flour
1 cup milk

Topping:
1 cup peanut butter
12-oz. pkg. chocolate chips
½ tsp. cooking oil

1. Cream together sugar, oil, salt, and vanilla. Add eggs and baking powder and mix well. Add flour and milk alternately and beat well.
2. Pour into greased 10" x 15" jelly roll pan.
3. Bake at 350° for 25 minutes. While still hot, spread peanut butter over top of cake. Chill in refrigerator.
4. Combine chocolate chips and oil in saucepan and melt over low heat. Spread on cool cake. Chill until chocolate sets and cut into bars. Serve.

Double Treat Bar Cookies

Sylvia Stoltzfus, Gap, PA
Mary Z. Stoltzfus, Gordonville, PA

Makes 24-36 bars

1 cup lard *or* shortening, softened
1 cup peanut butter
1 cup white sugar
1 cup brown sugar
2 eggs, beaten
½ tsp. salt
1 tsp. vanilla
2 tsp. baking soda
2 cups flour
6-oz. pkg. chocolate chips
¾ cup chopped nuts (optional)

1. Cream together shortening and peanut butter. Add sugars, eggs, salt, and vanilla and mix well. Add baking soda and flour and mix well. Fold in chocolate chips and nuts.
2. Spoon into greased 9" x 13" baking pan.
3. Bake at 350° for 15 minutes.
4. Cool and cut into bars.

Yummy Crunch Bars
Catherine Zimmerman
Ephrata, PA

Makes 24 bars

Bars:
½ cup butter *or* margarine
¾ cup sugar
2 eggs
1 tsp. vanilla
¾ cup flour
¼ tsp. baking powder
½ cup chopped nuts (optional)
2½ cups miniature marshmallows

Topping:
1 cup chocolate chips
1½ cups Rice Krispies
1 cup peanut butter

1. To prepare bars cream together butter and sugar. Beat in eggs and vanilla.

2. Combine flour and baking powder. Add dry ingredients to creamed ingredients and mix well. Fold in nuts. Spread mixture into greased 9" x 13" baking pan.

3. Bake at 300° for 15-20 minutes. Remove from oven and place marshmallows evenly over top. Return to oven for 2 minutes. Allow to cool 30 minutes.

4. Meanwhile prepare topping by melting chocolate chips in a saucepan over low heat. Stir in peanut butter and Rice Krispies.

5. Spread topping over bars and refrigerate. These bars are easier to cut after they have been refrigerated.

Cocoa Bars
Alice Whitman
Lititz, PA

Makes 24-36 bars

Bars:
8 Tbsp. margarine
1 cup sugar
1 egg
¾ cup sour milk
1 tsp. vanilla
1½ cups flour
½ tsp. baking soda
½ tsp. salt
½ cup cocoa

Icing:
⅓ cup margarine
⅓ cup cocoa
2 cups powdered sugar
1½ tsp. vanilla
5 Tbsp. milk
1 cup chopped nuts

1. To prepare bars cream together margarine, sugar, and egg. Add sour milk and vanilla and mix well.

2. Combine flour, baking soda, salt, and cocoa. Add dry ingredients to creamed ingredients and mix well. Spread into greased 9" x 13" baking pan.

3. Bake at 350° for 20-25 minutes.

4. To prepare icing combine margarine, cocoa, and powdered sugar and mix well. Beat in vanilla and milk until smooth and spreadable.

5. Frost cooled cake with chocolate icing and sprinkle with nuts. Cut into bars and serve.

Cherry Cheese Bars
Anna Z. Martin
East Earl, PA

Makes 24-36 bars

Crust:
1¼ cups flour
½ cup brown sugar, packed
½ cup butter-flavored shortening
1 cup walnut pieces
½ cup flaked coconut

Filling:
2 8-oz. pkgs. cream cheese, softened
⅔ cup white sugar
2 eggs
2 tsp. vanilla
21-oz. can cherry pie filling

1. Combine flour and brown sugar. Cut in shortening until fine crumbs form.
2. Coarsely chop ½ cup walnut pieces and set aside. Chop remaining walnuts into fine pieces and add to crust. Fold in coconut and mix well. Set aside ½ cup mixture.
3. Press remaining crumbs into bottom of greased 9" x 13" baking pan.
4. Bake at 350° for 12-15 minutes or until edges are lightly browned.
5. To prepare filling beat together cream cheese, sugar, eggs, and vanilla until smooth. Spread over hot, baked crust. Return to oven and bake 15 minutes longer.
6. Spread cherry pie filling over cheese layer.
7. Combine coarsely chopped walnuts and ½ cup reserved crumbs. Sprinkle evenly over cherries. Return to oven and bake 15 minutes longer. Cool and refrigerate several hours before serving.

Danish Apple Squares
Verna Douts
Quarryville, PA

Makes 24 squares

Squares:
3 eggs
2 cups sugar
1¼ cups cooking oil
3 cups flour
1 tsp. baking soda
3 cups chopped apples
1 tsp. vanilla

Topping:
8 Tbsp. margarine
1 cup light brown sugar
¼ cup milk
1 tsp. vanilla

1. Beat eggs. Add sugar and oil and mix well. Add flour and baking soda and beat well to blend. Fold in apples and vanilla. Spoon into greased 9" x 13" baking pan.
2. Bake at 325° for 1 hour.
3. To prepare topping combine all ingredients in saucepan and bring to a full, rolling boil. Boil for 2½ minutes. Spread over slightly cooled cake.

Golden Brownies

Jan Donnelly
Willow Street, PA

Makes about 36 brownies

2 cups flour
2 tsp. baking powder
1 tsp. salt
¾ cup butter, softened
¾ cup white sugar
¾ cup brown sugar, firmly packed
1 tsp. vanilla
3 eggs
12-oz. pkg. chocolate chips

1. In small bowl combine flour, baking powder, and salt. Set aside.
2. In large bowl cream together butter, sugars, and vanilla. Add eggs, one at a time, beating well after each addition. Gradually add dry ingredients and mix well. Fold in chocolate chips. Spread evenly into well-greased 10" x 15" jelly roll pan.
3. Bake at 350° for 30-35 minutes. Cool and cut into squares.

Amish Brownies

Maribelle M. Steffy
Leola, PA

Makes 24-36 brownies

¾ cup margarine *or* butter
½ cup brown sugar
½ cup white sugar
2 cups sifted flour
1 tsp. baking powder
¼ tsp. salt
3 eggs, separated
1 tsp. black walnut extract
1 cup brown sugar
1 cup chopped nuts
1 cup chocolate bits
1 cup coconut

1. Cream together butter, ½ cup brown sugar, and white sugar. Add flour, baking powder, salt, egg yolks, and black walnut extract and mix well.
2. Press evenly into greased 9" x 13" baking pan.
3. Beat egg whites until frothy. Add 1 cup brown sugar and mix well. Spread evenly over batter. Sprinkle nuts, chocolate bits and coconut evenly over egg white mixture.
4. Bake 325° for 40-45 minutes.
5. Cool and cut into bars.

Pecan Bars

Betty J. Hendricks
Lancaster, PA

Makes 24-36 bars

Bars:
¼-½ cup margarine, melted and cooled
½ cup light brown sugar, lightly packed
1 cup flour

Topping:
2 eggs
½ tsp. salt
1 cup light brown sugar, lightly packed
1 tsp. vanilla extract
1 Tbsp. flour
1 cup chopped pecans
½ cup flaked coconut

1. To prepare bars cream together margarine and sugar. Stir in flour until blended. Spread into bottom of well-greased 9" x 13" baking pan.
2. Bake at 350° for 10 minutes.
3. To prepare topping combine all ingredients and mix well. Spread topping over cake. Return to oven and bake 20 minutes longer.
4. Cool and cut into bars.

Chewy Apple Brownies

Marlene Weaver
Ephrata, PA

Makes 24-36 brownies

Brownies:
1 cup butter, softened
1¾ cups sugar
2 eggs, beaten
1 tsp. vanilla
2 cups flour
1 tsp. baking powder
1 tsp. baking soda
1 tsp. cinnamon
½ tsp. salt
2 cups chopped apples
½ cup pecans *or* walnuts

Glaze:
½ cup powdered sugar
1 Tbsp. hot water
¼ tsp. vanilla

1. In a large mixing bowl cream together butter, sugar, eggs, and vanilla.
2. Combine flour, baking powder, baking soda, cinnamon, and salt. Add to creamed ingredients and mix until flour is moistened. Fold in apples and nuts. Spread into greased 9" x 13" baking pan.
3. Bake at 350° for 45 minutes or until done. Cool.
4. To prepare glaze combine all ingredients and mix until smooth. Drizzle in a thin stream over top of cooled brownies, forming a woven pattern. Allow glaze to set before cutting into pieces for serving.

Desserts

Gourmet Apple Crisp

Diana Russell

Holtwood, PA

Makes 6 servings

9 fresh apples
1 cup flour
1 cup sugar
1 tsp. baking powder
Pinch salt
1 egg
4 Tbsp. butter
1 Tbsp. cinnamon

1. Slice apples into greased 7" x 11" baking dish.
2. Mix flour, sugar, baking powder, and salt. Break egg into mixture and continue to mix with hands. Spoon mixture over apples.
3. Melt butter in a saucepan and pour over apples. Sprinkle liberally with cinnamon.
4. Bake at 350° for 40-50 minutes.

Apple Betty

Elaine W. Good

Lititz, PA

Makes 6 generous servings

6-7 cups apple slices
6 Tbsp. orange juice
¾ cup flour
½ cup sugar
½ tsp. cinnamon
¼ tsp. nutmeg
Dash salt
¼ cup butter *or* margarine

1. Fill a deep 10-inch pie pan or 9-inch square pan heaping full with apple slices. Pour orange juice over slices.
2. Combine all remaining ingredients until crumbly. Spread over apples, covering as well as possible.
3. Bake at 375° for 45 minutes. Serve hot or cold with milk or ice cream.

Variation: Omit orange juice.
—Julia Mowrer, Quarryville, PA

Apple Crunch
Barbara Christ
Denver, PA

Makes 6-8 servings

4 cups peeled, sliced apples
½ cup water
1 tsp. cinnamon
¾ cup flour
1 cup brown sugar
½ cup butter

1. Arrange apples in deep, greased baking dish. Add water.

2. Combine cinnamon, flour, sugar, and butter with fork until crumbly. Spread evenly over apples.

3. Bake at 350° for about 30 minutes or until the crust is brown and apples are tender when pricked with a fork. Serve warm with ice cream or whipped cream.

Apple Roll-Up
Miriam E. Lefever
East Petersburg, PA

Makes 6-8 servings

Dough:
2 cups flour
2½ tsp. baking powder
½ tsp. salt
⅔ cup shortening
½ cup milk
2 Tbsp. butter, melted
½ cup brown sugar
½ tsp. cinnamon
6 medium apples, peeled and chopped

Sauce:
1½ cups brown sugar
1½ cups water
¼ tsp. cinnamon
¼ cup butter *or* less

1. To prepare dough sift together flour, baking powder, and salt. Cut in shortening until size of small peas. Sprinkle with milk and work only until dough holds together.

2. Roll out to ¼-inch thickness. Spread with melted butter and ½ cup brown sugar. Sprinkle with ½ tsp. cinnamon. Arrange chopped apples evenly over dough and roll up as for jelly roll.

3. Cut into 1¼-inch slices. Arrange in greased 9" x 13" baking pan.

4. To prepare sauce combine brown sugar, water, and cinnamon in saucepan and heat 5 minutes, stirring constantly. Remove from heat and stir in butter. Pour sauce over apple roll-ups in baking pan.

5. Bake at 375° for 35-40 minutes. Serve warm with milk.

Old-Fashioned Apple Dumplings
Marilyn Kay Martin
Manheim, PA

Makes 6 servings

Apple Dumplings:
6 medium baking apples
2 cups flour
2½ tsp. baking powder
½ tsp. salt
⅔ cup shortening
½ cup milk

Topping:
½ cup sugar
2 tsp. cinnamon

Sauce:
2 cups brown sugar
2 cups water
¼ tsp. cinnamon *or* nutmeg
4 Tbsp. butter

1. Peel and core apples, leaving them whole.

2. Sift together flour, baking powder, and salt. Cut in shortening until mixture is crumbly. Sprinkle with milk and work dough lightly, only enough to hold it together.

3. Roll out dough and cut into 6 equal squares. Place an apple on each square of dough.

4. Combine topping ingredients and fill cavity of each apple with mixture. Pat dough around apple to cover completely. Fasten edges securely on top of apple.

5. Arrange dumplings about an inch apart in a greased baking pan.

6. To prepare sauce combine brown sugar, water, and cinnamon in medium saucepan. Bring to boil and cook 5 minutes, stirring frequently. Remove from heat and add butter, stirring until melted. Pour sauce over dumplings.

7. Bake at 375° for 35-40 minutes. Baste occasionally during baking. Serve hot with milk or cream.

Apple Dumplings
Arlene Ruhl
Manheim, PA

Makes 12 servings

4 cups flour
4 tsp. baking powder
1 tsp. salt
4 Tbsp. sugar
1⅓ cups butter
1⅓ cups milk
12 apples

1. Combine flour, baking powder, salt, and sugar. Cut in butter. Gradually add milk and work until dough holds together.

2. Divide dough in half and roll as for a pie. Cut each half of dough into 6 wedges.

3. Peel and core apples, leaving them whole. Wrap an apple in each wedge of dough. Arrange on lightly greased cookie sheet.

4. Bake at 375° for 1 hour or until apples are soft.

5. Serve hot with cold milk.

Peach Cobbler
Rose Scantling
Ephrata, PA

Makes 6-8 servings

2½ cups sliced peaches
1 tsp. cinnamon
1 Tbsp. lemon juice
1 cup flour
1 tsp. baking powder
½ tsp. salt
3 Tbsp. butter
¾ cup sugar
½ cup milk
½ cup sugar
1 Tbsp. cornstarch
1 cup peach juice

1. Arrange peaches in bottom of 9-inch square greased baking dish. Sprinkle with cinnamon and lemon juice.
2. Sift together flour, baking powder, and salt.
3. Cream together butter and ¾ cup sugar. Add dry ingredients to creamed ingredients, alternating with milk and mixing thoroughly. Spread over peaches.
4. Sift together ½ cup sugar and cornstarch and sprinkle over top of batter.
5. Bring peach juice to a boil. Pour boiling peach juice over all very slowly.
6. Bake at 350° for 1 hour.

Blueberry Buckle
Elizabeth Anderson
Lancaster, PA

Makes 6-8 servings

Blueberry Buckle:
¾ cup sugar
¼ cup shortening
1 egg
½ cup milk
2 cups flour
2 tsp. baking powder
½ tsp. salt
2 cups blueberries

Crumb Topping:
⅓ cup flour
½ cup sugar
½ tsp. cinnamon
¼ cup soft butter

1. Cream together sugar, shortening, and egg. Stir in milk.
2. Combine flour, baking powder, and salt. Add dry ingredients to creamed ingredients, mixing well. Fold in blueberries. Spread into greased and floured 9-inch square pan.
3. To prepare topping combine flour, sugar, and cinnamon. Cut in butter until crumbly. Sprinkle over blueberry mixture.
4. Bake at 375° for 45-50 minutes. Serve warm.

Peach Crumble
Loretta Lapp
Kinzers, PA

Makes 8 servings

1 cup sugar
1 egg, beaten
1 cup chopped pecans
1 large pkg. instant vanilla pudding
1 cup milk
1 cup sour cream
2 cups sliced fresh peaches
1 cup whipped topping

1. Combine sugar, egg, and pecans. Arrange on greased, round pizza pan.
2. Bake at 350° for 18 minutes. Cool and crumble coarsely.
3. Combine pudding, milk, and sour cream and mix well.
4. In a serving dish alternate layers of crumbs, pudding mix, and sliced peaches.
5. Refrigerate until pudding sets. Top with whipped topping and serve.

Raisin Crisp
Alta M. Ranck
Lancaster, PA

Makes 12-15 servings

Raisin Mixture:
1 lb. raisins
2 Tbsp. cornstarch
$\frac{1}{2}$ cup white sugar
1 cup water
2 Tbsp. lemon juice

Crumbs:
1$\frac{3}{4}$ cups sifted flour
$\frac{1}{2}$ tsp. baking soda
1 cup brown sugar
$\frac{1}{4}$ tsp. salt

1$\frac{1}{2}$ cups uncooked oats
$\frac{3}{4}$ cup margarine *or* butter

1. In a saucepan combine raisins, cornstarch, sugar, and water. Cook until slightly thickened, stirring constantly.
2. Remove from heat, stir in lemon juice, and cool.
3. To prepare crumbs combine flour, baking soda, sugar, salt, and oats. Cut in margarine, making fine crumbs. Spread $\frac{1}{2}$ of crumbs into bottom of 9" x 13" baking pan. Pour raisin mixture over crumbs. Cover with remaining $\frac{1}{2}$ of crumbs.
4. Bake at 400° for 30 minutes. Cut into squares and serve.

Egg Custard
Barbara Hoffert
Denver, PA

Makes 4-6 servings

4 eggs
$\frac{1}{2}$ cup sugar
$\frac{1}{4}$ tsp. salt
3 cups milk
2 tsp. vanilla
1 tsp. cinnamon (optional)

1. In large mixing bowl beat eggs until fluffy and foamy. Add sugar, salt, milk, and vanilla and beat lightly until well mixed.
2. Pour into greased casserole dish and sprinkle with cinnamon, if desired. Place into pan of warm water on middle rack of oven.
3. Bake at 350° for about 50 minutes or until knife inserted in center comes out clean.

Pumpkin Custard
Ruth F. Hurst
Gordonville, PA

Makes 4-6 servings

1 cup cooked pumpkin
1 Tbsp. cornstarch
½ cup brown sugar
½ cup white sugar
1 cup milk
1 Tbsp. browned butter
1 tsp. cinnamon
2 eggs, separated

1. Combine all ingredients except egg whites and mix well.
2. Beat egg whites until soft peaks form. Fold into pumpkin mixture. Spoon into greased baking dish.
3. Bake at 375° for 40 minutes or until knife inserted in center comes out clean.

Pumpkin Coconut Custard
Miriam E. Lefever
East Petersburg, PA

Makes 4-6 servings

2 eggs, separated
1 cup mashed pumpkin
½ cup sugar
2 rounded Tbsp. flour
¼ tsp. ginger
2 cups milk
2 Tbsp. coconut
1 tsp. cinnamon

1. Beat egg whites until stiff peaks form.
2. Combine pumpkin, sugar, flour, egg yolks, ginger, and milk and beat until thoroughly blended. Pour mixture over beaten egg whites and blend together carefully.

3. Pour into greased 2-quart casserole dish and sprinkle with coconut and cinnamon. Set into pan of hot water.
4. Bake at 350° for about 50 minutes or until knife inserted in center comes out clean.

Spanish Cream
Miriam E. Lefever
East Petersburg, PA

Makes 8-10 servings

1 envelope unflavored gelatin
4 cups milk
3 eggs, separated
½ cup brown sugar
2 Tbsp. butter (optional)
¼ tsp. salt
1 tsp. vanilla

1. Dissolve gelatin in 1 cup milk.
2. Pour remaining 3 cups milk into heavy saucepan. Add gelatin mixture, beaten egg yolks, brown sugar, butter, and salt and bring to a boil. Remove from heat and add vanilla.
3. Beat egg whites until stiff peaks form. Pour hot mixture over egg whites and blend gently. Pour into serving dish.
4. Refrigerate and chill 24 hours to set.

A Local Diet

A major component of life in Lancaster County is gardening, so when I learned several years ago that a way to reduce waste was to go on a "local diet," my reflections underscored the bounty our area has to offer.

Of course, bananas and pineapple are readily available in local grocery stores and markets, but I have enjoyed consciously substituting them with fruits such as apples, peaches, and cherries which are grown in Lancaster County.

Living on a farm, I have found keeping the size of my garden manageable more of a problem than finding enough space. However, I hope if I ever live in an urban setting, I will still try to find creative ways to "go on a local diet."

—*Elaine W. Good, Lititz, PA*

Cracker Pudding

Anna N. Buckwalter, Ronks, PA
Elsie Houser, Lampeter, PA

Makes 10-12 servings

1 quart milk
2 cups coarsely crushed crackers
½ cup sugar
2 eggs, separated
½ cup coconut
1 tsp. vanilla

1. In a saucepan combine milk, crackers, sugar, egg yolks, and coconut and bring to a boil, stirring constantly. Remove from heat.
2. Beat egg whites until stiff peaks form. Fold into cracker mixture. Add vanilla and mix lightly. Serve either hot or cold.

Old-Fashioned Rice Pudding

Martha L. Stoner
Leola, PA

Makes 6-8 servings

½ cup uncooked long-grain rice
4 cups milk
¼ cup butter
3 eggs
¾ cup sugar
1 tsp. vanilla
¼ tsp. salt
½ tsp. nutmeg

1. In double boiler combine rice and 2 cups milk. Cook over boiling water until rice is tender and most of water has evaporated, about 45 minutes, stirring occasionally. Stir in butter.
2. In a bowl beat eggs. Add sugar, vanilla, salt, and remaining milk and mix well. Stir into the hot rice mixture. Pour into lightly greased 2-quart casserole and sprinkle with nutmeg.
3. Bake at 350° for 50 minutes or until firm.

Grapenut Pudding
Sara Newswanger
Narvon, PA

Makes 8-10 servings

1 quart milk
¾ cup sugar
2 egg yolks
½ scant cup flour
¼ tsp. salt
2 tsp. vanilla
8-oz. carton whipped topping
¾ cup grapenuts

1. Pour 3 cups milk into saucepan and add sugar, but do not stir. Heat on high until milk is scalding hot.
2. In small bowl mix together egg yolks, flour, and remaining 1 cup milk. Pour into scalded milk and lower heat, stirring constantly until thickened. Remove from heat and cool.
3. Fold in salt, vanilla, whipped topping, and grapenuts and serve.

Shredded Wheat Pudding
Jeanette Oberholtzer
Akron, PA

Makes 6-8 servings

4 large shredded wheat biscuits
2 eggs, beaten
2 cups milk
¾ cup molasses
1 tsp. cinnamon
¼ tsp. salt
1 Tbsp. butter *or* margarine
1 cup whipped topping

1. Crumble biscuits into greased 9-inch square baking dish.

2. In a bowl combine eggs, milk, molasses, cinnamon, and salt. Pour over biscuits. Dot with butter.
3. Bake at 350° for 45 minutes.
4. Cool and serve with whipped topping.

Date Pudding
Ruth H. Shank
Lititz, PA

Makes 4-6 servings

1 cup water
1 cup brown sugar
1½ Tbsp. butter
½ cup white sugar
1 cup flour
¼ lb. dates, chopped
½ cup chopped nuts
2½ tsp. baking powder
½ cup milk

1. In a saucepan combine water, brown sugar, and butter. Bring to a boil and cook 5 minutes, stirring frequently.
2. Combine white sugar, flour, dates, nuts, and baking powder and mix well. Add milk to make a stiff batter.
3. Pour hot syrup into 8-inch square baking pan. Spoon date mixture over syrup.
4. Bake at 350° for ½ hour. Serve warm with vanilla ice cream.

Peach Bottom

A dead-end road in the southwestern corner of Lancaster County leads to the tiny river community of Peach Bottom. Lining both sides of Peach Bottom Road, several rows of immaculate summer cottages look out over the Conowingo Reservoir on the Susquehanna River.

A mecca for recreational boaters, fishermen, and jet skiers, the Peach Bottom Marina and its uphill parking lot stay busy most days during the balmy summer months.

Upriver and within sight of the summer homes stands the imposing Peach Bottom Nuclear Power Plant. Owned by Philadelphia Electric Company, it uses water power from the Susquehanna to drive its nuclear plant and provide energy for customers throughout the region.

Butterscotch Pudding

Elsie M. Beachy
Lancaster, PA

Makes 10 servings

2 cups brown sugar
⅔ cup flour
4 eggs
1 quart milk
½ cup butter
1 Tbsp. vanilla

1. Combine brown sugar and flour in a saucepan and mix well. Add eggs and mix to a paste. Gradually add cold milk and stir well to avoid lumps.

2. Bring to a boil over medium heat, stirring frequently with a wire whisk. Add butter and continue cooking, stirring constantly. When thickened, remove from heat and stir in vanilla.

3. To assure smoothness, beat briskly with whisk after removing from heat. Chill and serve.

Crushed Oreo Pudding

Deb Ament
Lancaster, PA

Makes 12-15 servings

16-oz. pkg. Oreo cookies
1 large pkg. instant vanilla pudding
1 tsp. prepared instant coffee
16-oz. carton whipped topping

1. Crush Oreos in food processor (or put in a plastic bag and beat until crushed).

2. Prepare instant pudding according to directions. Stir coffee into pudding. Fold in ½ of whipped topping.

3. Layer ⅓ of crushed Oreos into large bowl. Top with ⅓ of pudding mix. Repeat layers 2 more times and top with whipped topping. Refrigerate and chill before serving.

Applesauce Cake Pudding
Eva Brubaker
East Earl, PA

Makes 8-10 servings

2 eggs
½ cup lard
1 cup sugar
1 cup applesauce
1 tsp. baking soda
½ cup raisins
2 cups flour
¼ tsp. cinnamon
Pinch nutmeg
Pinch ginger

1. Cream together eggs, lard, and sugar.
2. Combine applesauce and baking soda and add to creamed ingredients, mixing well. Fold in raisins.
3. Combine flour, cinnamon, nutmeg, and ginger and add to batter, mixing well. Spoon into 8-inch square baking dish.
4. Bake at 350° for 45 minutes. Serve warm with milk.

Fruity Lemon Pudding
Phyllis Gamber
Lancaster, PA

Makes 12-15 servings

1 large pkg. instant lemon pudding
12-oz. carton whipped topping
15¼-oz. can crushed pineapple, drained
15-oz. can mandarin oranges, drained
16-oz. can fruit cocktail, drained
1 cup miniature marshmallows

1. Combine all ingredients and mix well.
2. Refrigerate at least 1 hour before serving.

Cherry Watergate Pudding
Lena Mae Hoover
Leola, PA

Makes 12-15 servings

2 20-oz. cans crushed pineapple, drained
21-oz. can cherry pie filling
8-oz. carton whipped topping
14-oz. can condensed milk
2 cups miniature marshmallows

1. Combine all ingredients and mix well with a spoon.
2. Refrigerate and chill before serving.

Pink Pineapple Dessert
Traci Kreider
Lancaster, PA

Makes 15-20 servings

12-oz. carton whipped topping
14-oz. can condensed milk
21-oz. can cherry pie filling
20-oz. can crushed pineapple, drained

1. Combine all ingredients in large serving bowl.
2. Refrigerate until chilled and serve.

Cinnamon Pudding

Ruby Bontrager
Kinzers, PA

Makes 8 servings

Pudding:
1 cup white sugar
2 Tbsp. butter
1 cup milk
2 scant cups flour
2 tsp. baking powder
2 tsp. cinnamon
Pinch salt

Sauce:
2 cups brown sugar
1½ cups water

1. In a bowl combine all pudding ingredients and mix well.

2. In saucepan combine sauce ingredients and bring to a boil. Remove from heat and pour into 9-inch square baking pan. Pour pudding ingredients evenly over sauce.

3. Bake at 350° for approximately 45 minutes.

Apricot Tapioca

Emily Fleck
Elizabethtown, PA

Makes 10-12 servings

4 cups apricot nectar
6 Tbsp. minute tapioca
5 Tbsp. sugar
3-oz. pkg. apricot *or* orange gelatin

1. In a saucepan combine apricot nectar, tapioca, and sugar and bring to a boil over medium heat. Remove from heat and stir in gelatin. Stir until dissolved and pour into serving dish.

2. Chill in refrigerator until set. Serve with whipped topping.

Rhubarb Pudding

Pauline M. Gayman
Lancaster, PA

Makes 6-8 servings

1 quart diced rhubarb
1 cup sugar
½ cup butter, melted
1 tsp. vanilla
2 eggs, well beaten
1 cup flour
1 tsp. baking powder
½ cup sugar
¼ tsp. salt

1. Mix rhubarb and 1 cup sugar. Arrange in 2-quart baking dish.

2. Combine all remaining ingredients and mix well. Pour over rhubarb.

3. Bake at 375° for 35-40 minutes.

Rhubarb Tapioca

Diane K. Gehman, Stevens, PA
Doris Nissley, Bainbridge, PA

Makes 12-15 servings

4 cups cold water
1½ cups diced rhubarb
⅓ cup minute tapioca
1 scant cup sugar
3-oz. pkg. strawberry gelatin

1. In a saucepan combine water, rhubarb, tapioca, and sugar and bring to a boil, stirring occasionally. Boil for 8 minutes.
2. Remove from heat and stir in gelatin until it dissolves. Serve with vanilla ice cream.

Rhubarb Sauce

Mabel E. Weaver, New Holland, PA
Marilyn E. Weaver, New Holland, PA

Makes 4 quarts sauce

6 cups diced rhubarb
6 cups water
½ cup minute tapioca
6-oz. pkg. strawberry gelatin
2 cups sugar
1 quart fresh strawberries, chopped
  (optional)

1. Cook rhubarb with water and tapioca until rhubarb is soft and mixture has thickened. Remove from heat.
2. Stir in gelatin to dissolve. Add sugar and mix well.
3. When partly cooled, fold in strawberries if desired. Serve with waffles, ice cream, or cheesecake.

Rhubarb Fool

Doris Nissley, Bainbridge, PA
Rhoda H. Lind, Lititz, PA

Makes 10-12 servings

3 cups diced rhubard
¼ cup honey
½ tsp. ginger
1 large pkg. instant vanilla pudding
1 cup whipped topping
½ tsp. ginger

1. Cook rhubarb in water until softened. Drain and pour into blender or food processor. Blend together with honey. Remove from blender and stir in ginger.
2. Prepare vanilla pudding according to package directions. Stir in whipped topping.
3. Fold rhubarb into pudding mixture and pour into serving dish.
4. Chill and serve with cookies, ice cream, or fruit.

Prune Whip

Mabel E. Weaver
New Holland, PA

Makes 6-8 servings

½ cup seedless prunes
½ cup water
½ envelope unflavored gelatin
1 Tbsp. cold water
2 egg whites
½ cup sugar *or* less

1. In a saucepan cook prunes in water for 10 minutes. Remove from heat.
2. Soften gelatin in cold water and stir into prune mixture until dissolved. Let stand until completely cooled and slightly thickened.

3. Beat egg whites until soft peaks form, slowly adding sugar. Continue beating and add prune mixture, one Tbsp. at a time, beating until fluffy.

Apricot Pineapple Delight
Esther Becker
Gap, PA

Makes 12-15 servings

2 6-oz. pkgs. orange gelatin
2½ cups boiling water
29-oz. can apricots
20-oz. can crushed pineapple
½ cup sugar
2 heaping Tbsp. flour
1 egg, beaten
1 Tbsp. butter *or* margarine
1 cup whipped topping

1. Dissolve gelatin in boiling water.
2. Drain apricots and pineapple and reserve 1 cup juice. Stir remaining juice into gelatin mixture.
3. Chop apricots and add with crushed pineapple to gelatin mixture. Pour into 9" x 13" baking dish and chill to set.
4. In a saucepan combine 1 cup juice, sugar, flour, egg, and butter. Cook until thickened, stirring frequently.
5. Cool and fold in whipped topping. Spread over gelatin and serve.

Fruit Dessert
Lois Hoover
Ephrata, PA

Makes 8-10 servings

20-oz. can crushed pineapple
16-oz. can white cherries
10 large marshmallows
6-oz. pkg. lemon gelatin
2 cups hot water
4 Tbsp. sugar
3 Tbsp. pineapple juice
4 egg yolks, beaten
1 cup whipped topping

1. Drain pineapple. Reserve 3 Tbsp. juice. Drain and seed cherries.
2. Cut marshmallows. Combine pineapple, cherries, and marshmallows and mix well. Let stand several hours.
3. Dissolve gelatin in water and set aside until partially set.
4. Combine sugar, pineapple juice, and egg yolks in a saucepan and bring to a boil. Cook until thickened, stirring constantly. Remove from heat.
5. In large serving dish combine pineapple and cherry mixture, slightly thickened gelatin, and pineapple sauce. Refrigerate.
6. Immediately before serving, fold in whipped topping.

Orange Mallow Frost
Doris Becker
Manheim, PA

Makes 6 servings

3-oz. pkg. orange gelatin
1 cup boiling water
1 pint orange sherbet
11-oz. can mandarin oranges, drained
2 cups miniature marshmallows

1. Dissolve gelatin in boiling water. Add sherbet and stir until dissolved. Fold in oranges and marshmallows and pour into serving dish.
2. Chill until firm and serve.

Broken Glass Dessert
Marie Splain, Maytown, PA
Eva Brubaker, East Earl, PA

Makes about 15 servings

3-oz. pkg. lime gelatin
1½ cups boiling water
3-oz. pkg. cherry gelatin
1½ cups boiling water
3-oz. pkg. orange gelatin
1½ cups boiling water
2 cups graham cracker crumbs
½ cup margarine, melted
½ cup brown sugar
¼ cup cold water
1 envelope unflavored gelatin
1 cup pineapple juice
12-oz. carton whipped topping

1. Combine each of flavored gelatins with 1½ cups boiling water. Pour each into separate shallow dish to set. Refrigerate and let set overnight.

2. Combine graham crackers crumbs, margarine, and brown sugar and mix well. Reserve ½ cup crumbs. Pat remaining crumbs into bottom of 9" x 13" baking pan.

3. In a saucepan combine ¼ cup water, unflavored gelatin, and pineapple juice and heat to very warm so gelatin dissolves, stirring occasionally. Let cool. When cooled, fold in whipped topping.

4. Cut flavored gelatins into small cubes. Fold into pineapple and whipped topping mixture. Pour over graham cracker crust. Sprinkle with ½ cup reserved crumbs.

5. Refrigerate for at least 5 hours before serving.

Coffee Gelatin Dessert
Jeanette Oberholtzer
Akron, PA

Makes 4 servings

1 envelope unflavored gelatin
½ cup cold water
1 cup boiling hot strong coffee
⅓ cup sugar
⅛ tsp. salt
2 Tbsp. chopped walnuts
½ cup whipping cream

1. Soften gelatin in cold water and dissolve in hot coffee. Stir in sugar, salt, and walnuts. Refrigerate to set.
2. After mixture has set, break it up with fork or beater.
3. Beat whipping cream until stiffened. Fold into gelatin mixture. Serve for a refreshing summertime dessert.

Rothsville

From the ancient, dilapidated building which houses the post office to the renovated White Swan Hotel, Rothsville is a quiet village of frame houses and friendly people.

Its location, about halfway between the boroughs of Lititz and Ephrata, creates lots of traffic simply passing through on Highway 772. As they have for more than 200 years, some of those travelers occasionally stop to relax and have dinner at the White Swan. Established in 1790, this Rothsville landmark stands proudly on the corner of Newport Road and 772 and serves "dinner cooked to order."

Numerous churches, a fire company, a polo field, and a medical center provide other services to the small village and its surrounding rural community.

Finger Jello

Diana Russell, Holtwood, PA
Rosie Yeakel, Ephrata, PA

Makes many servings

4 envelopes unflavored gelatin
1 cup cold water
3 3-oz. pkgs. any flavor gelatin
½ cup sugar
4 cups boiling water
½ cup powdered sugar

1. Soften unflavored gelatin in cold water. Stir in three packages flavored gelatins, sugar, and boiling water and stir to dissolve.
2. Pour into 9" x 13" baking pan. Chill overnight in refrigerator to set.
3. Cut into small squares and roll lightly in powdered sugar before serving.

Strawberry Angel Food Layer Dessert

Darlene Rohrer-Meck
Lancaster, PA

Makes 6 servings

½ angel food cake
1 pkg. strawberry Danish dessert mix
10-oz. pkg. frozen strawberries, slightly thawed
2 cups whipped topping

1. Make angel food cake according to package directions and cut vertically in half. Freeze ½ for future use.
2. Tear remaining cake into bite-sized pieces.
3. Prepare Danish dessert according to package directions.
4. In a 2-quart serving dish layer ½ the pieces of cake, ½ of Danish dessert, ½ of strawberries, ½ of whipped topping. Repeat layers. Chill and serve.

Homemade Danish Dessert

Catherine Zimmerman
Ephrata, PA

Makes 10-12 servings

1 pkg. strawberry Kool Aid mix
7 cups water
1 cup sugar
¾ cup clear gel
1 cup water
6-oz. pkg. strawberry gelatin

1. In a kettle combine Kool Aid mix, 7 cups water, and sugar and bring to a boil. Stir in clear gel and 1 cup water. Boil for 1 minute and add strawberry gelatin and stir until dissolved.
2. Stir in choice of fruit and serve as a dessert.

Note: This recipe is an easy homemade version of the packaged Danish dessert mix.

Cherry Angel Delight

Florence Morrison
Lancaster, PA

Makes 4-6 servings

1 cup powdered sugar
3-oz. pkg. cream cheese
12-oz. carton whipped topping
1 angel food cake
21-oz. can cherry pie filling

1. Cream together sugar and cream cheese until fluffy. Fold in whipped topping.
2. Cut angel food cake into bite-sized pieces and add to cream cheese mixture, stirring until well mixed. Spoon into serving dish.
3. Top with cherry pie filling and serve.

Cool German Chocolate Dessert

Debra Hoover
Paradise, PA

Makes 12-15 servings

1 cup chocolate wafer crumbs
4 Tbsp. butter *or* margarine, melted
8 ozs. German sweet chocolate
⅓ cup milk
3-oz. pkg. cream cheese, softened
12-oz. carton whipped topping

1. Combine chocolate wafer crumbs and melted butter. Press firmly into bottom of 9-inch square pan.
2. Grate 2 ozs. chocolate. Set aside.
3. Heat remaining chocolate and milk in medium saucepan over low heat, stirring constantly until chocolate is melted. Using wire whisk, beat in cream cheese until smooth. Cool 5 minutes.
4. Fold 3½ cups whipped topping and grated chocolate into mixture. Spread over wafer crumb crust. Spread remaining whipped topping over chocolate layer.
5. Freeze at least 2 hours until firm. Cut into bars and serve.

Eclair Graham Cracker Dessert

Sandi Crills, Akron, PA
Cindy Bryan, Adamstown, PA
Twila D. Wallace, New Holland, PA

Makes 15-20 servings

Dessert:
1-lb. box graham crackers
2 small pkgs. instant vanilla pudding
3½ cups milk
8-oz. carton whipped topping

Frosting:
3 Tbsp. cocoa
2 tsp. light corn syrup
2 tsp. vanilla
3 Tbsp. butter *or* margarine, softened
1½ cups powdered sugar
3 Tbsp. milk

1. Line bottom of lightly greased 9" x 13" baking pan with graham crackers.
2. Mix pudding and milk together and beat until thickened. Fold in whipped topping. Pour ½ of pudding mixture over crackers. Add another layer of crackers. Cover second layer of crackers with remaining pudding mixture. Add another layer of crackers. Refrigerate for two hours.
3. Meanwhile prepare frosting by combining all ingredients and beating until smooth.
4. Spread chocolate frosting evenly over dessert. Refrigerate at least 12 hours before serving.

Dirt Dessert
Sandra L. Biondo, Reinholds, PA
Ruth Ann Becker, Manheim, PA
Loretta Lapp, Kinzers, PA

Makes 15 servings

1 cup powdered sugar
¼ cup butter, softened
8-oz. pkg. cream cheese, softened
2 small pkgs. instant vanilla pudding
3 cups milk
16-oz. carton whipped topping
1 tsp. vanilla extract
16-oz. pkg. Oreo cookies, crushed

1. Cream together sugar, butter, and cream cheese in large mixing bowl until light and fluffy.

2. In medium bowl combine pudding mix and milk until thick and smooth. Fold in whipped topping and vanilla. Add to creamed mixture and mix well.
3. In a new, sterilized flower pot layer ½ of cookie crumbs, all of pudding mixture, and remaining cookie crumbs. Chill until serving time.

Note: Be as creative as you desire with this dish. You may add gummy worms, silk flowers, and even a plastic shovel.

Chocolate Bash
Mabel Eshleman
Landisville, PA

Makes 12-15 servings

1 box Dark Dutch Fudge cake mix
½ cup hot, brewed coffee
2 large pkgs. instant chocolate pudding
16-oz. carton whipped topping
6 Hershey's Skor candy bars

1. Prepare cake mix according to directions and bake in 9" x 13" baking pan. Remove from oven and poke holes in cake. Pour coffee over cake and refrigerate to chill overnight.
2. Prepare pudding according to package directions.
3. Cut cake into bite-sized cubes.
4. Crush Skor bars into small pieces.
5. In very large glass serving bowl layer ⅓ of cubed cake, ⅓ of pudding, ⅓ of whipped topping, and ⅓ of crushed Skor bars. Repeat layers 2 more times.
6. Refrigerate to chill before serving.

Coconut Ice Cream Dessert
Anna Mae Weaver
Ephrata, PA

Makes 12-15 servings

60 Ritz crackers, crushed
8 Tbsp. butter, melted
½ gallon vanilla ice cream
1½ cups milk
2 small pkgs. instant coconut cream pudding
8-oz. carton whipped topping

1. Combine crackers and melted butter. Reserve ¼ cup crumbs. Pat remaining crumbs into bottom of 9" x 13" baking pan.
2. Let ice cream stand at room temperature for about ½ hour to soften. Add milk and pudding to ice cream and beat until smooth. Pour over cracker crumbs.
3. Refrigerate to chill and set. Immediately before serving, spread whipped topping over ice cream mixture. Sprinkle with reserved ¼ cup crumbs.

Striped Delight
Diana Russell
Holtwood, PA

Makes 12-15 servings

1½ cups graham cracker crumbs
¼ cup sugar
⅓ cup butter *or* margarine, melted
8-oz. pkg. cream cheese, softened
¼ cup sugar
2 Tbsp. milk
8-oz. carton whipped topping
2 small pkgs instant chocolate pudding
3½ cups cold milk
½ cup chopped nuts (optional)

1. Combine graham cracker crumbs, ¼ cup sugar, and melted butter. Press firmly into bottom of 9" x 13" baking pan.
2. Cream together cream cheese, ¼ cup sugar, and 2 Tbsp. milk until smooth. Fold in ½ of whipped topping. Spread over crust.
3. Using 3½ cups cold milk, prepare pudding as directed on package. Pour over cream cheese layer. Chill several hours or overnight.
4. Spread remaining whipped topping over pudding. Garnish with nuts if desired.

Banana Split Dessert
Barbara Christ, Denver, PA
Jennie Horst, Denver, PA

Makes 12-15 servings

2 cups graham cracker crumbs
½ cup butter, melted
2 cups powdered sugar
2 eggs
½ cup butter, softened
20-oz. can crushed pineapple, well
    drained
4 large bananas, sliced
12-oz. carton whipped topping
1 cup chopped nuts

1. Combine graham cracker crumbs and melted butter. Press into 9" x 13" baking pan.
2. Bake at 375° for 10 minutes.
3. In small bowl combine powdered sugar, eggs, and softened butter and mix well. Spread over graham cracker crust.
4. Return to oven and bake 12 minutes longer. Cool.
5. Spread pineapple, sliced bananas, whipped topping, and nuts over cooled cake. Serve.

Lemon Lush Dessert

Arlene Martin, Stevens, PA
Tammy Foltz, Mountville, PA
Betty Brightbill, Sinking Spring, PA
Linda Seldomridge, Gap, PA

Makes 12 servings

8 Tbsp. margarine
1 cup flour
8-oz. pkg. cream cheese
1 cup powdered sugar
2 cups whipped topping
2 small pkgs. instant lemon pudding
3 cups milk

1. Cut margarine into flour and mix well until blended. Pat into greased 9" x 13" baking pan.
2. Bake at 300° for 25 minutes. Cool.
3. Cream together cream cheese and sugar. Fold in 1 cup whipped topping. Spread over cooled crust.
4. Prepare pudding with milk. Spread over cream cheese mixture. Top with remaining whipped topping. Chill several hours before serving.

Pumpkin Torte

Sara Steffy
Ephrata, PA

Makes 12-15 servings

1¾ cups graham cracker crumbs
⅓ cup sugar
8 Tbsp. margarine, melted
2 eggs
¾ cup sugar
8-oz. pkg. cream cheese, softened
2 cups cooked pumpkin
3 egg yolks
½ cup sugar
½ cup milk
½ tsp. salt
1 tsp. cinnamon
1 envelope unflavored gelatin
¼ cup cold water
3 egg whites
¼ cup sugar
8-oz. container whipped topping

1. Combine graham cracker crumbs, ⅓ cup sugar, and melted margarine and pat into 9" x 13" baking pan for crust.
2. Beat together eggs, ¾ cup sugar, and cream cheese. Spoon over crust.
3. Bake at 350° for 10 minutes or until bubbly.
4. In a saucepan combine pumpkin, egg yolks, ½ cup sugar, milk, salt, and cinnamon and bring to a boil.
5. Dissolve gelatin in cold water. Add to pumpkin mixture and cool slightly.
6. Beat egg whites until stiffened. Gradually add ¼ cup sugar and beat well. Fold into pumpkin mixture. Spoon pumpkin mixture over cream cheese layer. Refrigerate.
7. Immediately before serving, top with whipped topping and cut into squares.

Pumpkin Roll Dessert

Patti Fisher, Mount Joy, PA
Karen Leisey, Akron, PA
Catherine Zimmerman, Ephrata, PA
Lois Hoover, Ephrata, PA

Makes 8-10 servings

Pumpkin Roll:
3 eggs, beaten
1 cup white sugar
²⁄₃ cup cooked pumpkin
¾ cup flour
1 tsp. baking soda
2 tsp. cinnamon

Filling:
8-oz. pkg. cream cheese
1 cup powdered sugar
4 Tbsp. butter
½ tsp. vanilla

1. To prepare pumpkin roll beat eggs for 5 minutes. Add sugar, pumpkin, flour, baking soda, and cinnamon and mix well. Pour into greased and floured 10" x 15" jelly roll pan.

2. Bake at 350° for 15 minutes.

3. Turn baked roll out onto long length of paper towel or cloth tea towel which has been sprinkled with powdered sugar. Roll the cake into towel, beginning with the narrow end. Let cool ½ hour.

4. Meanwhile beat together all filling ingredients until smooth.

5. Unroll cake and remove paper towel. Spread filling on cake roll and roll up again without towel.

6. Refrigerate to chill. Slice and serve.

Pumpkin Cheesecake

Nora Eberly
New Holland, PA

Makes 12 servings

Cheesecake:
4 Tbsp. margarine
1½ cups biscuit mix
2 Tbsp. sugar
8-oz. pkg. cream cheese, softened
¾ cup sugar
2 Tbsp. flour
1 tsp. cinnamon
¼ tsp. nutmeg
¼ tsp. ground ginger
¼ tsp. vanilla
3 eggs
16-oz. can pumpkin pie filling

Sour Cream Topping:
1½ cups sour cream
2 Tbsp. sugar
½ tsp. vanilla

1. Cut margarine into biscuit mix and 2 Tbsp. sugar and work until mixture resembles fine crumbs. Pat into 9-inch square baking pan.

2. Bake at 350° for 10 minutes.

3. Beat together cream cheese, ¾ cup sugar, and flour in large mixing bowl until creamy. Add spices, vanilla, eggs, and pumpkin and beat until smooth. Pour over crust.

4. Bake at 350° for 55 minutes or until knife inserted in center comes out clean.

5. Meanwhile prepare topping by combining all ingredients and beating until smooth. Spread topping over cheesecake immediately after removing from oven. Refrigerate at least 4 hours before serving.

Funnel Cakes at the Solanco Fair

Farm Women #15 was formed September 29, 1938 in the Kirkwood area of Lancaster County. Several years later six Farm Women Societies of southern Lancaster County, including #15, decided to sponsor a fall farmer's fair, which has been held each September since 1950. Since 1979 our society has operated a funnel cake stand at the Southern Lancaster County Community Fair, or the Solanco Fair as it has become widely known.

The first year we sold our funnel cakes from a tent, using iron skillets to prepare them. We have graduated to our own building and commercial equipment and still find it impossible to keep up with the demand. People stand in line, sometimes 30 deep, waiting for their funnel cakes.

—*Emily Linton Reath, Kirkwood, PA*

Cheesecake
Barbara Christ
Denver, PA

Makes 6-8 servings

1 cup crushed vanilla wafers
¼ cup margarine, melted
4 cups miniature marshmallows
⅓ cup milk
2 8-oz. pkgs. cream cheese, softened
2 Tbsp. lemon juice
1 tsp. vanilla
1 cup heavy cream

1. Combine vanilla wafer crumbs and melted margarine. Reserve ¼ cup for topping. Press remaining crumb mixture onto bottom of 9-inch springform pan.

2. Melt 4 cups miniature marshmallows with ⅓ cup milk in double boiler and stir until smooth. Chill until thickened.

3. Cream together cream cheese, lemon juice, and vanilla, beating until well blended and fluffy. Whip in marshmallow mixture.

4. Whip heavy cream until soft peaks form. Fold into cream cheese mixture. Pour over crumbs in springform pan. Sprinkle with ¼ cup reserved crumbs. Chill and serve.

Twice-Baked Cheesecake
Marie Splain
Maytown, PA

Makes 12-15 servings

1¼ cups graham cracker crumbs
½ cup butter *or* margarine, melted
3 8-oz. pkgs. cream cheese
¾ cup white sugar
1½ tsp. lemon juice
Pinch salt
2 large eggs
1 pint sour cream
½ cup white sugar
1 tsp. vanilla
Pinch salt

1. Combine graham cracker crumbs and melted butter. Press into bottom of 10" springform pan.

2. Cream together cream cheese, ¾ cup sugar, lemon juice, salt, and eggs until fluffy. Pour over graham cracker mixture.

3. Bake at 325° for 35-45 minutes. Remove from oven. Cool 1-2 hours.

4. Meanwhile combine sour cream, ½ cup sugar, vanilla, and salt. Pour over cheesecake.

5. Return to oven and bake 15 minutes longer.

Quick Pineapple Cheesecake
Alice Whitman
Lititz, PA

Makes 6 servings

½ cup graham cracker crumbs
4 Tbsp. butter, softened
2 Tbsp. sugar
2 eggs
2 8-oz. pkgs. cream cheese, softened
½ cup sugar
½ tsp. vanilla
2 cups crushed pineapple, drained
⅛ tsp. cinnamon
1 pint sour cream
3 Tbsp. sugar
1 tsp. vanilla

1. In small bowl cream together graham cracker crumbs, butter, and 2 Tbsp. sugar. Pat into greased 9-inch pie pan and refrigerate.
2. Combine eggs, cream cheese, ½ cup sugar, vanilla, pineapple, and cinnamon and blend thoroughly. Pour mixture into crust.
3. Bake at 350° for 30-40 or until knife inserted in center comes out clean. Let cool for 15 minutes.
4. Combine sour cream, 3 Tbsp. sugar, and vanilla and mix well. Spread sour cream mixture over cheesecake. Return to oven and bake 5 minutes longer. Cool for 15 minutes.
5. Refrigerate until ready to serve.

Mini Cheesecakes
Joy Layton
Quarryville, PA

Makes 2 dozen mini cheesecakes

2 dozen vanilla wafers
2 8-oz. pkgs. cream cheese
2 eggs
¾ cup sugar
1 tsp. vanilla
21-oz. can fruit pie filling, any flavor

1. Line muffin pans with cupcake papers. Put a vanilla wafer on bottom of each paper.
2. In a bowl combine cream cheese, eggs, sugar, and vanilla and beat until smooth. Fill each cupcake paper ½-⅔ full.
3. Bake at 350° for 15 minutes. While still hot, top with 1 tsp. pie filling.
4. Chill and serve.

Lemon Cheesecake
Jane Hess
Ephrata, PA

Makes 6 servings

8-oz. pkg. cream cheese, softened
2 cups milk
1 large pkg. instant lemon pudding
1 8" graham cracker crust

1. Cream cream cheese. Add ½ cup milk and mix until smooth and creamy. Add remaining milk and pudding mix and beat slowly for 1 minute.
2. Pour into prepared graham cracker crust. Chill and serve.

Quick Cherry Cheesecake
Orpha S. Kilheffer
Lititz, PA

Makes 10-12 servings

8-oz. pkg. cream cheese, softened
1 cup powdered sugar
1 tsp. vanilla
2 cups whipped topping
2 pkgs. Lady Fingers
21-oz. can cherry pie filling

1. Cream together cream cheese, powdered sugar, and vanilla. Fold in whipped topping.
2. Line a 9" x 13" baking pan with Lady Fingers. Spread ½ of cheese mixture over top. Add another layer of Lady Fingers. Spread remaining cheese mixture over top. Spread cherry pie filling over top.
3. Refrigerate and chill before serving.

Blueberry Cheesecake Delight
Ruth Houck
Stevens, PA

Makes 12-15 servings

Crust:
1¼ cups graham cracker crumbs
¼ cup butter, melted
¼ cup sugar

Filling:
4 cups whipped topping
2 cups powdered sugar
8-oz. pkg. cream cheese, softened
2 21-oz. cans blueberry pie filling

1. Combine crust ingredients. Press into 9" x 13" baking pan.
2. Bake at 375° for 8 minutes. Cool.

3. Combine whipped topping, powdered sugar, and cream cheese and mix well. Spread over cooled crust. Top with 2 cans blueberry pie filling.
4. Chill and serve.

Baked Fruit Compote
Elsie Kauffman
Stevens, PA

Makes 12 servings

2 16-oz. cans fruit cocktail
2 11-oz. cans mandarin oranges
15¼-oz. can pineapple chunks
16-oz. can sliced peaches
3 bananas
2 21-oz. cans pie filling, any flavor

1. Drain all fruit.
2. Slice 3 bananas and soak in pineapple juice for about 5 minutes and drain.
3. Mix all fruit together. Add pie filling. Spoon into lightly greased 9" x 13" baking pan.
4. Bake at 325° for 20 minutes.

Cream Cheese Fruit
Jane Hess
Ephrata, PA

Makes 8 servings

8-oz. pkg. cream cheese
4 Tbsp. pineapple juice
1 cup pineapple chunks
1 cup coconut
1 cup miniature marshmallows
11-oz. can mandarin oranges, drained

1. Cream together cream cheese and pineapple juice. Stir all remaining ingredients into cream cheese mixture and mix until fruit and marshmallows are coated.
2. Chill and serve.

Fruit Salad
Elaine Gibbel
Lititz, PA

Makes 20 servings

6 oranges
1 grapefruit
1 lb. red, seedless grapes
20-oz. can pineapple chunks
29-oz. can sliced peaches
29-oz. can pears
29-oz. can apricot halves
2 apples, diced
2 bananas, sliced

1. Peel oranges and grapefruit, dividing into segments and removing tough membrane. Cut oranges into small pieces.
2. Layer fruits except apples and bananas in order given in large glass or plastic container. Include all juices except apricot juice. Cover tightly and refrigerate overnight.
3. Immediately before serving, add apples and bananas and mix well.

Note: I divide into individual serving dishes and garnish each with a mint sprig, pomegranate seeds, or a fresh strawberry.

Fruit Float
Marion Witmer
Manheim, PA

Makes 6 servings

16-oz. can fruit cocktail
11-oz. can mandarin oranges
15¼-oz. can pineapple chunks
6 bananas, sliced
2 Tbsp. lemon juice
1 small pkg. instant lemon pudding

1. Combine all fruits with their juices. Add lemon juice and instant pudding and mix well.
2. Chill to set and serve.

Cranberry Sherbet
Lucy Moore Bomberger
Lancaster, PA

Makes 1 quart sherbet

4 cups cranberries
2¾ cups water
1 envelope unflavored gelatin
¼ cup cold water
2 cups sugar
⅓ cup lemon juice

1. Cook cranberries in water until skins pop open. Put through sieve.
2. Soften gelatin in cold water. In a saucepan combine cranberries, gelatin, and sugar and heat until dissolved. Cool and stir in lemon juice.

3. Pour into molds and freeze until firm, about 4 hours. Serve on hot summer day.

*H*omemade Vanilla Ice Cream
Erma J. Frey, Leola, PA
Tamara Lausch, Akron, PA

Makes 1 gallon ice cream

4 eggs, well beaten
2 cups sugar
5 cups milk
4 cups heavy cream
4½ tsp. vanilla
½ tsp. salt

1. Combine eggs, sugar, and 2 cups milk in double boiler and cook until thickened, stirring frequently. Cool mixture.
2. Combine thickened milk, 3 cups remaining milk, cream, vanilla, and salt and pour into ice cream freezer.
3. Freeze according to directions. Serve on hot summer day.

*B*utter Pecan Ice Cream
Audrey Brubaker
Lancaster, PA

Makes 1 gallon ice cream

Pecan Mixture:
6 Tbsp. butter, melted
1½ cups chopped pecans
¼ tsp. salt
2 Tbsp. sugar

Ice Cream:
1 cup brown sugar
½ cup white sugar
4 Tbsp. cornstarch
4 eggs, beaten

⅔ cup maple-flavored syrup
5 cups milk
2 cups heavy cream
4 tsp. vanilla

1. To prepare pecan mixture combine all ingredients and mix well. Spread, in single layer, on large, flat baking sheet.
2. Roast at 350° for 5-10 minutes. Stir and roast 10 minutes longer. Cool.
3. To prepare ice cream combine sugars, cornstarch, eggs, and syrup in double boiler. Gradually add milk and cook until mixture thickens, stirring frequently.
4. Remove from heat and chill several hours or overnight. Stir in roasted pecans, heavy cream, and vanilla. Pour mixture into ice cream freezer and freeze according to directions.
5. Let stand one hour before serving.

*H*omemade Coffee Ice Cream
June M. Charles
Lancaster, PA

Makes 2 quarts ice cream

2 cups milk
1 cup sugar
¼ tsp. salt
4 cups light cream
2 tsp. vanilla
¼ cup dry instant coffee

1. Scald milk. Add sugar and salt and stir until dissolved. Add cream. Stir in vanilla and coffee until dissolved. Cool.
2. Pour into ice cream freezer and freeze according to directions.

Candies

Peanut Butter Fudge
Sandra Kautz
Mount Joy, PA

Makes 20-24 servings

½ cup milk
2 cups sugar
12-oz. jar peanut butter
7-oz. jar marshmallow cream

1. In a saucepan stir together milk and sugar and bring to a boil. Boil 3 minutes and remove from heat.
2. Stir in peanut butter and marshmallow cream and blend well. Pour into greased 8-inch square baking pan. Let cool and cut into squares.

Chocolate Fudge
Fannie Ressler
Lititz, PA

Makes 20-24 servings

2 cups milk chocolate chips
1 cup semi-sweet chocolate chips
14-oz. can condensed milk
4 Tbsp. butter
1 cup chopped nuts

1. Mix all ingredients except nuts in a saucepan. Heat on low until melted, stirring constantly. Fold in nuts and spoon into greased 8-inch square pan.
2. Refrigerate and cut into squares.

Fudge Squares
Carolyn Burns
Lancaster, PA

Makes 24-36 servings

½ cup melted butter
1 cup sugar
2 eggs
½ cup chopped nuts
1 Tbsp. vanilla
2 squares melted chocolate
2 Tbsp. milk
½ cup + 2 Tbsp. flour

1. Pour melted butter into a 9-inch square baking dish, carefully spreading over bottom and sides.
2. In a large bowl combine all remaining ingredients and mix well. Spoon into prepared baking dish.
3. Bake at 350° for 25 minutes. Cut into small squares and serve.

Cream Cheese Mints
Ida Jane Zercher
Willow Street, PA

Makes about 130 mint roses

8-oz. pkg. cream cheese
2⅓ Tbsp. butter
½ Tbsp. oil of peppermint extract
2 lbs. powdered sugar
Dash salt
1 tsp. red food coloring
½ cup white sugar

1. Cream together cream cheese, butter, and flavoring. Gradually add powdered sugar and salt and knead with hands until like pie dough. Add powdered sugar until mixture is not sticky. (During hot weather you may need more than 2 lbs.) Mix in food coloring.
2. Roll into marble-sized balls. Dip each ball in white sugar and shape with rose molds. Unmold and arrange on waxed paper.
3. Store in plastic container, putting waxed paper between each layer of mints. They keep for weeks in the refrigerator.

Mints
Deloris J. Miller
Manheim, PA

Makes about 75 mints

1 lb. powdered sugar
8 Tbsp. butter
1 Tbsp. warm water
10 drops oil of spearmint extract
Food coloring (optional)

1. Combine all ingredients and knead by hand until well mixed. Roll into small balls. (Melon baller works well.)
2. Press down with fork and store in airtight container.

Fivepointville

*A*bout two miles north of Terre Hill in the northeastern part of Lancaster County, a village grew up around the spot where the present-day Fivepointville Road meets Maple Grove Road, Pleasant Valley Road, and the north and south points of Dry Tavern Road (Route 897). Probably once native American trails, the country roads that converge in Fivepointville are lined with the homes of old-time Pennsylvania Dutch folk, many of whom speak with a distinct dutchified accent.

A visit to almost any local establishment provides a linguistic treat. According to a receptionist, shoppers can find Weaver's Store "chust awtsite Fivepointville on 897." A bargain clothing, hardware, and housewares operation, Weaver's bustles with managers, clerks, and stockpersons, most of whom speak English with the unique inflections of people raised in the heart of Pennsylvania Dutch country.

A short distance south of Weaver's Store along Muddy Creek is Good's Mill, a fourth generation retail feed mill. Water-powered until 1938, the mill today runs with electric power, providing local farmers with feed for their animals.

Also home to the butchering Youndt families, well known for their sausage, hams, and scrapple, Fivepointville primarily serves as a sleepy, little haven where local folks come home to rest and relax.

Coconut Cream Eggs
Sarah Evans, Akron, PA
Alberta Gehman, Terre Hill, PA

Makes about 55-60 eggs

2 lbs. powdered sugar
2 Tbsp. butter
8-oz. pkg. cream cheese
1 tsp. vanilla
12 ozs. coconut
16-oz. pkg. chocolate chips
1 block paraffin

1. Cream together sugar, butter, and cream cheese. Add vanilla and coconut and mix well. Form into small, egg-shaped balls.
2. In a double boiler combine chocolate chips and paraffin and melt, stirring constantly. Dip eggs in melted chocolate to coat. Set aside to cool.

Butter Cream Eggs
Rhoda H. Lind, Lititz, PA
Teresa Burkhart, Brownstown, PA

Makes about 24-30 eggs

4 ozs. cream cheese
1 lb. powdered sugar
8 Tbsp. butter
1 tsp. vanilla
8 ozs. coating chocolate

1. Combine all ingredients except chocolate and mix until smooth. Form into small, egg-shaped balls. Chill in freezer before dipping.
2. Melt chocolate in double boiler. Dip each candy into melted chocolate and place on waxed paper or cookie sheet. Cool until chocolate sets.

*P*eanut Butter Eggs
Dawn J. Ranck
Strasburg, PA

Makes 2-3 dozen eggs

1 pint marshmallow cream
20-oz. jar peanut butter
1½ cups margarine
2 lbs. powdered sugar
8 ozs. coating chocolate

1. Cream together marshmallow cream, peanut butter, and margarine. Gradually add powdered sugar until well mixed. Shape into medium-sized, egg-shaped balls.
2. Melt chocolate in double boiler. Dip each egg in chocolate and place on waxed paper until cooled.

*C*reamy Peanut Butter Eggs
Alberta Gehman
Terre Hill, PA

Makes 8 dozen eggs

¾ cup peanut butter
¼ cup butter
1 tsp. salt
1 tsp. vanilla
14-oz. can condensed milk
4 cups sifted powdered sugar
1¾ lbs. light coating chocolate

1. Combine all ingredients except chocolate and mix well. Chill overnight in refrigerator.
2. Shape into small egg-shaped balls.
3. Melt chocolate in double boiler. Dip each egg in chocolate and set aside to cool and set.

*C*rispy Peanut Butter Eggs
Mary N. Nolt, New Holland, PA
Miriam and Sarah Horning,
Bowmansville, PA

Makes 3 dozen eggs

2 cups peanut butter
1 lb. powdered sugar
3 cups Rice Krispies
¼ cup butter, softened
4 ozs. German sweet chocolate
½ bar paraffin

1. Combine all ingredients and mix with hands until Rice Krispies sound crunchy.
2. Mold into tablespoon-sized egg shapes and arrange on waxed paper.
3. In a double boiler melt together chocolate and paraffin. Heat until smooth, stirring frequently. Remove from heat and dip each peanut butter egg into chocolate. Return eggs to waxed paper to cool.

Chocolate Caramel Bars

Mrs. James Zimmerman
Stevens, PA

Makes 2-3 dozen bars

2 cups cream
1¾ cups light corn syrup
2 cups sugar
¾ cup butter
½ tsp. vanilla
1 cup crushed peanuts
8 ozs. coating chocolate

1. Combine 1 cup cream, corn syrup, and sugar in a saucepan. Boil into a hard ball. Add remaining 1 cup cream and butter and cook slowly until soft ball stage. Stir in vanilla and pour into greased 8-inch square pan.

2. With greased hands, combine caramel and crushed peanuts and form mixture into 2-inch bars. Arrange small bars on cookie sheet and place in freezer while preparing chocolate.

3. Melt chocolate in double boiler. Dip each caramel bar in chocolate and store in cool place until ready to serve.

Hot Lunches in a One-Room School

When I taught in a one-room school near the borough of New Holland in the 1940s, my pupils and I often enjoyed a hot lunch on cold winter days. Each of us brought a scrubbed potato in our pails. These were placed in the ash pit of the coal furnace before classes started in the morning.

By lunch time the room was filled with the delicious aroma of baked potatoes. On certain days we also heated vegetable soup on an electric hot plate. Each one had his or her own ceramic cup in which I would serve the soup.

When the huge coal furnace in the room was replaced with an oil burner, our hot meals were history.

—*Ethel M. Brendle, Lititz, PA*

Peanut Butter Balls

Barbara Galebach
Ephrata, PA

Makes about 16-20 balls

¼ cup peanut butter
¼ cup skim milk
¼ cup raisins
4 2-inch graham crackers, crushed
1 tsp. vanilla
Dash cinnamon

1. Cream together peanut butter and 2 Tbsp. milk until well blended. Add all remaining ingredients and mix well.

2. Form into 1-inch balls and drop onto waxed paper. Store in freezer until ready to serve.

Intercourse

One of Lancaster County's most talked about villages stretches along Route 340 in the heart of Amish country. Called Cross Keys from 1754 when a tavern was established at a crossroads on the King's Highway, local landowner, George Brungard, changed the name to Intercourse in 1814 when he laid out and sold building lots around the point where the two roads met. Twenty-four years earlier in 1790, the first Amish settler of the Pequea Amish community, Christian Zook, had settled on a farm between the Cross Keys area and what is now the village of Gordonville.

More than two centuries later in 1993 a prosperous Old Order Amish community still surrounds and spills into the village of Intercourse. Several Amish farmers till fields within only a few hundred yards of the busy main highway which channels a mixture of local farmers and construction workers, Amish buggies, international visitors, tour buses, and shopkeepers through the village each day.

Today the 1882 Jason K. Eaby General Store houses an airy local fabric, crafts, and quilt store. At The Old Country Store Amish and Mennonite quilters buying fabric mingle with visitors buying their finished product. On its second floor the Store operates The People's Place Quilt Museum, which is dedicated to showing the quilt masterpieces created by Amish and Mennonite women in the late 1800s and early 1900s.

Many other shops and businesses—Zook's Dry Goods, The People's Place, W. L. Zimmerman & Sons, Kitchen Kettle, and Hoobers Farm Equipment—line Route 340. While traffic occasionally overwhelms the village, many visitors stop and sit on the front steps of one or another of the local stores to watch the mixture of life which shapes this unusual Lancaster County town.

Peanut Butter Candy

Jaci Rettew
Denver, PA

Makes 2-3 dozen balls

3 cups chocolate chips
3 cups peanut butter
1½ cups condensed milk
¾ cup powdered sugar

1. Combine all ingredients and mix well.
2. Form into 1"-2" balls and arrange on waxed paper. Chill and serve.

Hopscotch Candy

Janet L. Rynier
Gordonville, PA

Makes about 30 candies

6-oz. pkg. butterscotch morsels
½ cup peanut butter
3-oz. can chow mein noodles
2 cups miniature marshmallows

1. In a double boiler melt morsels over hot (not boiling) water. Stir in peanut butter and mix well.
2. Mix noodles and marshmallows together in large bowl. Add the butterscotch mixture. Mix thoroughly and drop by heaping teaspoonsful onto waxed paper-lined cookie sheets. Chill until set.

Caramel Candy Bars
Marcia Root
Manheim, PA

Makes 36 squares

14-oz. pkg. caramel candies
$\frac{1}{3}$ cup milk
2 cups flour
1 tsp. baking soda
$\frac{1}{2}$ tsp. salt
$1\frac{1}{2}$ cups brown sugar, packed
2 cups uncooked oats
1 egg
1 cup margarine, softened
6-oz. pkg. chocolate chips
1 cup chopped peanuts

1. Unwrap candies. Heat with milk in saucepan over low heat, stirring until smooth. Remove from heat.

2. In a large mixing bowl combine flour, baking soda, salt, brown sugar, oats, and egg and mix well. Stir in margarine with fork until mixture is crumbly.

3. Press half of the crumb mixture into greased 9" x 13" baking pan.

4. Bake at 350° for 10 minutes. Sprinkle with chocolate chips and peanuts. Drizzle with caramel mixture. Spread remaining crumb mixture over top.

5. Return to oven for another 20-25 minutes or until golden brown. Cool 30 minutes. Loosen edges from side of pan; cool completely. Cut into small bars.

Butter Chews
Rachel Pellman
Lancaster, PA

Makes 36 squares

$\frac{3}{4}$ cup butter
2 Tbsp. white sugar
$1\frac{3}{4}$ cups flour
3 eggs, separated
2 cups brown sugar
$\frac{3}{4}$ cup chopped pecans
$\frac{3}{4}$ cup coconut

1. Combine butter, white sugar, and flour. Pat mixture into 9" x 13" baking pan.

2. Bake at 325° for 20 minutes.

3. Meanwhile beat egg yolks thoroughly. Add brown sugar and mix well. Fold in pecans and coconut.

4. Beat egg whites until stiff and fold into batter. Spoon batter over baked crust.

5. Return to oven and bake 35-40 minutes longer. Do not overbake.

6. When cool, cut into squares and serve.

Peanut Brittle
Deloris J. Miller, Manheim, PA
June Hassel, Quarryville, PA

Makes 20-24 servings

2 cups white sugar
1 cup light corn syrup
$\frac{1}{4}$ cup cold water
2-$2\frac{1}{2}$ cups unroasted peanuts
2 tsp. baking soda
1 tsp. salt

1. In a double boiler bring sugar, syrup, and water to a boil. Boil until it spins a thread (about 25 minutes or until 280° on

candy thermometer).

2. Stir in unroasted peanuts and boil until mixture turns brown, about 8-10 minutes. Remove from heat.

3. Combine baking soda and salt. Stir into peanut brittle. Pour onto greased jelly roll pan and let set to harden.

4. Break into pieces and serve.

Coated Nuts
Dottie Donnelly
Willow Street, PA

Makes about 5 cups nuts

2 egg whites
1 cup white sugar
1½ cups walnuts
1 cup pecans
½ cup almonds
8 Tbsp. butter *or* margarine

1. Beat egg whites until stiff. Add sugar and beat until well mixed. Fold nuts into meringue until coated.

2. Melt butter on large baking sheet with sides. Spread coated nuts onto baking sheet.

3. Bake at 325° for ½ hour or until nuts are browned, stirring every 10 minutes.

Baked Caramel Popcorn
Ruth H. Shank, Lititz, PA
Mildred M. Ney, Columbia, PA

Makes 6 quarts popcorn

1 cup butter *or* margarine
2 cups brown sugar
½ cup light corn syrup
1 tsp. salt
½ tsp. baking soda
1 tsp. vanilla
6 quarts popped popcorn

1. Melt butter. Stir in brown sugar, corn syrup, and salt. Bring to a boil, stirring constantly. Boil, without stirring, for 5 minutes. Remove from heat and stir in baking soda and vanilla.

2. Pour popped popcorn into large, well-greased roasting pan. Pour caramel mixture over popcorn and mix well.

3. Bake at 250° for 1 hour, stirring every 15 minutes. Remove from oven and cool.

4. Break apart and store in tightly covered container.

Beverages

Tea Lemonade
Elaine Gibbel, Lititz, PA
Tina Snyder, Manheim, PA

Makes 6 quarts tea

2 cups sugar
5 cups water
1 large handful garden mint tea
1 cup orange juice
1 cup lemon juice
Water

1. Boil sugar in 5 cups water. Pour over tea leaves, cover, and steep for 1 hour.
2. Remove tea leaves. Add juices and refrigerate.
3. Before serving, dilute concentrate, using 1 part concentrate to 2 parts water. Add ice and serve on hot, summer day.

Note: I often freeze syrup and later add enough water to make a delicious winter treat.
—*Tina Snyder, Manheim, PA*

Delicious Iced Tea
Miriam Stoltzfus
Ronks, PA

Makes 1 gallon tea

2 cups boiling water
9 tea bags *or* more
1¾ cups sugar
Water
¼ cup frozen lemonade, thawed

1. In a medium bowl pour boiling water over tea bags. Steep for about 5-10 minutes.
2. Pour sugar into gallon-sized pitcher. Add brewed tea mixture and stir until dissolved. Add water to fill pitcher. Stir well. Add lemonade and mix well.
3. Serve with ice.

Adamstown

In Lancaster County the place to go antiquing is Adamstown. A modest residential village in the County's northeastern hills adjoining Berks County, Adamstown has become a mecca for antique lovers.

From the more than 700 vendors at Renninger's Antique Market, who begin to gather before sunrise on most Sunday mornings, to Heritage Antique Mall, which advertises "open every day," buyers search for everything from French country antiques to broken-down picture frames.

In 1991 one lucky collector purchased such an antique frame at one of the local establishments. Upon examining the frame more closely, the buyer discovered a priceless early copy of the Declaration of Independence hidden behind a rather nondescript painting.

On the edge of the village, Zinn's Diner and Stoudt's Black Angus Restaurant compete to whet the appetites of the numerous standholders, dealers, collectors, and browsers who descend on Adamstown most weekends of the year. Mom's Place Diner, at the foot of Main Street, attracts a more local crowd.

Hot Meadow Tea
Norma I. Gehman
Kinzers, PA

Makes 2-4 servings

3-4 cups boiling water
1 cup freshly picked spearmint
　　meadow tea
Honey *or* sugar

1. Steep tea in boiling water for about 5 minutes.
2. Remove tea leaves. Sweeten to taste and serve hot with freshly baked biscuits.

Fruit Punch
West Earl Fire Company Auxiliary
Brownstown, PA

Makes 2 gallons punch

2 quarts cranberry juice
1 quart orange juice
1 quart unsweetened pineapple juice
3 Tbsp. lemon juice
¾ cup sugar

1 quart 7-Up
1 quart pineapple sherbet (optional)

1. Chill all juices. Mix together in large punch bowl.
2. Add sherbet or ice and serve.

Summer Sparkle Punch
Carolyn Espigh
Terre Hill, PA

Makes 12-16 servings

2 3-oz. pkgs. strawberry gelatin
2 cups boiling water
2 12-oz. cans frozen lemonade, slightly
　　thawed
3 28-oz. bottles ginger ale
Ice cubes

1. Dissolve gelatin in boiling water. Stir in lemonade. Add ginger ale and stir until lemonade dissolves.
2. Add ice cubes and serve.

Easy Party Lime Punch

Dianna S. Ross, Akron, PA
Debra McComsey, Christiana, PA

Makes 12-16 servings

2 pkgs. lime-lemon Kool-Aid
2 cups sugar
2 quarts water
46-oz. can pineapple juice
1 quart ginger ale
1 quart lime sherbet

1. Combine Kool-Aid, sugar, and water. Add pineapple juice and mix well.
2. Refrigerate to chill. Immediately before serving, stir in ginger ale and lime sherbet.

Coffee Punch

Marcia Root
Manheim, PA

Makes 12 servings

¼ cup instant coffee powder
1 cup sugar
1½ quarts hot water
1 quart milk
1½ tsp. vanilla
3 ozs. chocolate syrup
½ gallon vanilla ice cream

1. Stir coffee and sugar into hot water until dissolved. Add milk, vanilla, and chocolate syrup and chill overnight.
2. Immediately before serving, pour into punch bowl, add vanilla ice cream, and mix well.

Banana Crush

Rhoda H. Lind
Lititz, PA

Makes 2 gallons punch

3 cups sugar
6 cups water
Juice of 2 lemons
Juice of 5 oranges
5 bananas, mashed
46-oz. can unsweetened pineapple juice
4 quarts ginger ale *or* 7-Up

1. Combine sugar and water and bring to a boil. Boil for 5 minutes, stirring frequently. Remove from heat and add all remaining ingredients except ginger ale or 7-Up, stirring until well mixed.
2. Pour into 4 1-quart containers and freeze.
3. Remove from freezer about 1 hour before serving. Spoon into punch bowl. Add 1 quart ginger ale or 7-Up for each quart frozen crush and serve.

Mincemeat Fund Raiser

At the Colemanville United Methodist Church, the mincemeat making and pie bake is our largest annual fund raising project. Begun in 1934 at the height of the Depression, the event has grown to where we make 540 gallons of mincemeat and 2000 pies. The cost of each pie—25 cents in 1934—has also gone up considerably. Each year this community event is shared by the women of our church, their families, and many friends.

—*Ida Jane Zercher, Willow Street, PA*

Terre Hill

The view from almost anywhere in Terre Hill is spectacular. Perched on top of a Welsh Mountain foothill in northeastern Lancaster County, Terre Hill overlooks the lush Conestoga Valley. Scores of farmsteads spread south across the countryside between Terre Hill and New Holland. Only an occasional tiny village like Reidenbach or Blue ball or Weaverland interrupts the densely populated farm country where many people operate cottage industries to supplement their income from the land.

The fried scrapple at Dell's Family Restaurant on Main Street adds pizzazz to a breakfast of eggs and homefries and melts in the mouth. A local folks' place, Dell's offers friendly service and good food.

Signs proclaiming, "Terre Hill has many children, but none to spare," pointedly warn approaching motorists to drive carefully. Several churches, a quick market, a pizza place, and a concrete manufacturing plant occasionally appear among the rows of frame houses with rail-fence porches.

Instant Friendship Tea

Alta M. Ranck
Lancaster, PA

Makes many servings

½ cup dry lemonade mix
2 cups Tang
1¼ cups white sugar
½ cup instant tea mix
1 Tbsp. cinnamon
½ Tbsp. ground cloves

1. Combine all ingredients and store in airtight container.
2. To serve stir 2 heaping teaspoons mix into each cup hot water.

Hot Chocolate Mix

Teresa Burkhart
Brownstown, PA

Makes many servings

8-quart carton powdered milk
1-lb. carton instant chocolate mix
8-oz. jar coffee mate
1 cup powdered sugar

1. Mix all ingredients together and store in airtight 5-quart container.
2. To serve combine ¼ to ⅓ cup mix with 1 cup boiling water.

Breakfast Foods

Baked Eggs
Alice Whitman
Lititz, PA

Makes 6-8 servings

9 eggs, beaten
$\frac{1}{2}$ cup sour cream
$\frac{1}{2}$ cup milk
1 tsp. salt
Dash pepper
1 Tbsp. chopped onion tops
2 Tbsp. margarine

   1. Mix together eggs, sour cream, milk, salt, and pepper. Add chopped onion tops.
   2. Melt margarine in 8-inch square baking pan. Pour egg mixture into pan.
   3. Bake at 325° for 45 minutes.

Variation: Sprinkle crisp, crumbled bacon or chopped ham over egg mixture before baking.

Egg, Potato, and Cheese Casserole
Loretta Lapp
Kinzers, PA

Makes 6-8 servings

6 medium potatoes
8 eggs
2 Tbsp. water
Salt and pepper to taste
1 cup grated cheese

   1. Cook potatoes until soft. Cool, peel, and grate. Spread over bottom of greased 9-inch square baking pan.
   2. Combine eggs, water, salt, and pepper. Pour egg mixture over potatoes. Spread cheese over egg mixture.
   3. Cover and bake at 350° for 30 minutes. Uncover and bake another 15 minutes. Let stand 10 minutes before serving.

Overnight Egg Casserole
Pam Nussbaum
Reinholds, PA

Makes 6-8 servings

8 slices bread, cubed
¾ lb. cheddar cheese, shredded
1½ lbs. bulk sausage
4 eggs
2½ cups milk
1 Tbsp. prepared mustard
10¾-oz. can cream of mushroom soup
¼ cup chicken broth

1. Arrange bread cubes in greased 9" x 13" baking dish. Sprinkle with cheese; set aside.
2. In a skillet brown sausage over medium heat. Drain all excess fat. Crumble sausage over cheese and bread.
3. In a bowl beat together eggs, milk, mustard, soup, and broth. Pour over sausage. Cover and refrigerate overnight or at least 2-3 hours before baking.
4. Bake at 350° for 50-60 minutes or just until set.

Variation: Omit cream of mushroom soup and chicken broth. Arrange in 7" x 11" baking pan. Bake at 375° for 45 minutes.
—Emma King, Gordonville, PA

Bacon and Egg Casserole
Donella King
Cochranville, PA

Makes 10-12 servings

6 slices white bread
12 eggs
2 cups milk
1 cup sour cream
1 tsp. salt

1 lb. cooked ham, bacon, *or* sausage
½ lb. cheddar cheese, grated

1. Arrange bread slices in greased 9" x 13" baking pan.
2. In large bowl beat together eggs, milk, and sour cream. Add salt and cooked meat and mix well. Pour mixture over bread and sprinkle cheese over other ingredients. Refrigerate overnight.
3. Bake at 350° for 50-60 minutes.

Miniature Quiche
Marcia Root
Manheim, PA

Makes 24 servings

½ cup butter
3-oz. pkg. cream cheese
1 cup flour
1 egg
½ cup milk
¼ tsp. salt
1 cup grated Swiss cheese
5 slices bacon

1. Cream together butter and cream cheese. Work in flour. Chill about ½ hour.
2. Roll into 24 balls and press into greased miniature muffin tins.
3. In a bowl combine egg, milk, and salt. Set aside.
4. Sprinkle cheese evenly into each of the unbaked cream cheese shells in miniature muffin tins. Pour egg mixture evenly over cheese.
5. Fry, drain, and crumble bacon. Sprinkle bacon evenly over each miniature quiche.
6. Bake at 350° for 30 minutes. Can be frozen on cookie sheet and stored in freezer. Reheat at 325° for 15 minutes.

Quarryville

*I*n 1775 Martin Barr purchased the land surrounding the present-day site of Quarryville. Within several years he began mining the area for limestone. By 1858 Quarryville, as it was being called, had twelve quarries and produced 600,000 bushels of lime a year, employing more than 100 people.

While the introduction of commercial fertilizers eventually put the quarries out of business, the borough of Quarryville became the largest town in the southern end of Lancaster County.

Today, farming is the lifeblood of the region and many Solanco (an acronym for southern Lancaster County) families trace their roots to the eighteenth century settlers. In the 1940s many Amish families from other parts of the County began buying the fertile and more affordable farms, and Amish farmers have become a major force in the Solanco farming community.

Chartered as a borough in 1892, the town of Quarryville has numerous businesses, including Newswanger Furniture, Howard E. Groff Fuel Oil, Nickel Mine Floor Coverings, Good's Store, and the Quarryville Presbyterian Home.

Ham and Egg Casserole

Elsie Stoltzfus
Gap, PA

Makes 10-12 servings

6 eggs, beaten
6 slices ham, cubed
6 slices bread, cubed
2 cups milk
1 cup grated cheese
Salt and pepper to taste
½ tsp. dry mustard
1 tsp. minced onion

1. Combine all ingredients in greased 9" x 13" baking pan.
2. Bake at 350° for 45 minutes.

Note: This dish may be refrigerated overnight if needed.

Breakfast Pizza

Lena Mae Hoover
Leola, PA

Makes 4 servings

4 eggs
2 Tbsp. milk
½ tsp. salt
Dash pepper
1 Tbsp. butter
4 slices bread, toasted
4 Tbsp. ketchup
½ cup shredded cheese

1. In a bowl combine eggs, milk, salt, and pepper.
2. Melt butter in a skillet and pour in egg mixture. Cook over low heat until eggs are thickened but still moist. Stir gently.
3. Spread ketchup evenly over hot, toasted bread. Place toast on baking sheet and spoon scrambled eggs onto each piece. Sprinkle cheese on top of eggs.
4. Broil at 500° until cheese melts.

Potato Pancakes
Vera Nolt
Leola, PA

Makes 4-6 servings

2 medium potatoes, cooked and peeled
4 egg whites
½ cup lowfat yogurt
¼ cup grated onion
1 Tbsp. parsley flakes
1 Tbsp. whole wheat flour
Pepper to taste
Cooking oil

1. Grate potatoes into egg whites. Add all remaining ingredients and mix well.
2. Heat cooking oil in skillet. Pan fry potato cakes, turning to finish on both sides.

Egg Dogs
Ruth Weaver
Reinholds, PA

Makes 6-8 servings

6 hot dog rolls
12 eggs
¼ cup minced green onion
Salt and pepper to taste
½ cup grated cheese

1. Separate each hot dog roll into two pieces. With a fork dig out the center of each piece, forming a hollow shell. Save for future use as bread crumbs. Arrange the half buns in a greased baking pan.
2. Break one egg into the hollow of each half bun. Sprinkle each with 1 tsp. onion. Salt and pepper lightly.
3. Bake at 325° for 15-20 minutes until desired doneness. Sprinkle with grated cheese for the last 5 minutes of baking time. Serve.

Cornmeal Mush
Betty Pellman
Millersville, PA

Makes 4 servings

1 quart water
¼ tsp. salt
1½ cups cornmeal

1. Bring salted water to a brisk boil. Slowly add cornmeal, stirring constantly. Reduce heat and continue to stir until lumps are gone and mixture is thick and smooth.
2. Serve with molasses.

Note: Cornmeal mush may also be poured into loaf pans and refrigerated. Slice and fry in oil before serving.

Waffles
Jane Groff
Lancaster, PA

Makes about 20 medium waffles

4½ cups flour
8 tsp. baking powder
1 tsp. salt
2 Tbsp. sugar
4 eggs, separated
4 cups milk
½ cup butter, melted

1. Combine flour, baking powder, salt, and sugar. Add egg yolks, milk, and melted butter and mix well.
2. Beat egg whites until stiffened. Fold into waffle batter.
3. Preheat waffle iron. Pour batter onto hot waffle iron and follow directions for making waffles. Serve.

Paradise

Many Lancaster Countians avoid Route 30 east of Lancaster. Known for its motels, chain restaurants, and tourist attractions, the highway is perpetually crowded and congested. Just east of the main tourist strip, Amish farms jut against the busy truck thoroughfare, and the highway passes through villages like Soudersburg, Paradise, Leaman Place, Vintage, and Kinzers. Single-file rows of homes stretch along both sides of the road and the villages meet each other at their east and west ends.

In Paradise the Historic Revere Tavern still carries on its centuries-old tradition of providing sleeping accommodations, food, and drink to weary travelers. Built in 1740 at the point where Pequea Creek crossed the Lancaster-Philadelphia turnpike, the tavern today houses a Best Western motel, a fine restaurant, and a dinner theater.

Several churches, a children's home, a truckstop, and a car dealership mingle with ordinary middle-class residences, whose inhabitants have long since learned to sleep undisturbed in spite of the truck and train traffic rumbling through Paradise at all hours of the day and night.

Breakfast Waffles

Janet Rettew
Denver, PA

Makes 10 medium waffles

2 cups sifted flour
3 tsp. baking powder
½ tsp. salt
2 Tbsp. sugar
2 eggs
1½ cups milk
4 Tbsp. cooking oil

1. Combine flour, baking powder, salt, and sugar.
2. Beat eggs and milk together. Add dry ingredients and oil and blend batter thoroughly.
3. Pour batter onto hot waffle iron and follow directions for making waffles. Serve with syrup.

Molasses Breakfast Cake

Loretta Lapp
Kinzers, PA

Makes 10-12 servings

4 cups flour
2 cups sugar
Dash salt
¾ cup margarine *or* shortening
2 tsp. baking soda
½ tsp. vinegar
1 cup molasses
2 cups boiling water

1. Combine flour, sugar, and salt. Cut in margarine until crumbly. Reserve 1½ cups crumbs.
2. Dissolve baking soda in vinegar.
3. To remaining crumbs add molasses, boiling water, and baking soda. Stir well and spoon into greased 9" x 13" baking pan. Spread reserved crumbs evenly over batter.
4. Bake at 350° for 35-45 minutes.

Baked Oatmeal

Miriam E. Lefever, East Petersburg, PA
Louise Weaver, Denver, PA
Helen Stoltzfus, Gap, PA

Makes 4 servings

⅓ cup cooking oil
½ cup sugar
1 large egg, beaten
2 cups uncooked oats
1⅓ tsp. baking powder
1 tsp. salt
⅔ cup milk

1. Combine oil, sugar, and egg. Add oats, baking powder, salt, and milk. Pour into greased casserole dish.

2. Bake at 350° for 30-35 minutes. Serve warm with milk and cinnamon or vanilla ice cream.

French Breakfast Puff

Mary Louise Kurtz
Ephrata, PA

Makes 8-10 puffs

⅓ cup shortening
½ cup sugar
1 egg
1½ cups flour
1½ tsp. baking powder
½ tsp. salt
¼ tsp. nutmeg
½ cup milk
½ cup sugar
1 tsp. cinnamon
½ cup butter, melted

1. Cream together shortening, ½ cup sugar, and egg. Stir in flour, baking powder, salt, and nutmeg, alternating with milk.

2. Fill greased medium muffin cups ⅔ full.

3. Bake at 350° for 20-25 minutes.

4. Mix ½ cup sugar and cinnamon.

5. Immediately after baking, dip top of hot muffin into melted butter and then into sugar and cinnamon mixture. Serve hot.

Orange Brunch Cake

Kathy Reilly
Lancaster, PA

Makes 8 servings

Cake:
6-oz. can frozen orange juice
2 cups flour
1 cup sugar
1 tsp. baking soda
1 tsp. salt
¼ lb. butter *or* margarine
½ cup milk
2 eggs
⅓ cup chopped nuts

Topping:
⅓ cup sugar
¼ cup chopped nuts
1 tsp. cinnamon

1. In a bowl combine ½ cup orange juice concentrate with flour, sugar, baking soda, salt, butter, milk, and eggs. Pour into blender and blend at low speed for 30 seconds. Beat 3 minutes at medium speed. Fold in nuts. Pour into greased and floured 9" x 13" baking pan.

2. Bake at 350° for 30-40 minutes. Drizzle remaining orange juice concentrate over warm cake.

3. To prepare topping combine all ingredients and sprinkle over cake. Serve warm with coffee.

Honey Nut Granola
Mary King
Leola, PA

Makes 6 cups granola

2½ cups uncooked oats
½ cup brown sugar, packed
½ cup chopped nuts
⅓ cup honey
⅓ cup butter, melted
¼ cup wheat germ
1 tsp. cinnamon
1 tsp. vanilla

1. Combine all ingredients and mix well. Pour into greased baking pan.
2. Bake at 325° for 20-25 minutes, stirring occasionally.
3. Serve with cold milk.

Granola Bars
Vera Nolt
Leola, PA

Makes about 40 bars

1½ lbs. marshmallows
4 Tbsp. margarine
¼ cup cooking oil
½ cup honey
¼ cup peanut butter
10-oz. box Rice Krispies
5 cups toasted oatmeal
1½ cups raisins
1 cup coconut
1 cup M&Ms *or* chocolate chips
1 cup peanuts
1 cup crumbled graham crackers

1. In double boiler melt together marshmallows and margarine. Add oil, honey, and peanut butter and mix well.

Remove from heat and stir in all remaining ingredients.
2. Spread onto large greased baking pan or cookie sheet. When cool, cut into squares and store in airtight container.

Homemade Grapenuts
Sara Newswanger
Narvon, PA

Makes about 3 lbs. grapenuts

3½ cups whole wheat *or* graham flour
2 cups buttermilk *or* sour milk
1 cup molasses
1¼ tsp. baking soda
1 tsp. salt
3 Tbsp. shortening
1 tsp. vanilla

1. Combine all ingredients and mix well. Spoon into 9" x 13" baking pan.
2. Bake at 400° for 35-40 minutes. Remove from oven and cover with a towel to cool.
3. When cooled, crumble by hand. Return to oven. Bake at 200° for 1-1¼ hours until dry and crisp.
4. Store in a tightly-closed container.

The Brown Porcelain Cup

One of my favorite lunches as a child in Lancaster County during the 1920s and 1930s was a soft-boiled egg which my mother always served in a special brown porcelain cup with white interior. She also often cut a piece of buttered bread cut into narrow strips. I loved dipping the bread into the egg for each bite.

—*Betty Pellman, Millersville, PA*

Condiments and Relishes

𝒫epper Relish
Rene E. Scheuing
Maytown, PA

Makes 4 pints

12 large peppers
6 medium onions
Boiling water to cover
1 tsp. mustard seed
1 tsp. celery seed
1 tsp. salt (not iodized)
1 cup sugar
1½ cups vinegar
1 cup water

1. Chop peppers and onions in food chopper or processor. Pour boiling water over vegetables and let stand for 5 minutes. Drain.

2. Combine spices, sugar, vinegar, and water in a saucepan and bring to a boil. Stir in well-drained peppers and onions and boil for twenty minutes.

3. Sterilize pint jars. Pour hot relish into hot jars and seal.

The Fall Fairs

Life in Lancaster County comes alive in the fall of the year when various communities take turns hosting their annual farmers' or street fairs. Floats and bands, pumpkins and chocolate cakes, and beautiful handmade quilts all mingle in the sights and sounds of the fairs. The distinct odors of French Fries and cotton candy float across crisp cool evenings. The whirr of amusement rides, the moos and baas and oinks of the animals, and the grunts of the local firemen working hard at a rope pull blend with the music of high school marching bands. From Manheim to Quarryville and New Holland to Ephrata, a night out at the fair becomes a favorite memory for many a Lancaster County child.

—Tina Snyder, Manheim, PA

Zucchini Pepper Relish

Emily Fleck, Elizabethtown, PA
Janice Horning, Mohnton, PA

Makes 8 pints

10 cups coarsely ground zucchini
4$\frac{1}{2}$ cups coarsely ground onions
$\frac{1}{2}$ cup salt
3 red peppers, chopped
3 green peppers, chopped
2$\frac{1}{4}$ cups vinegar
6 cups sugar
1 tsp. dry mustard
2 tsp. cornstarch
2 tsp. turmeric
2 tsp. celery seed

1. Pour ground zucchini and onions into large bowl. Sprinkle salt evenly over top. Let stand overnight. Wash and strain two times in cheesecloth. Let drain in colander.
2. Add chopped peppers to onions and zucchini.
3. In a saucepan bring vinegar, sugar, mustard, cornstarch, turmeric, and celery seed to a boil. Stir in zucchini and pepper mixture and cook for 15 minutes.
4. Sterilize pint jars. Pour hot mixture into hot jars and seal.

Zucchini Relish

Irene Shirk
Akron, PA

Makes 10 pints

4 quarts coarsely ground zucchini
4 large onions, coarsely ground
$\frac{1}{2}$ cup salt
3 cups vinegar
$\frac{1}{2}$ tsp. dry mustard
2 Tbsp. mustard seed
5 cups sugar
1 tsp. turmeric
1 Tbsp. celery seed

1. In large bowl combine zucchini and onions. Pour salt over mixture and let stand for 20 minutes. Drain thoroughly.
2. Combine all remaining ingredients in large kettle and bring to a boil. Add drained zucchini and onion mixture and boil for 7 minutes.
3. Pour into hot, sterilized jars and seal.

Zucchini Chow Chow

Mabel E. Weaver
New Holland, PA

Makes 8 quarts

Chow Chow:
4 quarts diced zucchini
2 medium heads cauliflower, diced
2 cups diced carrots
2 cups diced celery
6 medium onions, chopped
3 red peppers, chopped
Water to cover
$\frac{1}{2}$ cup salt

Syrup:
4 cups vinegar
8 cups sugar

2 cups water
$\frac{1}{2}$ tsp. turmeric
1 tsp. garlic salt
$\frac{1}{2}$ tsp. celery seed
1 tsp. alum

1. In large container combine zucchini, cauliflower, carrots, celery, onions, and red peppers. Cover with salt water and soak at least 3 hours. Drain well.
2. To prepare syrup combine all ingredients in large kettle and bring to a boil. Add drained vegetables and boil 3-5 minutes.
3. Spoon into sterilized quart canning jars and seal.

Mustard Beans
Elsie Kauffman
Stevens, PA

Makes 8 pints

8 pints yellow string beans
2 cups sugar
2 cups vinegar
$\frac{1}{2}$-$\frac{3}{4}$ cup prepared mustard
1 Tbsp. salt *or* less
1 tsp. pepper

1. Wash and blanch string beans.
2. In a saucepan combine all remaining ingredients. Gently stir in string beans and bring to a boil. Cook about 10 minutes.
3. Spoon into hot, sterilized jars and seal.

Spiced Watermelon
Millie Eisemann
Ephrata, PA

Makes 8 pints

2 lbs. watermelon rind
4 cups water
$\frac{1}{2}$ cup salt
4 cups sugar
2 cups vinegar
2 cups water
1 drop oil of cinnamon
1 drop oil of cloves

1. Peel green off watermelon rind and cut into desired-sized pieces. Soak overnight in 4 cups salt water.
2. In the morning drain water. In a saucepan bring drained watermelon rind to a boil. Reduce heat and cook 15 minutes. Drain again.
3. In separate kettle combine sugar, vinegar, 2 cups water, and spices and bring to a boil. Pour rind into vinegar mixture and cook 3 minutes longer.
4. Put into sterilized jars and seal.

Seven-Day Sweet Pickles
Marilyn Kay Martin
Manheim, PA

Makes 10 pints

7 lbs. medium-sized cucumbers
Water to cover
1 quart vinegar
8 cups sugar
2 Tbsp. salt
2 Tbsp. pickling spices

1. Wash cucumbers and cover with boiling water. Let stand for 24 hours, then drain. Repeat this process each day for 4 days, using fresh water each time.

2. On the fifth day, cut cucumbers into ¼-inch slices. In a kettle combine vinegar, sugar, salt, and spices. Bring liquid to a boil and pour over sliced cucumbers. Let stand 24 hours.

3. On sixth day drain and reserve syrup, bringing to a boil again. Pour over cucumbers. Let stand 24 hours.

4. On the seventh day drain and reserve syrup, bringing to a boil again. Add cucumber slices to kettle and bring to boil.

5. While still hot, pack into sterilized jars and seal.

Generation Sour Pickle
Florence Nolt
New Holland, PA

Makes 5 quarts

5 quarts whole small cucumbers
4 cups vinegar
4 cups water
2 cups sugar
1 tsp. salt

1. In a large kettle bring vinegar, water, sugar, and salt to a boil. Add cucumbers and boil only until fresh green color disappears.

2. Spoon pickles and syrup into hot, sterilized jars and seal.

Christmas Pickles
Reba I. Hillard
Narvon, PA

Makes 1 gallon

1 gallon small to medium cucumbers
4 Tbsp. alum
4 Tbsp. pickling spices
4 Tbsp. salt
4 cups vinegar
Water to cover
6 cups sugar
2 cups water

1. In late July or early August (at the height of cucumber season) wash and pack cucumbers in a gallon jar. Add alum, pickling spices, salt, and vinegar. Fill jar with water to cover and seal. Store in basement until mid-December.

2. Drain vinegar water off pickles. Reserve water, remove spices, and pour into large container. Slice pickles into large bowl.

3. Add sugar and 2 cups water to vinegar water and stir a little. Pour over the sliced pickles. Cover and store in refrigerator until crisp.

Note: These pickles go well with a Christmas dinner and will keep for months in the refrigerator.

Salsa California-Style
Cindy Bryan
Adamstown, PA

Makes 1 pint

5 small very ripe tomatoes
2-3 finely chopped jalapeño peppers
1 small onion, chopped
1 tsp. chopped parsley
$\frac{1}{2}$ tsp. salt
$\frac{1}{2}$ tsp. sugar
$\frac{1}{4}$ tsp. pepper

1. Combine all ingredients in small bowl and mix well. Store in refrigerator for 10 days. (Flavor improves with time.)
2. Serve as a dip or garnish.

Hot Bacon Dressing
Teresa Burkhart
Brownstown, PA

Makes 3-4 cups

$\frac{1}{2}$ lb. bacon
2 cups water
$\frac{3}{4}$ cup vinegar
1 cup sugar
1 heaping Tbsp. prepared mustard
3 eggs
3-4 Tbsp. flour

1. Fry, drain, and crumble bacon.
2. Combine all remaining ingredients in a saucepan. Bring mixture to a boil. Lower heat, stirring until mixture thickens. Remove from heat and stir in bacon pieces.
3. Serve warm over lettuce.

Sweet and Sour Dressing
Ruth Houck
Stevens, PA

Makes about 3 cups

1 cup cooking oil
$\frac{2}{3}$ cup ketchup
$\frac{1}{2}$ cup vinegar
$\frac{1}{2}$ tsp. Italian seasoning
$\frac{1}{2}$ cup water
1 cup sugar
1 tsp. salt
$\frac{1}{2}$ Tbsp. minced onion

1. Blend all ingredients in blender.
2. Serve with fresh, tossed salad.

Georgetown

Along Route 372 west of Christiana, travelers come upon a sleepy, little village surrounded by Amish farms. Like several other southern Lancaster County towns, it has a bit of a split personality. Many people call Georgetown "Bart." After all, it is home to the Bart Fire Company and the Bart Post Office. Since the post office in Rawlinsville is called Holtwood and the one in Wakefield is called Peach Bottom, the confusion of names is not completely unusual. However, no one calls Wakefield "Peach Bottom" or Rawlinsville "Holtwood," making Georgetown's problem unique.

According to local history, Georgetown was named after George Baughman, a landowner who laid out the village in the early 1800s. When the town was awarded a post office, it was renamed Bart to avoid confusing it with Georgetown in Beaver County, Pennsylvania. However, local folks never stopped calling their village by its original name. Many out-of-towners, on the other hand, do talk of going to Bart to the annual spring sale, in spite of the fact that they will spend all of their time in the heart of Georgetown.

Several businesses—Fisher's New and Used Furniture, Village Dry Goods and Country Store, and a chiropractor's office—huddle around the crossroads square. With its surrounding Amish population, Georgetown is the kind of place where horses pulling buggies pace long lines of patient, lazy Sunday afternoon drivers.

Salad Dressing

Janet Pickel
Lancaster, PA

Makes 2 cups

¾ cup sugar
1 tsp. dry mustard
1 tsp. salt *or less*
1 small onion, grated
⅓ cup vinegar
1 cup cooking oil
1 tsp. celery seed

1. Beat all ingredients except celery seed in blender. Blend a few seconds.
2. Add celery seed and stir to mix. Pour into container and refrigerate.

French Dressing

Miriam Stoltzfus
Ronks, PA

Makes 1 quart dressing

1 cup sugar
1 cup ketchup
1½ tsp. celery seed
1½ tsp. salt
1½ tsp. paprika
1½ tsp. grated onion
1½ tsp. cooking oil
½ cup vinegar

1. Combine sugar, ketchup, celery seed, salt, paprika, and onion and blend well. Add oil and vinegar alternately and blend well.
2. Refrigerate until ready to serve.

Quick Salad Dressing
Julia C. Herman
Leola, PA

Makes about 1 quart

1 cup mayonnaise
1 cup vinegar
1 cup water
1 cup sugar

1. Combine all ingredients in a blender or jar and blend or shake until thoroughly mixed.
2. Serve with sliced cucumbers or tossed salad.

Favorite Barbecue Sauce
Joyce E. Imhoff
Akron, PA

Makes 1 cup

1 medium onion, chopped
2 Tbsp. butter
2 Tbsp. vinegar
2 Tbsp. lemon juice
2 Tbsp. brown sugar
2 Tbsp. prepared mustard
1/2 cup water
3 Tbsp. Worcestershire sauce
Dash salt and pepper

1. Sauté onion in butter. Add all remaining ingredients and simmer at least 15-20 minutes.
2. Serve with leftover beef, chicken, turkey, or pork.

Zesty Barbecue Sauce
Valerie Voran
Ephrata, PA

Makes about 2½ cups

1/2 cup butter
1/2 cup wine vinegar
1/2 cup lemon juice
1/2 cup ketchup
3/4 cup brown sugar
1/4 tsp. dry mustard
Dash garlic powder
Dash celery salt

1. In a saucepan melt butter. Add all remaining ingredients and heat through, stirring frequently.
2. Serve with chicken or beef.

Barbecue Sauce
Diana Russell
Holtwood, PA

Makes 1½ cups

1/2 cup chopped onions
1 green pepper, chopped
1 Tbsp. butter
1 Tbsp. sugar
2 Tbsp. prepared mustard
1 Tbsp. vinegar
1 tsp. salt
1 cup ketchup
1/2 tsp. ground cloves

1. Sauté onions and green pepper with butter. Add all remaining ingredients and heat through, stirring occasionally.
2. Pour sauce over choice of prepared meat and heat. Serve.

Making Jellies with Fruit Pits

When seeding sour cherries for canning or freezing, save the pits. Pour pits into a kettle and almost cover with water. Bring to a boil and boil for ten minutes. Strain pits from water. To make Cherry Pit Jelly follow directions on a package of Sure Jell.

When peeling peaches for canning or freezing, save the pits and skins. Pour mixture of pits and skins into kettle and almost cover with water. Bring to a boil and boil for ten minutes. (If skins have turned slightly brown, it doesn't matter, although the sooner they are cooked the better.) Strain pits and peelings from water. To make Peach Pit Jelly follow directions on a package of Sure Jell.

—Erma Wenger, Lancaster, PA

Quick and Easy Barbecue Sauce
Stacey Rettew
Denver, PA

Makes 1½ cups

½ **cup mayonnaise**
½ **cup ketchup**
¼ **cup Worcestershire sauce**
¼ **cup prepared mustard**
¼ **cup brown sugar, firmly packed**

1. In a bowl whisk together all ingredients until smooth.
2. Marinate and baste choice of meat, turning frequently.

Meatloaf Topping
Margie Jones
Lancaster, PA

Makes ¼ cup

3 **Tbsp. brown sugar**
¼ **cup ketchup**
1 **tsp. dry mustard**

1. Combine all ingredients and mix well.
2. Pour over meatloaf and bake according to directions.

Spaghetti Sauce
Anne Nolt
Reinholds, PA

Makes 7 pints

12 **large tomatoes**
2 **green peppers, diced**
1 **cup finely chopped celery**
2 **medium onions, finely chopped**
1 **tsp. oregano**
1 **tsp. dry mustard**
2 **cups sugar**
1½ **cups vinegar**

1. Cut tomatoes into large kettle. Add all remaining ingredients and bring to a boil. Lower heat and simmer for 2 hours.
2. Spoon into sterilized pint jars and seal.

Hot Pepper Jelly
Patti Smith
Columbia, PA

Makes about 4 pints

½ cup diced hot peppers
¾ cup diced bell peppers
1¼ cups cider vinegar
6 cups sugar
6 ozs. liquid Certo
Several drops red *or* green coloring

1. Put peppers in blender with ¼ cup vinegar and purée. Mix with sugar in large saucepan.
2. Pour remaining vinegar into blender and blend to wash blender. Add to sugar and bring mixture to a boil. Boil for 2-3 minutes. Skim off foam.
3. Stir in Certo and cook 2 more minutes. Add food coloring and pour into jars. Cool.
4. Serve with crackers and cream cheese.

Peanut Butter Sauce
Esta M. Ansel
Reamstown, PA

Makes 1½ cups

1 cup brown sugar, packed
⅓ cup milk
¼ cup light corn syrup
1 Tbsp. butter
½ cup creamy peanut butter

1. In a saucepan combine all ingredients except peanut butter and cook over medium heat, stirring constantly. Cook until sugar is dissolved and butter is melted.

2. Remove from heat and stir in peanut butter. Beat until smooth. Cool.
3. Serve with ice cream.

Coating Mix for Chicken
Marilyn Langeman
Akron, PA

Makes 1 quart mix

2 cups fine bread *or* cracker crumbs
2 cups flour
2 Tbsp. salt
2 Tbsp. sugar
1½ Tbsp. paprika
1 tsp. onion powder
1 tsp. garlic powder
2 Tbsp. cooking oil

1. Mix all ingredients well. Store in airtight container in refrigerator.
2. To use, coat chicken pieces with mixture.
3. Bake chicken at 350° for 1 hour.

Note: This recipe equals about 10 purchased packages. Also you may experiment with other herbs and spices such as thyme, dill seed, and parsley flakes.

Large Quantity Recipes

Potato Salad
Dorothy Galebach
Manheim, PA
Penryn Fire Company

Makes 150 or more servings

Salad:
50 lbs. potatoes, boiled, peeled, diced
6 cups chopped celery
3-4 dozen hard-boiled eggs, diced

Dressing:
12 cups white sugar
2 cups brown sugar
2½ cups flour
12 eggs
½ cup dry mustard
2 tsp. turmeric
2 cups butter
6 medium onions, chopped
10 cups vinegar
4 cups water
4 Tbsp. salt
2 tsp. black pepper
3 Tbsp. celery seed

1. Gently combine cooked potatoes, chopped celery, and diced eggs.
2. In a large kettle combine all dressing ingredients and bring to a boil, stirring constantly. Cook until mixture turns thick and clear. Cool slightly.
3. Pour dressing over potato mixture and stir gently but thoroughly.
4. Refrigerate 6-12 hours for flavors to mix.

Note: This recipe has been used for serving wedding receptions and buffets.

Frozen Slaw

Mary Ella Herr
Quarryville, PA
Quarryville Fire Company

Makes about 150 servings

5-7 medium heads cabbage, shredded
6 carrots, grated
6 sweet peppers, chopped
5 tsp. salt
5 cups vinegar
1½ cups water
5 lbs. sugar
5 tsp. celery seed
5 tsp. whole mustard seed
3 tsp. garlic powder

1. In large container mix together cabbage, carrots, peppers, and salt. Let stand for 1 hour. Squeeze out juice.

2. In a kettle combine all remaining ingredients and bring to a boil over medium heat. Boil for 1 minute, stirring constantly. Cool.

3. Pour dressing over cabbage mixture. Spoon into desired-sized containers and freeze.

Note: We make this coleslaw ahead of time and serve it at our annual fall Roast Chicken Supper.

Chicken Corn Soup

Arlene Ruhl
Manheim, PA
Mastersonville Fire Company

Makes 80 servings

6 large *or* 10 small chickens
5 gallons hot water
½ cup salt
Pepper to taste
Saffron to taste
8 quarts creamed corn
10 quarts whole kernel corn
1 lb. thin crushed noodles
8 eggs
10 cups flour

1. Cook chickens in water to cover until meat is soft. Remove from broth. Cool, debone, and cut into bite-sized pieces.

2. In a large iron kettle combine 5 gallons hot water, diced chicken, chicken broth, salt, pepper, and saffron and bring to a full, rolling boil.

3. Stir in creamed corn and whole kernel corn. Add crushed noodles.

4. In a bowl combine eggs and flour and work with hands to make rivels. Sprinkle rivels slowly through fingers into boiling soup, stirring constantly.

5. Heat through and serve.

Note: We have served this recipe at public auctions for over 40 years. Usually we make several large iron kettles of soup at a time and sell it by the bowl, quart, or gallon.

Chicken Pot Pie

Dorothy Galebach
Manheim, PA
Penryn Fire Company

Makes 20-24 servings

8-lb. whole chicken
4 quarts water
6 cups flour
3 Tbsp. margarine, softened
6 eggs
3 tsp. salt
⅛ cup water
½ tsp. baking powder
2½ quarts chicken broth
5 quarts water
2 quarts peeled, diced potatoes
Pinch saffron

1. Cook chicken in 4 quarts water until meat is tender. Reserve 2½ quarts broth. Cool and debone.

2. Meanwhile combine flour, margarine, eggs, salt, ⅛ cup water, and baking powder with a large spoon. Mix well, then form into 5 separate balls by hand.

3. Let dough rest 20-30 minutes. Roll out each ball of dough. Cut into squares.

4. Combine chicken broth, 5 quarts water, potatoes, and saffron and bring to a boil. Drop squares of pot pie dough into boiling liquid, keeping squares separated until they are partially cooked. Cook about 20 minutes.

5. Immediately before serving, add cooked chicken and heat through.

Note: Each year the Penryn Firemen have a Chicken Pot Pie fund raiser in September while the women have one in February. Lots of kidding about whose pot pie turns out the best enlivens the day spent raising funds for the local fire hall.

Creamed Chicken Patties

Ida Jane Zercher
Willow Street, PA
Colemanville United Methodist Church

Makes about 50 servings

Chicken Mixture:
2 medium stewing chickens
6 hard-boiled eggs, diced
5 cups minced celery

White Sauce:
5 Tbsp. butter *or* margarine
1¼ cups flour
3 cups chicken broth
5 cups milk
Salt and pepper to taste

Patty Shells:
1 lb. shortening
2 lbs. flour
2 Tbsp. salt
1 cup water

1. To prepare creamed chicken cook chicken in 5-6 cups water. Cool, debone, and dice. Skim and reserve chicken broth.

2. To prepare white sauce melt butter in large saucepan. Stir in flour until bubbly. Gradually add chicken broth and milk, stirring constantly until sauce thickens. Add diced chicken, hard-boiled eggs, and celery and heat through, stirring until well mixed. Add salt and pepper and mix well.

3. To prepare patty shells cut shortening into flour and salt. Add water and mix by hand to consistency of pie dough. Roll out dough and press small pieces into tart pans.

4. Bake at 400° about 15 minutes.

5. Fill each patty shell with the creamed chicken and serve.

Note: We serve this recipe each year at our annual cafeteria supper. Used as a fund raiser, we began doing this in 1955.

Chicken Casserole

Esther W. Sensenig
New Holland, PA

Makes 24-30 servings

2 4-lb. whole chickens
32 slices bread
2 cups chopped onion
2 cups chopped celery
2 cups chopped green peppers
    (optional)
6 eggs
6 cups milk
1 Tbsp. salt
1 tsp. pepper
2 cups mayonnaise
4 10¾-oz. cans cream of chicken soup
2 cups grated cheese

1. Cook whole chickens until meat is soft. Cool, debone, and dice meat.

2. Cut bread into 1-inch squares. Put ½ of bread into bottom of large, greased baking pan. Add chicken pieces, onion, celery, and green peppers. Add remaining bread cubes.

2. Combine eggs, milk, salt, pepper, and mayonnaise. Beat well and pour over chicken and bread cubes. Let stand 1 hour or overnight.

3. Immediately before baking, pour cream of chicken soup over all.

4. Bake at 325° for 1 hour. Remove from oven and sprinkle cheese over top. Bake ¼-½ hour longer.

Note: I have made this recipe many times for large, extended family get-togethers.

Beef Barbecue

Anna Mae Conley
Mount Joy, PA
Silver Spring Fire Company

Makes 120 servings

17 lbs. ground beef
3 large stalks celery
12 green peppers
12 large onions
7-lb. can ketchup
1½ cups brown sugar
¾ cup vinegar
3 Tbsp. dry mustard
4 Tbsp. Worcestershire sauce
Salt and pepper to taste
120 hamburger rolls

1. Brown ground beef in a large skillet and drain.

2. Chop vegetables in a food processor or blender.

3. In a large electric roast pan or kettle combine chopped vegetables and all remaining ingredients. Stir in ground beef and mix thoroughly.

4. Bring to a full, rolling boil. Reduce heat and simmer for 1 hour.

5. Serve on hamburger rolls.

Note: This popular quick dish sells well at the foodstands our Ladies' Auxiliary occasionally sets up at public auctions.

Sauerbraten

Helen E. Keener

Rheems, PA

Makes 100 servings

3 8-lb. boneless beef pot roasts
3 quarts vinegar
5 quarts water
2 gallons tomatoes
5½ cups brown sugar
7 tsp. salt
½ cup dry mustard
¼ cup whole cloves
2 Tbsp. cinnamon
2 Tbsp. allspice
2 Tbsp. nutmeg
1½ quarts chopped onions
1½ quarts chopped celery
3½ cups chopped carrots
¼ cup chopped garlic

1. Combine all ingredients except meat in very large container and mix well. Pour over meat in very large kettle. Cover kettle and store in walk-in cooler for 72 hours.

2. To prepare sauerbraten boil meat in its pickling solution until meat is tender.

3. Immediately before serving, remove and slice meat. Prepare a gravy or sauce with pickling solution.

New Holland

More than 5000 people call the borough of New Holland home. They live in homes stretching from Yoders Country Market and Restaurant on the northeast side of town to Good's Furniture Store on the southwest. Highway 23 passes directly through the center of town, and the numerous traffic lights which connect side streets to the highway create the illusion of a much larger town.

Kauffman's Hardware and a Dollar General Store face each other on Main Street at the center of the borough. The Dollar Store makes its home in the old Rubinson's Department Store building, a longtime New Holland establishment. During its mid-1900s heyday, Rubinson's stocked shoes, fabric, clothing, books, and toys, as well as many other items appropriate for the plain people who frequented the store.

In the 1970s and 1980s a strip mall at the west end of town and fast-food places such as Pizza Hut, Burger King, and MacDonalds lured shoppers away from the downtown part of the borough. The arrival of Dollar General, along with the reopening of the Ritz Theater occasionally bring folks back to the once-bustling corner of Main and Railroad Avenues.

An old Conrail line passes along the southern rim of the borough. Two major corporations provide employment for many New Hollanders and trace their humble beginnings to small plants located near the rail line. New Holland Machine, home of the New Holland baler and other patents for farm equipment, became Ford New Holland when it was bought out in the 1980s. Weaver's Chicken Plant, widely recognized for quality chicken products, became a division of Tyson Foods in the late eighties. The many other businesses in New Holland include everything from funeral homes and insurance companies to drugstores and restaurants.

Bread Filling

Joyce Eby
Denver, PA
Fivepointville Fire Company

Makes 50 servings

5 large loaves bread
12 eggs
2 12-oz. cans evaporated milk
2 cans water
½ gallon milk *or* **more**
1 large onion, diced
2 quarts chopped celery
2 tsp. salt
Pepper to taste
1 cup margarine *or* **more**

1. Tear bread into small pieces. (Day-old bread works well.)
2. Blend eggs, evaporated milk, water, and milk. Stir into bread until nice and moist. Add onion and celery and mix well. Add seasoning to taste and mix well.
3. Spoon bread mixture into greased baking pans and dot with margarine or butter.
4. Cover and bake at 325° for 2-2½ hours. Uncover and bake another ½ hour.

Potato Filling

Dorothy Galebach
Manheim, PA
Penryn Fire Company

Makes 30 servings

10 lbs. potatoes
½ cup chopped onions
1 cup chopped celery
2 Tbsp. butter
12 ozs. dry bread cubes
6 eggs
Pinch saffron
½ cup hot water
2 quarts milk
Salt and pepper to taste
4 Tbsp. butter

1. Peel potatoes and cook until soft. Mash them.
2. Sauté onions and celery with 2 Tbsp. butter until onions are translucent.
3. Put all ingredients except 4 Tbsp. butter in a large pan, adding milk, a little at a time. Mix well.
4. Spoon into 3 large greased casserole dishes. Allow at least 1 inch of space at top of each dish. Dot with 4 Tbsp. butter.
5. Bake at 350° for about 45 minutes.

Note: Most of the fund-raising dinners at the Penryn Fire Hall feature this potato filling. For many years we called it Lebanon County Filling because the woman who introduced the recipe to us came from Lebanon County.

Baked Lima Beans
Helen E. Keener
Rheems, PA

Makes 36 servings

5 lbs. dry lima beans
3 lbs. bacon
3 pints tomato juice
3 cups ketchup
3 cups brown sugar
3 cups dark corn syrup
3 onions, chopped
6 tsp. prepared mustard
2 tsp. ginger

1. Prepare and cook beans according to package directions. Drain ½ of water.
2. Fry, drain, and crumble bacon.
3. Combine all ingredients and mix well. Pour into large roaster or baking pan.
4. Bake at 350° for 1-2 hours, stirring frequently.

Baked Beans
Emma Reiff
Ephrata, PA
Farmersville Fire Hall

Makes 36 servings

1½ lbs. bacon
¼ cup chopped onions
2 gallons Great Northern beans
4 cups ketchup
3½ cups molasses
2½ cups brown sugar

1. Fry, drain, and crumble bacon. Sauté onions in 2 Tbsp. bacon drippings.
2. Drain about ½ of liquid from beans.
3. Combine all ingredients in large roaster or baking pan. Refrigerate overnight.
4. Bake at 350° for 2 hours.

Sour Cream Cookies
Darlene Redcay
Goodville, PA

Makes more than 20 dozen cookies

2 Tbsp. baking soda
1 quart buttermilk
1½ Tbsp. vanilla
1 cup sour cream
6 cups sugar
2 cups shortening, melted
15 cups flour

1. Dissolve baking soda in buttermilk and mix well. Add vanilla, sour cream, and sugar and stir to mix. Add melted shortening and stir until sugar is dissolved.
2. Stir in 8 cups flour and mix well. Add remaining 7 cups of flour and mix well. Refrigerate overnight.

3. Drop by large teaspoonsful onto floured cookie sheet.

4. Bake at 350° for 8-10 minutes.

5. If desired, ice cookies with favorite vanilla icing recipe.

Shoofly Pies by the Dozen

Anna Mae Conley
Mount Joy, PA
Silver Spring Fire Company

Makes 12 9" pies

12 cups flour
9 cups brown sugar
2 cups butter, softened
¼ cup baking soda
3 quarts hot water
12 eggs
1 8-lb. can King syrup
12 9" unbaked pie shells

1. Mix together flour, brown sugar, and butter until crumbly. Reserve 8 cups crumbs for topping.

2. Dissolve baking soda in 1 quart hot water.

3. In a very large bowl beat together eggs, syrup, remaining hot water, and baking soda water. Combine with crumb mixture. Spoon mixture evenly into 12 unbaked pie shells.

4. Sprinkle ⅔ cup reserved crumbs on top of each pie.

5. Bake at 400° for 10 minutes. Reduce oven temperature to 375° and bake another 25 minutes.

Church Apple Butter Pies

Lydia Smoker
Gordonville, PA
Gordonville Fire Company

Makes 40 8" pies

2 gallons apple butter
4 gallons applesauce
2½ cups tapioca
5 cups sugar *or* more
1 Tbsp. cinnamon
1 Tbsp. nutmeg
80 8" unbaked pie shells

1. Combine all ingredients except pie shells in very large container and mix well.

2. Pour mixture evenly into 40 unbaked pie shells. Cover with top crusts, fluting edges. Cut slits in tops of each pie.

3. Bake at 425° for 15 minutes. Reduce oven temperature to 350° and bake another 30 minutes.

Note: A traditional Lancaster County Old Order Amish church meal includes Schnitz Pies. This is a quick substitute for the long process of drying apples. Today some Amish women use this recipe when preparing for church at their homes.

Index

About the Authors

Louise Stoltzfus, a native of Lancaster County, grew up in a large Amish family where good food was an expected part of every family get-together.

Stoltzfus is the co-author of *Favorite Recipes from Quilters, The Central Market Cookbook, The Best of Mennonite Fellowship Meals,* and *Lancaster County Cookbook.*

Jan L. Mast comes from Lancaster County and lives near the village of Smoketown, Pennsylvania. She grew up in a Mennonite family with a long tradition of Pennsylvania Dutch cooking styles.

She is the author of *The School Picnic, Amish Doll Patterns,* and co-author of *An Amish Nativity: Complete Projects and Instructions.*

Mast is manager of The People's Place, an Amish and Mennonite heritage center in the village of Intercourse.